Contents

Preface

We live in a time in which everyone seems to have a relationship with Jimmy. It may seem odd, and perhaps impertinent, to deploy a name used by his closest friends and family, yet there seems to be that level of intimacy among those who have reclaimed Jimmy as their own—their teacher, prophet, inspiration, and friend. The man who was panned by critics (literary and political, black as well as white) in the late '60s, '70s, and '80s as being out of touch and past his prime, has now returned to the public arena in such a way that not a day goes by that his voice does not ring out on a social media platform, his name is not invoked on a news program, or a news piece (academic or popular) does not drop with a presumably *new* take on his life and work. On one level, this Baldwin resurgence should be praised. As David Baldwin recounted in the 1990 documentary "James Baldwin: The Price of the Ticket," Jimmy wanted to be found again, to prove himself useful, long after he passed. David Baldwin remembers his brother as saying:

> I pray I've done my work so, that when I've gone from here . . .
> through the wreckage and rumble . . . when someone finds themself
> digging through the ruins . . . I pray that somewhere in that wreckage
> they'll find me. Somewhere in that wreckage, that they can use some-
> thing that I left behind. And if I've done that, then I've accomplished
> something in life.[1]

One need not belabor the point that we live in a time of "turmoil" and "wreck-age," one in which we are struggling to find, and sustain, life in the "ruins" left by capitalism, anti-blackness, and cisheteronormativity. And in the midst of that devastation, Jimmy's speaking again, calling us to follow his gospel.[2]

But we must acknowledge that we lost something with the advent of the soundbite Jimmy, the Jimmy of popular culture. Take for instance, the 2016 release of the documentary "I am Not Your Negro." After walking out of my first viewing, although filled with joy to see my hero on the big screen, being viewed by some for the first time, I knew that something was amiss; something of Jimmy had been erased in the film. Soon after my viewing, a number of excellent articles, reviews, and reflections were written that gave voice to my discomfort,[3] and my suspicions were confirmed sometime later as I participated in a panel discussion on the film, organized by a local Black Lives Matter organization in central Indiana. After I offered my comments on the problematic erasure of Baldwin's queerness/sexuality in the film, a man stood up—a professor at a prestigious university in the Midwest—and said something along the lines of, "Listen, we just need to bracket the sexuality stuff. We need to focus on the main thing, which was Baldwin's critique of race. Yes, he was gay, but that wasn't as important as his critique of white supremacy." Following this professor's comment, a black woman raised her hand and offered, "I agree, let's stick to the point. My child isn't menaced because of his sexuality, but because of his race." There is much I could say about these comments, but what is most important for our purposes here is that these statements made clear that if we are going to claim a closeness with Jimmy, if we are going to profess him as our teacher, prophet, and friend, we cannot have a piecemeal Jimmy. We cannot have a Jimmy in whom we only engage those parts that we find palatable, sexy, and easily digestible. We need Jimmy in his complexity, or what Douglas Field calls "the shifting and developing James Baldwins."[4] We need a Jimmy who never discussed race in the United States without also pointing to the ways in which white supremacy is bolstered by an intersecting sexual, gender, and *religious* ideology that can only be deconstructed and combated *together*. This book, which engages Jimmy's faith specifically, and his engagement of religion broadly, will demonstrate that to discuss Jimmy's faith is also to discuss the theological regime which contributed to the birth of whiteness; to discuss Jimmy's faith is to discuss Western Christianity's attempt to police and control the sexual body through the creation and (re)entrenchment of heteronormativity; to discuss Jimmy's faith and religion is to understand the sacrament that is (queer) sexuality; to discuss Jimmy's faith is to understand Baldwin's sociopolitical vision for a society freed from the shackles of anti-blackness and cisheteronormativity—a reality he calls "the New Jerusalem."[5] This book is one small, and inadequate, attempt to *see* Jimmy in his complexity, to *find* Jimmy in the wreckage.

JIMMY'S FAITH

Introduction[1]

As Douglas Field notes in his 2015 work, *All Those Strangers: The Art and Lives of James Baldwin*, examinations of Baldwin's relationship to religion are a "glaring absence" in Baldwin scholarship, with only a handful of full-length monographs being dedicated to the topic.[2] This book attempts to add to the growing body of work on Baldwin's deeply complex relationship to black religion. Why did Baldwin, a man who spoke often of having left the church as a teenager, seem unable to leave the symbols and language, the church-talk and indeed the god-talk,[3] of Christianity behind? Clarence Hardy is correct in pointing out that, unbeknownst to many of those who have only been exposed to the Baldwin of popular culture, the literature of James Baldwin, in its entirety, remains "captive to . . . [the] rhythms, language, and themes" of black religious expression in the United States—particularly black Christianity.[4] *Jimmy's Faith will explore this primary question: What is Baldwin doing with, and through, his literary deployment of religious language and symbols?*

Jimmy's Faith is by no means the first text to raise this question, as the scholarship of Clarence Hardy, Douglas Field, Josiah Ulysses Young, Michael Lynch, and El Kornegay, among others, can attest. However, this study demonstrates that in Baldwin's literature one does not find either a rejection ("counteridentification") or an embrace ("identification") of Christianity, but rather a strategic "disidentification"—disidentification in the manner articulated by queer theorist José Esteban Muñoz.[5] According to Muñoz, disidentification "works on, with, and against a cultural form,"[6] and is a means of "transfiguring" or "recycling" a phenomenon which is typically hostile to the queer person, recreating it as a space of queer imagination, "survival," and at times empowerment.[7] In my reading, Baldwin disidentifies with Christian theology, for although he publicly

1

rejects the faith of his upbringing, he continues to speak through the framework of black church music, language, and symbols in order to challenge and restructure their meaning in articulating his own, unique black religious vision, a vision rooted in the possibility that individual humans, and the culture at large, can be radically transformed.

A (Queer) Theory of Disidentification

In order to offer a more robust understanding of disidentification as it will be utilized in this project, we turn now to the queer of color critique[8] of theorist José Esteban Muñoz. Muñoz builds his distinct understanding of disidentification through a complex blending of various theories including, but not limited to, Michel Pêcheux's theory of disidentification which is inspired by the Marxist analysis of Louis Althusser,[9] and the "political strategy" of disidentification found in the work of radical feminists of color, particularly Cherríe Moraga and Gloria Anzaldúa's work *This Bridge Called My Back: Writings by Radical Women of Color.*[10] In essence, these diverse theories coalesce in offering a "hermeneutic" of disidentification which allows one to explore how the queer person/community takes "a moment, object, or subject that is not culturally coded to 'connect' with the disidentifying subject," and remakes that social phenomenon in a way that "invest[s] it with new life."[11] According to Muñoz:

> Disidentification is about recycling and rethinking encoded meaning. The process of disidentification scrambles and reconstructs the encoded message of a cultural text in a fashion that both exposes the encoded message's universalizing and exclusionary machinations and recircuits its workings to account for, include, and empower minority identities and identifications. Thus, disidentification is a step further than cracking open the code of the majority; it proceeds to use this code as raw material for representing a disempowered politics or positionality that has been rendered unthinkable by the dominant culture.[12]

In other words, disidentification is the means through which marginalized subjects, which for Muñoz are those queer persons who exist at the intersections of class, gender, sexual, and racial oppression, strategically utilize hostile cultural phenomena in a fashion that acknowledges their oppressive / "exclusionary machinations," while also reworking and reimagining them in such a way as to create the possibility for a "disempowered politics."

Therefore, disidentification is "a hermeneutic, a process of production, and a mode of performance."[13] As a hermeneutic, disidentification presupposes the ability to "read" cultural phenomena in way that excavates their underlying meanings. In addition, as a form of production, disidentification serves as a means of queer "worldmaking."[14] Muñoz, in his opening reflection on the legacy of performance artist Jack Smith, posits: "Smith once claimed that important acting did not change the actor but instead transformed the world. Smith made worlds during his performances; he recycled schlock culture and remade it as a queer world."[15] This quote not only speaks to the productive capacities of disidentification, but also to its performative aspects, for Muñoz's text seeks to theorize disidentification as a "modality of performance," exploring how queer performance artists create their own distinct queer worlds.[16]

However, disidentification is not limited to performance art, and Muñoz claims that "one of the most compelling examples of the process and effects that I discuss here as disidentification," is found in the literature of James Baldwin.[17] Muñoz's own reading of Baldwin's practice of disidentification, which served as a direct inspiration for my own reading of Baldwin, is helpful in offering a concrete example of how Muñoz's theory functions. He explores one passage from *The Devil Finds Work* as an example of Baldwin's disidentifying practice. In this passage, Baldwin recounts his father's consistent claim that Baldwin was "the ugliest boy he had ever seen," an insult based in the presumed ugliness of Baldwin's, and his mother's, "frog-eyes."[18] However, this common trope of Baldwin's father is troubled the first time a young James Baldwin sees the actor, Bette Davis. Baldwin states:

> So, here, now, was Bette Davis, on that Saturday afternoon, in
> close-up, over a champagne glass, pop-eyes popping. I was astounded.
> I had caught my father, not in a lie, but in an infirmity. For, here,
> before me, after all, was a *movie star: white:* and if she was white and a
> movie star, she was *rich:* and she was *ugly.* . . . Out of bewilderment,
> out of loyalty to my mother, probably, and also because I sensed some-
> thing menacing and unhealthy (for me, certainly) in the face on the
> screen, I gave Davis's skin the dead-white greenish cast of something
> crawling from under a rock, but I was held, just the same, by the tense
> intelligence of the forehead, the disaster of the lips: and when she
> moved, she moved just like a nigger.[19]

According to Muñoz, Baldwin found "something both liberatory and horrible" in the image of Davis on the big screen.[20] For here was a rich and white movie star, a woman of untold cultural and financial capital, who had the same ugly "frog-eyes" as Baldwin, the very object of his father's scorn. Baldwin troubles his father's claim that he is in fact ugly by strategically seeing himself in the actress, an actress that not only bore Baldwin's eyes, but "moved like a nigger." However, Davis cannot serve as a definitive source of identification for Baldwin, for her whiteness signifies a danger, something "menacing and unhealthy."[21] Therefore, Baldwin cannot *identify* with Davis, nor does he choose to *counter-identify* with her, but he strategically *disidentifies* with Davis in an attempt to revalue his own appearance. Muñoz posits:

> The example of Baldwin's relationship with Davis is a disidentification insofar as the African-American writer transforms the raw material of identification (the linear match that leads toward interpellation) while simultaneously positioning himself within and outside the image of the movie star. For Baldwin, disidentification is more than simply an interpretive turn or a psychic maneuver; it is, most crucially, a survival strategy.[22]

This book builds on, yet moves beyond, Muñoz's engagement of Baldwin and disidentification. I will demonstrate that Baldwin's unique disidentificatory practice is far more extensive than this brief reflection on the appearance of a Hollywood actor, for disidentification became the primary means through which Baldwin engaged the Christian tradition throughout his adult life. What will be shown is that Baldwin places himself "within and outside" of Christian language and symbols.[23] For despite Christianity's perceived failures, Baldwin's literary and political vision remains inundated with the symbols of black Christian faith, particularly that of the sanctified/Pentecostal tradition.[24] Rather than rejecting the symbols of the Pentecostal church in a totalizing manner, Baldwin queers them, disidentifying with and transfiguring their meaning so as to signify the flourishing of life for the very people those symbols were once used to exclude.[25] Baldwin, although he left the church as a teenager, continues to find its language and symbols efficacious, not only in leveling his devastating critique of the anti-black, anti-sex regime of white (Christian) supremacy, but he also utilizes those same symbols in his own attempt at imagining and building a new world.[26]

Autobiography as "Rehearsal for Fiction"[27]

In addition to the method of disidentification, I will also utilize a biographically informed reading strategy in exploring both Baldwin's nonfiction and fiction. This strategy seeks to avoid the temptation of drawing what Baldwin calls "one-on-one relationships between" himself and his literary creations,[28] while also acknowledging that Baldwin's fiction and its characters are a profound source for understanding Baldwin's relationship to Christianity. Once again, the work of José Esteban Muñoz proves invaluable in articulating this project's reading strategy.

Muñoz claims that Baldwin not only utilizes a praxis of disidentification *in* his fiction and nonfiction writings, but that he also disidentifies with the genre of fiction itself, understanding "nonfiction, or, more nearly, autobiography, [as] a rehearsal for fiction."[29] Muñoz roots this claim in the fact that Baldwin understood his nonfiction/autobiographical essay, *The Devil Finds Work* as a prelude to what would be expressed in his final novel *Just Above My Head*.[30] Muñoz highlights this passage from David Leeming's biography of Baldwin to exhibit the autobiographical connection between *The Devil Finds Work* and *Just Above My Head*. Leeming explains:

> He told Mary Blume that the book [*The Devil Finds Work*] "demanded a certain confession of myself," a confession of his loneliness as a celebrity left behind by assassinated comrades, a confession of compassion and hope even as he was being criticized for being passé, a confession of his fascination with the American fantasy, epitomized by Hollywood, even as he condemned it. It was "a rehearsal for something I'll deal with later." That something, *Just Above My Head*, would be the major work of his later years.[31]

Therefore, Baldwin understood *The Devil Finds Work* as space in which to express a personal "confession," which would be more fully fleshed out in his last work of fiction *Just Above My Head*. This language of confession is important, as will be shown in Chapter 1, for it signifies the act of revealing a truth about one's own life. Thus, confession presumes the autobiographical, the revelation of who one is.

Muñoz also claims that "Baldwin's fiction did not indulge the project of camouflaging an authorial surrogate. Instead, he produced a fiction that abounded with stand-ins."[32] He goes on to argue:

> With this posited, we begin to glimpse an understanding of fiction as a "technology of the self." This self is a disidentificatory self whose relation to the social is not overdetermined by universalizing rhetorics of selfhood. The "real self" who comes into being through fiction is not the self who produces fiction, but is instead produced by fiction. Binaries finally begin to falter and fiction becomes the real; which is to say

that the truth effect of ideological grids is broken down through Baldwin's disidentification with the notion of fiction—and it does not stop here: fiction then becomes a contested field of self-production.[33]

In other words, Muñoz is arguing that Baldwin queers and troubles the line between autobiography and fiction, between the authorial "real self" and the "real self" that is constructed through fiction. Therefore, in order to understand Baldwin's relationship to religious rhetoric and symbols, we must engage "both Baldwins," the Baldwin *producing* works of literature and the *Baldwin being produced* through his literary output.

Baldwin biographer David Leeming argues that Baldwin's "semiautobiographical approach" to his literature was "his method since *Go Tell It on the Mountain*."[34] This is confirmed by Baldwin himself in a 1976 interview with Jewell Handy Gresham. In response to the question "Did you write that out of personal experience?," Baldwin explains:

> That's a very good question. You're talking about *Go Tell it On the Mountain*, my first novel, which concerns itself with John, his father and mother and the church people. The point of the book, in a way, is what experiences shaped his aunt, his father, his mother. All of these lives were shaping John's life. *His* choices are defined by things that have happened to other people, not him. Not yet. In short he's walking into his ancestors' lives and experiences. Obviously at some point in my life that was my situation. And in order for me to assess and surmount it, I had to face it. *That's why you write any book, in a sense, to clarify something.* Not merely for yourself. What I have to assume is that if it happened to me it happened to someone else. You have to trust your own experience, which is all that connects you to anyone else.[35]

This relationship of autobiography to fiction, which Baldwin highlights above, offers a reading strategy through which I will engage Baldwin's corpus and his disidentification with religious symbols. As both Muñoz and Baldwin make clear, Baldwin's sense of self can be gleaned from his fiction, and I extend this idea in saying that Baldwin's sense of self *in relation to religion* can be gleaned from his fiction. Baldwin is both producing and being produced by his fiction, as he writes "to clarify" things that remain unsettled in his personal life. With this in mind, one could argue that Baldwin likewise continues to engage and reimagine religious symbols out of an attempt to clarify religion's meaning both for himself and others.[36] Thus, Baldwin's fiction and nonfiction should be read in tandem, with one genre being used to illuminate the other, both shedding light on Baldwin's distinct religious vision.

James Baldwin's Religion

In engaging the question of religion in relation to Baldwin's literature, it is important to be explicit about the disciplinary location of this text, which sits at the intersections of black studies, black religious studies, and black theological discourses. As for the meaning of "black religion" as I understand it, I borrow from, and build on, the scholarship of Anthony Pinn. According to Pinn, black religions in the United States, whether Christian, Muslim, or humanist, were and continue to be, birthed out of a shared historical struggle against white supremacy, and are at their core, reflective of the human "quest for complex subjectivity."[37] As he puts it:

> This quest means a desired movement from being corporeal object controlled by oppressive and essentializing forces to becoming a complex conveyor of cultural meaning, with a complex and creative identity. . . . This subjectivity is understood as complex in that it seeks to hold in tension many ontological possibilities, a way of existing in numerous spaces of identification as opposed to reified notions of identity that mark dehumanization.[38]

In other words, diasporic black persons have been subjected to a process of "thingafication,"[39] or reification, as varying socio-political, economic, linguistic, and theological structures sought to (re)create and "*fix*"[40] black people in an image created by white supremacy, with blackness conceived as the embodiment of subhumanity, and to use more theological language, sin. It is within this existential situation that black religion arises, which is "the creative struggle in history for increased agency, for a fullness of life."[41]

Pinn argues that black Christian appeals to being made in the "image of God" and the Nation of Islam's claims for "the black person as 'god'" are attempts at building a sense of "fullness" and meaning in the world.[42] He goes so far as to call this experience, this desire for complex subjectivity, a "mystical experience,"[43] reflective of that "deeper, elemental impulse, an inner stirring, that informs and shapes religion as practice and historical structure."[44] In essence, Pinn understands religious experience, this quest for complex subjectivity, as an answer to "the crisis of identity that constitutes the dilemma of ultimacy and meaning."[45] I argue that this framework of complex subjectivity provides a helpful lens through which to discuss Baldwin's relationship to black religion.

However, we must be careful in utilizing the language of "subjectivity," for I am not signifying what scholar Ashon Crawley calls the "liberal logics of subjectivity,"[46] or what he names elsewhere as that "perfectable" and "enclosed subject."[47] For he is correct, as articulated in his work *Blackpentecostal Breath: The Aesthetics of Possibility*, in a section on Immanuel Kant, that the subject/subjectivity is rooted in the "aversion" to, and the fleeing of, the social.[48] He states, "Kant's theory of Enlightenment was founded upon the escape from sociality and sociability. . . . The scholar, the philosopher, *the subject* would emerge when that individual thinks for himself without the aid of others."[49] Black religion, however, is always and already about a movement into/toward the social, as will be shown in Chapter 5. Therefore, it would be more appropriate to speak of complex *asubjectivity*, which Crawley defines as "the subjectivity in the commons, an *a*subjectivity that is not about the enclosed self but the open, vulnerable, available, enfleshed organism."[50]

According to Baldwin, the human is "resolutely indefinable [and] unpredictable." He adds:

> In overlooking, denying, evading his complexity—which is nothing more than the disquieting complexity of ourselves—we are diminished and we perish; only within this web of ambiguity, paradox, this hunger, danger, darkness, can we find at once ourselves and the power that will free us from ourselves.[51]

Therefore, in centering the complexity of the human (and we will see in Chapter 4 that Baldwin's understanding of "the human" needs to be thoroughly interrogated), persons can find the "power" to free themselves from the myopic visions and identities which are placed upon them. Baldwin then argues that "this power of revelation," the power to show humanity who it truly is as complex (a)subjects, "is the business of the novelist," and one could argue the artist in general.[52] Utilizing the framework of Pinn, Baldwin's work and public "witness" should be conceived as a religious quest, for he is seeking to create a world in which humans are free from the confines of fixed identity constructs

It is also important to note that in examining Baldwin's literature as articulating a distinct religious critique and vision, I will be in conversation with black theological discourses. However, I am using "theology" in a very specific, and indeed unconventional way. I return again to Anthony Pinn and his work *Varieties of African American Religious Experience*:

> . . . theology is deliberate or self-conscious human construction focused upon uncovering and exploring the meaning and structures of religious experience within the larger body of cultural production. . . . Conceived in this way, African American theology's only obligation, then, is the uncovering of meaning and providing of responses to the

questions of life that explain experience, assess existing symbols and categories, and allow for healthy existence.[53]

In other words, Pinn understands theology as a means for exploring the "meaning and structures," the "symbols and categories," of varying "quests for complex subjectivity"—i.e., various expressions of religion.[54] Therefore, inspired by Pinn's distinct take on theology, this project is not a constructive theology, nor is it "comparative"[55] as is Pinn's in *Varieties*. It is, in fact, exploring Baldwin's *theological* "responses to the questions of life." This is not "god-talk" proper, and it will be shown later that theology as an academic and often confessional enterprise cannot adequately *hold* Baldwin, but this book moves through and is influenced by theological discourse in seeking to explicate the *meaning* and liberating potential of Baldwin's vision for those on the margins of, or outside of, traditional religious spaces, whether due to transgressive religious identities (black skeptics, agnostics, humanists, or nontheists), or because of nonnormative sexual or gender identities and expressions (i.e., queer and trans persons). However, this book's relationship to theology remains intentionally unsettled, and this work must examine Baldwin and black religion with and, to borrow Crawley's phrase, *"against* theology."[56]

An (A)theological Paradigm

As previously stated, this book stands at the intersection of black theological and black religious studies discourses, deploying a hermeneutic stemming out of queer theory. In a similar fashion to works written in the traditions of black and womanist theologies and black religious studies, I, like Baldwin, am concerned with exploring black life as source material for teasing out black religions' role in bolstering or hindering the cause of black liberation and survival in an anti-black world. However, Baldwin's work, and praxis of disidentification, also provides an opportunity for engaging black theological and religious studies in a *queer* fashion, transgressing the bounds of what Ashon Crawley, in his work *Blackpentecostal Breath: The Aesthetics of Possibility*, calls "categorical distinction" that stalks under the surface of theology as a discourse.[57]

Teasing out the meaning of this phrase, Crawley raises the question, "what does it mean—to riff on, and thus off, Immanuel Kant—to orient oneself in thinking . . . *theologically* and *philosophically*?"[58] In answering this question, Crawley claims that these two modes of inquiry, theology and philosophy, are the product of an epistemological striving for "pure thought" / "pure difference" that arose with modernity.[59] Crawley states:

What does it mean to place oneself into a conceptual zone and category of distinction and think from such a "place"? How does thought emerge from that which has been deemed, a priori, a categorically distinct modality of thought? And just what desires for purity undergird such a drive toward thinking from the categorically distinct zone? Air, the impure admixture, had to be let out of thought, had to be evacuated. . . . The possibility for distinction that is categorical, that is in the end pure, is the *problem* of Enlightenment thought. Pure difference. This is what theological and philosophical thought attempt to achieve.[60]

In other words, Crawley is pointing out that the Enlightenment project was/is an attempt "to organize knowledge,"[61] generating categorical distinction / "pure difference"[62] through the *exclusion* of that which was/is deemed "other," or "*other* thought."[63] Therefore, this Enlightenment drive to categorize, to create zones of pure difference, is according to Crawley, "the grounds for racism, sexism, homo- and transphobia, classicism and the like."[64]

Crawley gives special attention to race, positing that in the Enlightenment, the categorical distinction that is race was thought and produced *out of* theological and philosophical discourses, a reality of which Baldwin was particularly aware and will be discussed in Chapter 2 of this work.[65] Crawley claims:

In a word, provocative though it may be: to think theologically, to think philosophically, is to think racially. It is to produce thought through the epistemology of western constructions. To attend to the necessary antiblackness of raciality is to summon us to be attentive likewise to the necessary antiblackness of theological-philosophical thought.[66]

In other words, theological and philosophical paradigms utilized aesthetic markers of blackness, framed as "an entire range of sensual experiences—sound, smell, touch," in demarcating blackness as the marker of "pure difference" and as "other"—i.e., as radically distinct from, and deficient to, whiteness.[67] Therefore, because categorical distinction is the modern western[68] enterprise, then theological discourse, as an Enlightenment project, participates in creating and maintaining racial/categorical distinction.

Crawley raises the question: If theology participates in the creation of the categorical distinction that is racialization, can one theorize about blackness and black life from the "zone" of the theological?[69] In answering this question, Crawley explores the notion of the "blues body" as articulated by Kelly Brown Douglas in her work, *Black Bodies and the Black Church: A Blues Slant*. According to Crawley, Douglas interrogates the lives of "blues women," arguing that "the blues body, the black woman body, is a disruption to notions of civility and decorum; the more this body performs its wildness—the more one accepts one's conditions of fleshiness—the more disruptive and in need of coercive control."[70] That control is rendered through the respectability politics that continue to plague the black church.[71] It is here that Crawley raises the question of whether the blues (and hence blackness) can be examined *within* the discourse of theology.[72] The aesthetic markers of blackness, including "sound," were conceived as "pure difference" (read distinct from and deficient to whiteness) through theological and philosophical discourses. So how can those same discourses be used to interrogate the blues, and benefit from assimilating the blues into its project? Crawley asks, "How is theology antiblack, and, thus, antiblues?"[73] He continues:

> Blues are nonnormative, and Douglas's blues bodies would be likewise. Such that if the blues does anything—and Douglas's attentiveness to the refusal of distinction between sacred and secular in the songs and lives of blues folks is instructive—it compels us to rethink the efficaciousness of the categorical distinction. That is, Douglas ends up reproducing the logic of exclusion by forcing the blues into to the hermeneutic work of theology . . . [74]

To put it slightly differently, the blues, in and of itself, is "a critique of the capacity to make something theological, which is to say the capacity to make the pure distinction, the purely different."[75] Blackness, reflected in what Crawley calls "black tone,"[76] is "a destabilizing force against the project of racial purity, of aesthetic distinction,"[77] which in turn makes blackness a destabilizing force in theological discourse.

Again, in a fashion similar to Crawley, this book explores black religion with and "*against*" theology."[78] To read against theology is to imagine the study of black religion and theological discourse "otherwise" than theology's role in bolstering normative Christian claims and in creating and maintaining the categorical distinction. By otherwise, I am pointing to Crawley's understanding of "otherwise possibilities." Crawley offers:

> Otherwise, as word—otherwise possibilities, as phrase—announces the fact of infinite alternatives to what *is*. And what *is* is about being, about existence, about ontology. But if infinite alternatives exist, if otherwise possibility is a resource that is never exhausted, what *is*, what exists, is but one of many.[79]

Thus, *Jimmy's Faith* is a work of theoretical "possibility," of articulating alternatives to "what *is*," for it moves in, with, and against theology as a discipline in pushing the boundaries of "what counts . . . [as] theological thought."[80]

I am reading against dominant forms and understandings of doing theology which seek to delimit the boundaries of theology as a "pure discourse," as "pure thought," which presumes the hard and fast distinction between its discourse/discipline and others. In essence, I want to trouble the lines of distinction and disrupt disciplinarity. This quote from Crawley is helpful in highlighting the questions that I hope to raise through my engagement with Baldwin's literature:

> . . . if the sacred/profane split is a result of enlightened thought, that split is also always racialized, gendered, classed, sexed. But if dualism is actually *not*, if categorical distinction of sacred from profane is unsettled through otherwise epistemologies, then what is thought that can be considered categorically as "theological" over and against other modalities of thought? If theology is "god talk," as is often colloquially offered, but talk in blackness is never categorically distinct or pure, what does it mean to do, think or be theology or theological?[81]

Therefore, this book is an interdisciplinary work in such a way as to blur the lines of distinction between pure thought, pure modes of thinking the theological and the religious. As Crawley states, "Imagination is necessary for thinking and breathing into the capacities of infinite alternatives."[82] Therefore, *Jimmy's Faith* is a work of the imagination, a project which seeks to "think" and "breathe" theology and black religious studies "otherwise."

However, and most importantly, apart from the methodology undergirding this project, I will show that Baldwin's queering of religious symbols and language, and his narration of characters who queerly exist both within and outside traditional religious bounds, is *also* a clear example of Crawley's "otherwise possibilities." Baldwin's disidentification with, and queering of, religious language and symbols muddies the purity of categorical distinctions, for Baldwin's praxis is simultaneously theological and "*a*theological," philosophical and "*a*philosophical,"[83] and proceeds to trouble other categories of pure distinction, including those of white / black, Christian / non-Christian, saved / unsaved, heteronormative / queer. Baldwin pushes the boundaries of religious language, stretching theological symbols in such a way as to tear at their fabric, creating a porosity which allows an "impure admixture"[84] to contaminate the purity of the categories. For despite Baldwin's disavowal of Christianity and its god, he understands religious symbols to bear an "energy,"[85] an energy able to shift and change culture, an energy able to support and sanctify complex expressions of the human person, especially those vilified and marginalized within US American culture. Baldwin is, in fact, seeking to imagine religion "otherwise," and his method of doing so has the potential to reshape how we understand black religion, or perhaps even gesture toward the religion that is blackness.[86] *Jimmy's Faith* is an attempt to examine the shape of Baldwin's vision.

Organizational Structure

Through an examination of *The Amen Corner* and *Just Above My Head*, Chapter 1 will explore James Baldwin's disidentification with Christian conversion. In *The Amen Corner*, Baldwin "transfigures" or "recycles" the meaning of conversion from signifying a person's dedication to the Christian faith and community, to more appropriately denoting the necessity of leaving Christianity in pursuit of a truly loving mode of being.[87] While in *Just Above My Head*, conversion is reinterpreted through the medium of queer sexual expression, which simultaneously sanctifies queer sexuality, while also marking the sex act as a generative space for reimagining god, the sacred, and salvation. In essence, Baldwin consistently returns to the experience of conversion, not in an attempt to bolster the Christian faith, but in disidentifying with its symbols, he seeks to imagine both religion and the world "otherwise."

Chapter 2 will examine Baldwin's disidentification with notions of "people-hood." In order to do that, we must first engage Baldwin's understanding of white identity—a political, theological, and discursive creation that links racial whiteness with Christianness.[88] In addition, Baldwin claims that as whiteness created itself, it also required/needed the simultaneous creation of a racialized "Other," understood in modernity as the Negro/the nigger, a "fantasy" of the white "Christian mind."[89] Therefore, as Baldwin sets out to deconstruct white notions of peoplehood in relation to a kind of pristine Christian identity, he also seeks to radically reassess, if not undermine, normative understandings of the Negro, for Baldwin clearly recognized that the Negro functions as a theological construct, one conflated with "evil . . . sin and suffering."[90]

However, Baldwin does not stop at examining white Christians and their alterity creating[91] practices. The second portion of Chapter 2 engages Baldwin's critique of the ways in which black sanctified churches also create a kind of (theological) identity and community in relation to an Other, a "sinful" and "unredeemed" Other.[92] In other words, Baldwin is keenly aware of the ways in which understandings of salvation and sanctification served as the means by which a sense of peoplehood was established in the Christian community of his childhood, while at the same time that identity was knit together in opposition to an Other, those conceived as being in need of Jesus's saving work. For

Baldwin, this form of alterity creation, this exclusivism, was a truly death-dealing and life-denying reality, for to be "unsaved" in Baldwin's community was to exist in a deficient mode of being. Although both white and black expressions of Christianity reveal a tendency toward alterity-creating practices, there are very real differences between the outcomes of those practices. Yet, Baldwin feels compelled to confront this tendency within black and white expressions of Christianity in his attempt at dismantling the fictive notions of color, salvation, and "divine peoplehood."[93]

Lastly, building on the work of Ed Pavlić and Ashon Crawley, I will show that, rather than rooting notions of black peoplehood in the logics of race or theology, Baldwin grounds black communal identity in *tone*—what Pavlić calls "a tonal narrative"[94] and Crawley a "black tone."[95] In other words, black art broadly, and black music in particular, somehow, mysteriously, provides the avenue through which black community is created and a genuine sense of peoplehood established, for it is in black sound and song that the narrative of black suffering and joy is communicated and shared.

Chapter 3 explores Baldwin's message of hope, which I argue is centered in his oft-repeated notion, borrowed from the Christian tradition, of "the New Jerusalem."[96] However, before exploring Baldwin's understanding of hope, Chapter 3 will first examine the underside of Baldwin's optimism, which is the struggle of, and for, black existence in a world of white supremacy. In other words, Baldwin's language of hope must be framed in relation to the possibility of black despair, articulated in one place as the threat of "suicide, or death , or madness."[97] Baldwin's 1964 piece, "The Uses of the Blues," is essential for understanding Baldwin's notion of despair, for in it the blues serves as a "metaphor" for the "pain" and "anguish" of black existence in an anti-black world.[98]

In light of this struggle against black despair, Baldwin offers a vision of hope through the language of "the New Jerusalem" and other similar variations on this general theme. He is disidentifying with this Christian eschatological symbol, queering it in such a way as to signify his vision of a world made new, a world defined by justice. In order to understand the meaning of Baldwin's disidentification with this eschatological symbol of "the New Jerusalem," we must understand its meaning in the Christian scriptures, in addition to Jürgen Moltmann's understanding of eschatology as rooted in the notions of "hope" and "promise."[99] Lastly, Chapter 3 will explore Baldwin's "metaphor" of "the kid" or "the child"[100]—the black child to be exact[101]—for in conversation Josiah Ulysses Young's work *James Baldwin's Understanding of God*, which was essential in pointing out "the hopes [Baldwin] had for the next generation,"[102] I will build on, and extend, Young's argument in showing that the black child is the one who must usher in "the New Jerusalem," a world set free from the confines of militarism, white supremacy, and cisheterosexism.[103] This is clearly seen in Baldwin's essays, but also his novels *Tell Me How Long the Train's Been Gone* and *If Beale Street Could Talk.*

Baldwin's disidentification with the category "Man"[104]/the human being will be examined in Chapter 4. However, unlike previous chapters, most of Chapter 4 is committed to exploring the ways in which Baldwin *fails* to disidentify with the dominant understanding of "Man" in the West. Baldwin's failure to disidentify with "Man" stems from his "universalizing impulse,"[105] which privileges what is "shared" between humans in opposition to that which marks humans as different.[106] The work of queer theorist Matt Brim reveals how Baldwin's universal human is, potentially, "nothing," a "meaningless" construct that "moves in a dangerous direction."[107] However, Chapter 4 will move beyond Brim, for through an engagement with the work of Sylvia Wynter it will become apparent that Baldwin's human is far from "nothing," but in fact presumes a troubling gender binary reflective of what Wynter calls the "descriptive statement" of the human found in the West.[108] Therefore, Baldwin's literature displays a deeply sexist capitulation to a definition of the human already established by US American culture's "descriptive statement," its understanding of "Man."[109]

Chapter 4 will then turn toward an in-depth analysis of Baldwin's problematic ideas concerning masculinity, women, and the feminine in his literature. Baldwin is consistent in arguing that the emasculation of the black man is the most damaging outcome of white supremacist oppression in the black community.[110] With that, Baldwin consistently presents femininity as a space of deficiency, a space that black men must emphatically reject in a reclamation of their manhood. The chapter then moves into an examination of Baldwin's public dialogues with Nikki Giovanni and Audre Lorde, for they offer the strongest pushback to Baldwin's misogynoir. We end the chapter by raising the question of whether Baldwin's misogynoiristic worldview was challenged and changed in any way by the critiques of black feminists late in his life. In answering that inquiry, we will explore one of Baldwin's final essays "Freaks and the American Ideal of Manhood." In it, he engages in a radical troubling of, and disidentification with, gender norms, as he calls for a profoundly queer gender expression—the "androgynous."[111]

The fifth and final chapter will examine Baldwin's disidentification with "god," while refusing to place Baldwin within the thought world of Christian theological discourse. Baldwin, apophatically, refuses to engage in god-talk, going so far as to consistently argue that god is a construct of the human imagination.[112] What Chapter 5 will demonstrate is that Baldwin's understanding of the sacred should be understood as a kind of *mysticism*, one committed to the deeply sensual experience of an "unnamed"[113] *something*.[114] Baldwin's mysticism is a matter of *feeling* or affect[115]—feeling in the sense of a deeply embodied experience, as opposed to belief in god. This chapter will first examine why Baldwin rejects the construct "god," followed by an exploration of the unique mysticism of Baldwin's thought, putting Baldwin into a substantive conversation with the affective, aesthetic, and agnostic black mysticism or mysticism "otherwise"[116] of Ashon Crawley. What will be demonstrated is that Baldwin's mysticism, like that of Ashon Crawley, is in fact about *sociality*.[117]

1

Jimmy's Queer "Threshing-Floor":[1] Transformation and the Role of Disidentification in Baldwin's Fiction

James Baldwin's famous conversion experience, recounted in *The Fire Next Time* and fictionalized in *Go Tell It on the Mountain*, has rightly received considerable attention from religious studies scholars and literary critics, for it highlights Baldwin's dramatic entry into the world of black Christianity. In *The Fire Next Time*, Baldwin describes falling under the influence of a divine power, bringing about an intense feeling of "anguish" that he describes as "the strangest sensation I have ever had in my life—up to that time, or since."[2] It was this moment of conversion, at the age of fourteen, which would serve as the pivotal event of his young life, an event which would forever change his relationship to the Christian church and the world.

As previously mentioned, Baldwin scholars have rightly noted the importance of conversion for both Baldwin's life and literary output. Clarence Hardy, in *James Baldwin's God*, argues that Baldwin "brought the initiation rite of conversion to the center of his critical and artistic reflections."[3] In a similar fashion, Douglas Field posits that "this experience of conversion, I would suggest, had a profound effect on Baldwin's writing; the experience on the threshing floor is described without irony and there is an acknowledgement of the power of the Holy Spirit."[4] Even Michael Lynch, an early commentator on Baldwin and religion, posits that "Baldwin's whole career is a meditation on the meaning of conversion."[5] Thus, in order to understand Baldwin's relationship to the Christian religion and the ways in which he disidentifies with and queers black religious rhetoric and symbols, we must begin with what might be called a theological foundation of Baldwin's religious vision—the experience of conversion. In this one event, which Hardy calls Baldwin's "fixation,"[6] Baldwin paradoxically sees both the "promise"[7] and failure of the Christian faith, while holding in it a mystical possibility that human beings can indeed change—can in fact "be better than we are."[8]

After a brief examination of the historic roots of the conversion experience in African American Protestantism and its importance in the life and literature of Baldwin, this chapter will engage a select number of Baldwin's fiction works including, but not limited to, *The Amen Corner* and *Just Above My Head*, to show the ways in which Baldwin continually returns to this early religious experience, disidentifying with and queering the theme of conversion.[9] In *The Amen Corner* conversion is, to borrow Muñoz's language, thoroughly "transformed," "rethought," and "re-formed."[10] Traditionally, conversion marks the start of a new convert's life of faith and introduction into the Christian community. However, Baldwin reimagines true conversion/salvation as the rejection of Christian beliefs and the church, for a life found outside the confines of a restrictive religion, a space where true love can be experienced and expressed. In *Just Above My Head*, conversion/transformation is "recircuited" or "reconstructed"[11] as Baldwin reveals black and queer sexuality as holy (repositioning/revaluing queer bodies as sites of religious meaning), and as a site for experiencing the sacred and salvation.[12] In essence, Baldwin lays the groundwork for a novel religious vision. These symbols, now reimagined, take on new theological meaning and life, ceasing for all intents and purposes to be "Christian," but reflecting a reimagined black and truly queer religious worldview.

Conversion as the Foundation for Baldwin's Religious (Re)Imagination

As Hardy makes clear, the conversion experience has played an important role in the history of African American Protestantism.[13] Its roots reach back to the antebellum period as, according to Albert Raboteau, white Christian missionaries, and to a lesser extent planters, sought to justify the colonization and enslavement of African peoples under the guise of missionizing "the heathen."[14] Raboteau demonstrates that, although initial attempts at missionizing enslaved Africans "was blocked by major obstacles," (due to early resistance on the part of planters out of fear that baptism would alter the status of the enslaved and/or create "rebellious" slaves) with the arrival of the "revivalist" sentiments of the so-called "Great Awakening" enslaved Africans began to increasingly embrace Christianity.[15] Within this historic moment of revival, Raboteau shows that the newfound emphasis on the "*experience*" of conversion came to the fore,[16] a phenomenon marked by "the *experience* of conviction, repentance, and regeneration."[17] This move away from an understanding of conversion as being a matter of "literacy and religious learning," "a process of careful nurture and slow growth" as articulated by groups like the Anglicans, to an *experience* of conversion, brought enslaved Africans quickly into the fold of "salvation," and led to increased conversions among enslaved African peoples.[18] This evangelical tradition, rooted in the experience of conversion, would become and remain a significant, if not the predominant, foundation of black Protestantism in the United States. Hardy states:

> Even where a singular conversion experience was not emphasized, black religious communities still placed a high importance on the palpable immediacy of sacred presence and the acceptance of various forms of religious ecstasy that the metered singing, preaching, and rhythms of folk liturgical life often helped to engender. These aspects of black worship life demonstrate the extent of evangelicalism's sway on nearly all practitioners of Afro-Protestantism.[19]

This is also true of the sanctified/Pentecostal tradition within which Baldwin would come of age, one which sometimes blended the rite of conversion with ecstatic religious experiences.

According to Baldwin biographer David Leeming, Baldwin converted to the Christian faith within the Harlem ministry of "Mother" Rosa A. Horn.[20] Horn's ministry, in particular, is essential for understanding Baldwin's relationship to the Christian church, for although as a child, according to Hardy, Baldwin sometimes attended the Abyssinian Baptist Church with his father,[21] he would have his famous conversion experience (recounted in *The Fire Next Time* and dramatically retold through the character John Grimes in *Go Tell It on the Mountain*) as a result of Horn's ministry. Therefore, it was Horn and her particular black Pentecostal religious tradition that would mark Baldwin's religious experience, and his time as a young preacher, in the black church.[22]

Horn's church community, the Mount Calvary Assembly Hall of the Pentecostal Faith Church, was part of a tradition of black Christian faith conceptualized by Cheryl Sanders under the banner of the "Sanctified church," which includes "Holiness, Pentecostal, and Apostolic churches.[23] Although the churches encapsulated under this banner hold to divergent theological beliefs, they are, according to Sanders, all marked by the identity of being "saved, sanctified, and filled with the Holy Ghost."[24] This identity was bestowed largely through the rite of conversion and the ecstatic experience of being "filled" with the Holy Spirit. According to Sanders:

> To be saved means that one has repented, asked forgiveness of sins, and confessed Jesus Christ as Savior and Lord. This experience

imparts a basic "entry level" of liturgical identity that distinguishes the
saint from the unbeliever. To be sanctified is to receive some second
form of blessing that conveys upon the believer a distinctive ethical
identity of being set apart for God, literally to be made holy.[25]

These two movements are present in Baldwin's recounting of his conversion
experience—both the acknowledgment of the Lordship of Christ and the
second movement of being filled with the Holy Spirit with the goal of being
"made holy."

In *Go Tell It on the Mountain*, Baldwin offers a dramatic portrayal of his
own conversion experience. At the novel's opening, we meet fourteen-year-old
John Grimes on his birthday, which also turns out to be the day of his conversion to the Christian faith.[26] Baldwin, too, would begin what he called "a prolonged religious crisis" during the summer in which he turned fourteen.[27] This
"crisis" was a struggle for identity, acceptance, and love—for on the one hand,
John/Baldwin had the church, the community of saints called to live a holy
and "set-apart" life over and against the world (in Baldwin's religious community, "holiness" included sexual repression and the rejection of all forms of
artistic expression not directly connected to the church).[28] On the other hand,
John/Baldwin was inwardly pulled toward the arts, particularly music, plays,
movies, and works of literature.[29] Thus, he was plagued by feelings of guilt over
his "sinful" and "depraved" nature.[30] John, like Baldwin, found himself on that
day brought under "the power of the Lord" on the floor of the church.[31] The
narrator states, "And something moved in John's body which was not John. He
was invaded, set at naught, possessed."[32] The event itself is retold as having
taken place both in front of the worshippers witnessing and praying over the
prostrate body of John, but also in sight of John's ancestors and untold others
who are bearing witness to this child's entry into the religious community.[33]
Hardy highlights that this conversion moment is, in fact, "a ritual of 'becoming'
and adulthood before an expectant religious community," and scholars such
as Keri Day note that in Pentecostal worship, particularly in tarry services like
the one John attended, conversions are a communal affair, "midwifed" by the
broader community.[34] John rises from the floor of the church, empowered to
a new life as a Christian.

Even in this moment of seeming triumph in *Go Tell It on the Mountain*,
there is an uncertainty as to the effectiveness of this conversion moment. John
himself, when speaking to Elisha, who is also the object of John's burgeoning
adolescent queer desires, states: "'Elisha,' he said, 'no matter what happens to
me, where I go, what folks say about me, no matter what *any*body says, you
remember—please remember—I was saved.'"[35] This view is supported by literary

critic Michael Lynch, who also understood the conversion narrative in *Go Tell It* as "ambiguous," for John "feels profound doubts about his ability to pursue his artistic vocation in the church."[36]

Years after the publication of *Go Tell It*, in *The Fire Next Time* Baldwin explicitly problematizes this conversion experience. Rather than marking his entry into a community which would love and embrace him, Baldwin came to realize that his hope for community was based on a lie. Not only was the Christian god not a loving being, but the community itself was a community marked by a palpable fear that often translated into suspicion and intolerance for the "Other," and any and all considered to be outside of the fold of the sanctified community.[37] In addition, and this will be discussed at length in Chapter 2, for Baldwin, conversion ushers black Christians into what Hardy calls a "symbolic universe" in which their very own blackness is conflated with sin, depravity, and evil.[38] For Baldwin, black "self-hatred" becomes the very ground upon which Christian identity is constituted.[39] The failure of the conversion moment lay in the fact that the experience promised transformation, yet the domestic violence of his ordained father, the community's suspicion of those outside the fold of the tradition, and the repressive sexual atmosphere of the religious community all attested to the fact that true transformation had not materialized.[40]

Despite Baldwin's ultimate rejection of his personal experience of conversion, I would argue that much of Baldwin's literary corpus is an attempt to deal with the promise and failure of this ecstatic moment. Baldwin, in his articulation of a moral vision for a society unable to contend with its own violent history of racial injustice and repressed sexual desire, is searching for a means to bring about the transformation[41] and redemption promised by the religious ritual.[42] Baldwin states, "If I were still in the pulpit which some people (and they may be right) claim I never left, I would counsel my countrymen to the self-confrontation of prayer, the cleansing breaking of the heart which precedes atonement."[43] And although he goes on to say that "this is, of course, impossible," for conversion is not possible *en masse*, the potential for transformation remains an ever present possibility in Baldwin's corpus.[44] Although Baldwin problematizes Christian conversion, he still finds the symbol and language efficacious for articulating his moral vision.

Therefore, rather than counteridentifying with the symbol of conversion, Baldwin takes that very symbol and disidentifies with it, giving it "new life"[45] and reimagining it in ways that make visible and create possibilities for black queer modes of being and alternative ways of creating and glimpsing change within culture. The remainder of this chapter will be dedicated to this purpose, offering a brief snapshot into the ways in which Baldwin disidentifies with and queers Christian symbols, particularly conversion, through his fictional characters, with the goal of pulling out of those stories distinct themes of a Baldwinian religious expression. This glimpse into Baldwin's work is far from comprehensive and will only offer a summary and introductory exploration into Baldwin's disidentificatory practice, which will receive further explication in the coming chapters.

The Amen Corner:
Calling, Conversion, and Salvation Reimagined

According to literary critic Michael Lynch, Baldwin's play *The Amen Corner* should be read as the conclusion of the narrative that Baldwin began with *Go Tell It on the Mountain.* Lynch believes that Baldwin wanted to clarify the ambiguous ending of *Go Tell It,* firmly establishing the fact that the tentative conversion of John at the close of the novel could not last within the confines of his repressive Christian community.[46] Lynch states, "Baldwin knew that John would not be able to remain in the church indefinitely any more than he would be able to stay for long in his stepfather's house after acquiring a fundamental affirmation of his worth and identity from the Lord."[47] In other words, and I am in agreement with Lynch, *The Amen Corner* brings *Go Tell It on the Mountain* to a close, powerfully showing John's fate through the character David and his inevitable departure from the church. It is in examining the meaning of David's departure that we can begin to see the ways in which Baldwin takes a number of Christian theological symbols—"calling," "conversion," and "salvation"—and turns them on their heads. In essence, Baldwin disidentifies with these theological symbols, putting forth the idea that true conversion and salvation require leaving the church for the higher call of love and/or the world of black artistic expression.

The Amen Corner is the story of a small, sanctified black church and a pastor fighting to keep her family and congregation afloat. The church itself is inspired by the church in which Baldwin first converted to the Christian faith, and the lead character Margaret was inspired by the Harlem Renaissance figure, "Mother" Rosa A. Horn.[48] In the play, Baldwin juxtaposes the "sanctified," yet conniving and manipulative elders of the church with the "backslidden" David and "sinful" Luke. The character Margaret, for most of the play, remains in the camp of the "sanctified," only to be "saved" at the play's end through the evangelistic witness of Luke. At the beginning of the play, Margaret's and David's lives are turned upside down by the return of Luke, Margaret's husband and David's father, who was estranged from the family when David was still a young child. According to both the elders of the church and Margaret, Luke stands as a dramatic symbol of "the world," for he is a trumpet player in a jazz band and a man known for his willingness to indulge in "worldly"/sinful acts. Luke, although debilitated by sickness throughout most of the play, signifies the threat of the non-Christian life, a life that both Margaret and the church members fear that David, a talented musician like his father, will soon enter.

Baldwin's framing of allegedly sinful persons such as Luke as threatening to the religious community is a historic reality in sanctified church spaces, for the sanctified churches of Baldwin's Harlem were, in fact, obsessed with keeping their members pure from the "poisons" of worldliness. According to Cheryl Sanders, not only were sanctified churches marked by a particular theology which stressed the utmost importance of "the experience of Spirit baptism," but that act of spiritual empowerment enabled parishioners to live out an "ascetic ethic," one devoid "of alcohol, tobacco, and other addictive substances, gambling, secular dancing and the wearing of immodest apparel," to name only a few of its moral prohibitions.[49] In a sermon entitled "What is Holiness? A Complete Life in Christ," Horn, who is, again, the inspiration for the main character Margaret, discusses sanctification, stating:

> Now then, we are born again, washed and circumcised—converted, cleansed, sanctified. After we have been converted we must be sanctified and set apart from the world of sin; card-playing, dancing for the devil, telling lies, joking, hatred, malice, strife, heresy, busy-bodies always meddling in other men's matters, trouble-makers, truce-breakers, false accusers, respect of person, swearing, jealousy, back-biting your neighbors, and all other uncleanness, as mentioned—tobacco is also an unclean habit.[50]

In the play itself, Margaret's conflict with Brother Boxer over his desire to gain employment driving an alcohol delivery truck, which Margaret forbids as sinful, signifies the stringent nature of holiness morality within black sanctified churches.[51] Margaret, in the play's opening sermon, states:

> This way of holiness is a hard way. I know some of you think Sister Margaret's too hard on you. She don't want you to do this and she won't let you do that. Some of you say, "Ain't no harm in reading the funny papers." But children, *yes*, there's harm in it. While you reading them funny papers, your mind ain't on the Lord. And if your mind ain't stayed on Him every hour of the day, Satan's going to cause you to fall.[52]

Baldwin's critique of, and disidentification with, the sanctified church arises in the midst of this ascetic cultural milieu, which fuels his particular condemnation of the Christian faith as a religion obsessed with "safety."[53]

This brings us now to the character Luke who allows us to see Baldwin's disidentifying praxis come to the fore. In my reading, Luke's character serves as a paradoxically evangelical figure, a man answering a type of "Macedonian call" to aid his wife and son as their lives stand on the precipice of change and transformation.[54] As mentioned previously, Luke's return marks a moment of existential upheaval for both Margaret and David. On the one hand Margaret soon comes to face a threat to her leadership from the elders of the congregation who resent her authoritarian rule. David, on the other hand, hears the call of the streets, the call of the world of black music and artistic expression which begins to pull him away from the church. Luke returns to usher Margaret and David into these spaces of transformation; or to put it slightly differently, Luke returns with a Baldwinian message of good news, one which sparks Margaret's and David's conversion to a new mode of existence. Therefore, Luke serves as the bridge which takes Margaret and David away from the life-denying space of the church into the very world which the church fears.

What is the content of Luke's message? In essence, Luke seeks to convert[55] Margaret and David to his blues-inflected "religion of love."[56] In a fashion reminiscent of New Testament declarations of the good news, Luke must first confront Margaret with the truth of her spiritual need: it is not, in fact, he that needs "saving," but she. Baldwin captures the bitter irony of Luke's and Margaret's confrontation in this scene:

> Margaret: I can't do no more. Before God, I done my best. Your blood can't be required at my hands.
> Luke: I guess I could have told you—it weren't *my* soul we been trying to save.[57]

The meaning of salvation is being thoroughly queered at this moment. Baldwin could have chosen to reject the symbol of "salvation," wholly problematizing the category in and of itself. However, he instead chooses to disidentify with the symbol, bending and stretching its meaning in such a way as to reveal Margaret's "lost" mode of being. *Margaret is lost not in spite of her Christian identity, but because of it.*

The play later reveals that Margaret's "lost" state of being stems from the traumatic death of her unborn child years before the narrative of the play takes place.[58] Margaret is convinced that the death of her and Luke's child was punishment from god for their "godless" lifestyle, a life of happiness marked by their deep love for one another and also their lack of any explicit religious commitments. Margaret states, "We'd been living like two animals like—like two children, never thought of nothing but their own pleasure. In my heart, I always knew we couldn't go on like that—we was too happy."[59] Later, Margaret laments:

When they laid my baby in the churchyard, that poor little baby girl what hadn't never drawn breath, I knowed if we kept on a-going the way we'd been going, He weren't going to have no mercy on neither one of us. And that's when I swore to my God I was going to change my way of living.[60]

Again, Margaret believes that her lifestyle with Luke left god with no other choice than to kill their unborn child, a drastic yet necessary action meant to save their souls.

Margaret's god, which is the very god with whom Baldwin would fight and question in his own life and literature, is a vindictive god who is willing to kill children in order to maintain a person's loyalty. The depths of this troubling theology in Margaret's life and ministry are also seen in her inter-action with the character Mrs. Jackson who comes to the church asking for prayer for her sick child at the beginning of the play.[61] After questioning the woman, Margaret learns that Mrs. Jackson's husband is not in good standing with the church.

> Margaret: Maybe the Lord wants you to leave that man.
> Mrs. Jackson: No! He don't want that!
> (Smothered giggles among the women.)
> Margaret: No, children, don't you be laughing this morning. This is serious business. The Lord, He got a road for each and every one of us to travel and we is got to be saying amen to Him, no matter what sorrow he cause us to bear. (To Mrs. Jackson) Don't let the Lord have to take another baby from you before you ready to do His will.[62]

This god, the god of both Margaret and the young Baldwin, is indifferent to and/or the cause of human suffering. Baldwin would later explicitly discuss this god in The Fire Next Time, stating:

> And if one despairs—as who has not?—of human love, God's love alone is left. But God—and I felt this even then, so long ago, on that tremendous floor, unwillingly—is white. And if His love was so great, and if He loved all His children, why were we, the blacks, cast down so far? Why?[63]

Baldwin is making it clear that in the void left by a lack of human love, like the void left in Margaret's life by the death of her child and her subsequent abandonment of her partnership, one is left with few options, one of which is to fill that void with the love of god.[64]

However, for Baldwin, the decision to exchange the love of human beings for the love of god is a trap—for to love this god requires the death of the self. Margaret is, in fact, lost. The loving woman she once was died in her pursuit of the love of god.[65] This exchange between Margaret and Luke highlights Margaret's loss of self after the death of her child and her decision to give her life to the church:

> Margaret: Luke. That's all past. (*She sits on the edge of the bed.*) Luke, it been a long time we ain't seen each other, ten long years. Look how the Lord done let you fall. Ain't you ready to give up to Him and ask Him to save you from your sins and bring peace to your soul?
> Luke: Is you got peace in your soul, Maggie?
> Margaret: Yes! He done calmed the waters, He done beat back the powers of darkness, He done made me a new woman!
> Luke: Then that other woman—that funny, fast-talking, fiery little thing I used to hold in my arms—He done done away with her?
> Margaret (*Rises*): All that's—been burned out of me by the power of the Holy Ghost.[66]

This "new woman," reflective of Margaret's status as "saved, sanctified, and filled with the Holy Ghost"[67] is transfigured in Baldwin's religious imagination, being revealed as a tragic mode of being, signifying the loss of one's ability to love both the self and the other. The Margaret that once lived has been "burned out" by the Holy Spirit, along with the love she had for Luke, leaving only a toxic religion and "tyrannical" faith.[68]

Baldwinian salvation requires that Margaret reject the false love of the vindictive god of her faith and return to the loving arms, not of her savior Jesus, but of her partner Luke. Luke attempts to remind Margaret of this reality, pointing out that their marriage, their partnership, was rooted in their love for one another, not their love for god. Luke truly believes that their love was salvific, and that their love for each other was all that was necessary to save their souls:

> Luke: Maggie, don't fight with me. I don't want to fight no more. We didn't get married because we loved God. We loved each other. Ain't that right?
> Margaret: I sure can't save your soul, Luke.
> Luke: There was a time when I believed you could.[69]

Tragically, Margaret comes to see that Luke was right, but only just before he succumbs to tuberculosis. Her love for Luke, the love that Margaret believed the Lord had "burned out," had never truly died. Luke's return, and Luke's challenge to her, opened the door for Margaret to embrace that dormant love which was the key to her salvation. Margaret exclaims, "It's an awful thing to think about, the way love never dies!"[70] Yet, that awful love of which she speaks is the only reality that makes life worth living. Margaret, through the witness of Luke, has come to see that she had, in fact, "throwed away [her] life," that it was not the Lord who needed her love, but her son and partner.[71] Margaret's new confession of faith, *her moment of conversion*,[72] only comes when she is able to reconnect to that repressed love for her partner. She states, "Maybe it's not possible to stop loving anybody you ever really loved. I never stopped loving you, Luke. I tried. But I never stopped loving you."[73] In this moment Margaret has indeed found herself and her salvation. Baldwin states:

> Her triumph, which is also, if I may say so, the historical triumph of the Negro people in this country, is that she sees this finally and accepts it, and, although she has lost everything, also gains the keys to the kingdom. The kingdom is love, and love is selfless, although only the self can lead one there. She gains herself.[74]

Moving now to a discussion of the character David, we find in David's narrative of leaving the faith a story most like Baldwin's own.[75] Unlike Luke who never converted or embraced the Christian religion, or Margaret who leaves the church and church leadership but maintains some semblance of Christian faith, David lives most of his life steeped in the church, only to have a moment of extreme crisis in which he comes to embrace nonbelief as a mode of being. As stated previously, per Michael Lynch, David should be read as an extension of John in *Go Tell It on the Mountain*. Thus, it should be assumed that David was a young man of deep belief (at least early on), yet always unsure of whether he would be able to remain in the church and pursue his call to the arts. In a conversation with his father, the last conversation they would have, David recounts his journey away from the Christian faith:

> David: A few months ago some guys come in the church and they
>   heard me playing piano and they kept coming back all the time.
>   Mama said it was the Holy Ghost drawing them in. But it wasn't.
> Luke: It was your piano.
> David: Yes. And I didn't draw them in. They drew me out. They setting up a combo and they want me to come in with them. That's when I stopped praying.[76]

David continues on, arguing that as he stopped praying, something both "terrible" and "wonderful" began in him, and he began to "see" the "church—like

I was seeing it for the first time." Although David is not specific as to what he "saw" in the church with this newfound sight, what is clear is that this sight, this revelation if you will, caused a sudden rupture in his faith commitments. There is shocking abruptness to this change, for David states in regard to his faith: ". . . I stopped believing—it just went away."[77]

It is important to note, yet again, that Baldwin is disidentifying with the conversion experience in this play, for we see all the hallmarks typically found in narratives of conversion—"evangelism" (the musicians and Luke coming to deliver a message); "conflict" (the "terrible" and "wonderful" change David speaks of); "repentance" (David's claim that he saw "for the first time"); and "a new life of faith" (discipleship in the world of black art). In addition, the category of "calling" is particularly important here. Within the Christian symbolic universe, "calling" can refer to a distinct sense of god's call to a particular ministerial work. However, for David, this calling is the world of black music.[78] Luke reflects on the gravity of this call to music, stating: "Music's what you *got* to do, *if* you got to do it."[79] The play shows clearly that music is exactly what David *has* to do, and it is that world of music that pulls David away, giving him the ability to see the church for what it is, and what it is not.

Shifting slightly from David to Baldwin himself, Baldwin's biography makes clear that he, too, was called away from the church by the lure of the arts. He recounts the beginning of the destruction of his faith: "It happened, as things do, imperceptibly, in many ways at once. I date it—the slow crumbling of my faith, the pulverization of my fortress—from the time, about a year after I had begun to preach, when I began to read again. I justified this desire by the fact that I was still in school, and I began, fatally, with Dostoevski [sic]."[80] It is also not by chance that on the day that Baldwin left both his ministry and church behind, he "tip-toed" out of the church to attend a Broadway matinee with his best friend.[81] What Baldwin ironically refers to as a "leap," a leap of faith *away* from the Christian faith, was accompanied by a newfound commitment to center the rest of his life on being a writer.[82] Thus, we see here one primary theme which shall be revisited in Chapter 2 of this book: the world of artistic expression does in fact serve as a space of *religious* meaning and value in Baldwin's work.[83] Baldwin's disidentification with conversion is not simply about signifying the movement out of the black church, but it seeks to reveal a movement into that space where black life bubbles over—the world of black art, particularly black music. As Douglas Field notes:

> Baldwin's writing on music points to the transformative qualities of music, a force all the more powerful for being not only democratic (jazz clubs, streets, records) but also an experience that can be shared.

Although his writing about the transformative powers of music is written in a suggestively spiritual way, Baldwin hints through his iconoclastic character, Luke, that spirituality need not be restricted to the church.[84]

In many ways, music, for Baldwin, as shown through the characters Luke and David, comes to signify what religion *could* and perhaps *should* be. Clarence Hardy argues that for Baldwin, "it is music that sanctifies religion and not religion that sanctifies music."[85] Literary critic Saadi Simawe makes a similar claim, arguing that, as opposed to religion, "music" is "the only medium that constantly eludes the reach of repression" in Baldwin's view.[86] Therefore, music in *The Amen Corner* is a reality not unlike religion.

As with religion, one is called to the arts, or perhaps even fated, for Baldwin speaks of the musician as one who has a message to give to the world. David's call to the sacred task of music is clearly seen in this statement to his mother:

> If I stayed here—I'd end up worse than Daddy—because I wouldn't be doing what I know I got to do—I *got* to do! I've seen your life—and now I see Daddy—and I love you, I love you both!—but I've got my work to do, somethings happening in the world out there, I got to go! I know you think I don't know what's happening, but I'm beginning to see—something. Every time I play, every time I listen, I see Daddy's face and yours, and so many faces—who's going to speak for all that, Mama? Who's going to speak for all of us? I can't stay home. Maybe I can say something—one day—maybe I can say something in music that's never been said before. Mama—*you* knew this day was coming.[87]

As stated earlier, David is a reflection of the character John in *Go Tell It on the Mountain*, and in that novel, during John's conversion, John experienced a vision of the masses: "They were the despised and rejected, the wretched and the spat upon, the earth's offscouring; and he was in their company, and they would swallow up his soul. . . . And their dread testimony would be his!"[88] It is safe to assume that David is speaking of these very same masses when he claims to have seen "so many faces."[89] David's calling, this need to bear witness, is not to be given through the religion of the church, but through the religious medium of music. David must share his gift with the world, and he must share the story of black life through his piano. Thus, through David's choice to leave the confines of the Pentecostal church, the religion of the institutional church is shown to be lesser than the religion of the arts. As Simawe claims, ". . . music in *The Amen Corner* becomes the only religion worth practicing, primarily because it lends full expression to the deepest human desire and feeling."[90]

However, before bringing this section to a close, it is important to note that although Luke and David are, and come to be, positioned outside of the church and Christianity, Margaret seemingly remains a Christian, even as she leaves the confines of the institutional church. Margaret's final sermon to her congregation illustrates this point:

> Children. I'm just now finding out what it means to love the Lord. It ain't all in the singing and the shouting. It ain't all in the reading of the Bible. (*She unclenches her fist a little.*) It ain't even—it ain't even— in running all over everybody trying to get to heaven. To love the Lord is to love all His children—all of them, everyone!—and suffer with them and rejoice with them and never count the cost![91]

Baldwin is not writing off Christianity wholesale in this play, for Margaret's character reveals the possibility of maintaining faith in the Christian god while embracing a life of freedom and love. In other words, one can be both a disciple of Jimmy's gospel, and Jesus's. However, Baldwin seems unrelenting in his claim that Christian or not, a life of freedom and authenticity can only be discovered outside of the confines of the institutional church.[92] It is not by chance that Margaret's salvation must be ushered in through the witness of the "sinful" character Luke, again reflective of Baldwin's disidentifying reversal.[93] Josiah Ulysses Young, in *James Baldwin's Understanding of God*, posits: "Baldwin thus stages an ironic development. Salvation is at work between Luke, a dying, 'heathen' musician, and his son who wants to play jazz like his father. Condemnation is at work in the church above them, where the saints scorn Sister Margaret's holy, miserable life."[94] As Baldwin states in an interview with Margaret Mead: "So, in my case, in order to become a moral human being, whatever that may be, I have to hang out with the publicans and sinners, whores and junkies, and stay out of the temple where they told us nothing but lies anyway."[95] Hence, Baldwin is again signifying that "salvation"/conversion must come through the act of leaving the church.

Sexual Rebirth in *Just Above My Head* and *If Beale Street Could Talk*

In Baldwin's final novel, *Just Above My Head*, he offers what might be the most complete portrait of his gospel,[96] one in which the flesh of black queer bodies introduces his audience to a new understanding of the ecstatic moment of conversion—found not only in the song of the black community, but also in the sexual expression of black queer persons with one another. One scene in particular highlights Baldwin's disidentification with conversion, provocatively mingling the lyrics of a well-known spiritual with an erotic scene of queer sex.[97] El Kornegay, in his work *A Queering of Black Theology: James Baldwin's Blues Project and Gospel Prose*, also engages this scene in his chapter entitled: "Conversion: Queer Theory and Black Theology." Kornegay's interpretation of the theological richness of this moment served as an inspiration for my own reading of this sexual encounter in *Just Above My Head*, and I will spend some time later explaining how my own reading differs from his in significant ways. It is also important to note that scholars such as Douglas Field rightly state that "while a handful of critics have noted how Baldwin infuses his descriptions of sex with religious language, little work has been done on this important area."[98] This section will attempt to engage that "important area" by offering a type of deep reading of the scene, highlighting the ways in which Baldwin disidentifies with and queers conversion and the sacred in this moment of queer sexuality. In addition, other sexual encounters from both *Just Above My Head* and *If Beale Street Could Talk* will be examined.

At a pivotal moment in *Just Above My Head*, one finds the book's protagonist Arthur Montana, the gospel singer who later becomes a soul singer, as a teenager who is about to engage in his first sexual encounter with his best friend Crunch, who is also a singer in the traveling quartet to which they both belong. In a fashion similar to, though markedly different from, *The Amen Corner*, Baldwin frames this moment as a type of religious experience, a conversion— one which contains confession, an encounter with the sacred, terror and deliverance, and a born-again newness to life. The confession of this religious experience is initiated as the two characters find themselves in an empty room, suddenly faced with the naked bodies of the other.[99] This nakedness is new and serves as a confession in that this moment of nakedness, unlike all others before, speaks a sexual truth about their queer subjectivity that had not previously been known.[100] In Christian theology, confession speaks to the need for human beings to bring an unvarnished truth to the surface. Oftentimes, that confession is related to some concealed sin. However, this particular confession, which Baldwin is narrating, speaks to Arthur and Crunch's queer desire, which is not sinful in Baldwin's estimate, but is in fact salvific.[101] Again, it is their nakedness *together* that is the confession, and it is nakedness that Baldwin argues must be "received" by the other, welcomed and embraced or rejected and "despised."[102] Kornegay offers a similar take on the meaning of "nakedness" in this scene, positing:

> Self-discovery happens in nakedness. In *Just Above My Head*, Baldwin, writes about how nakedness is transformed when nakedness as a presentation, an offering of an uncloseted, unclothed body coupled with

sexual desire is an invocation of the sacred. For example, Baldwin identifies nakedness via the initial sexual interaction between the characters Crunch and Arthur, as a "confession" or a "vow."[103]

Returning to the sexual encounter, Baldwin narrates that the room is charged with an erotic and spiritual energy, which leads to an encounter with the sacred, one provocatively initiated by Arthur's licking and taking of Crunch's penis into his mouth (perhaps reminiscent of the receiving of the Eucharist into one's mouth).[104] However, before proceeding to discuss the sacred, it is important to note that in Christian theology and practice the confrontation with the self that comes with confession is often accompanied by fear and terror,[105] the realization of who one *truly* is in the sight of god. In other words, confession sometimes requires a reckoning with the sin and depravity that marks one's life. This queer moment of confession bears some of the hallmarks of Christian confession, for although Crunch and Arthur are not concerned with the supposed "sin" of their lives, the terror of openly expressing their queer subjectivity to one another is almost too much to bear. As Arthur begins to fellate Crunch, this moment of confession is marked by the accusing voice of an "enemy." That enemy is not the voice of Satan, as is often found in Christian theology, but the voice of internalized self-hatred, a type of queerphobia which taunts the young men with the aspersion "cocksucker." "Cocksucker" signifies for Crunch and Arthur a debased form of existence, a deficient mode of (queer) being only worthy of being despised.[106]

However, Crunch and Arthur overcome their fear together. Baldwin states:

> He had never done this before. In the same way that he knew how Crunch feared to be despised—by him—he knew, too, that he, now, feared to be despised by Crunch. *Cocksucker.*
>
> Well. It was Crunch's cock, and so he sucked it; with all the love that was in him, and a moment came when he felt that love being trusted, and returned. A moment came when he felt Crunch pass from a kind of terrified bewilderment into joy. A friendly, a joyful movement, began. *So high, you can't get over him.*[107]

In this moment, with the juxtaposition of a well-known gospel song with the sexual encounter, we see Baldwin's queering of conversion and the sacred through his method of disidentification.[108] The lyrics of the song, as recorded by Baldwin, state: "So high, you can't get over him. . . . So low . . . you can't get under him. . . . So wide. You can't get around him. . . . You must come in at the door."[109] Powerfully, what once signified the height, depth, and width of god's love and god's transcendent nature, is now being deployed to signify, not only the overwhelming nature of Crunch's flesh,[110] but the height, depth, and width of their expression of love, a black queer love.[111] This moment of fellatio can only be described as a conversion, one marked by a startling encounter with the sacred that brings about a transformation.[112] The sacred, for Baldwin, *is* the other, *is* the flesh of another human being, and in Baldwin's religious imagination, one does not have to look *beyond* the act of sexual expression to encounter that which gives human life meaning. Sexuality, queer sexuality, reveals that which is larger than the individual and yet requires the individual, it is the touchpoint for the sacred rooted in human relationships.[113]

Baldwin is also clear that this moment is transformational, a *true* conversion. Just as the apostle Paul's encounter with the risen Christ on the road to Damacus forever changed his life, Arthur's lovemaking with Crunch "was setting Crunch free."[114] At the moment of sexual climax, both Crunch and Arthur were forever changed. Baldwin states:

> Curious, the taste, as it came, leaping, to the surface: of Crunch's prick, of Arthur's tongue, into Arthur's mouth and throat. He was frightened, but triumphant. He wanted to sing. The taste was volcanic. This taste, the aftertaste, this anguish, and this joy had changed all tastes forever. The bottom of his throat was sore, his lips were weary. Every time he swallowed, from here on, he would think of Crunch, and this thought made him smile as, slowly, now, and in a peculiar joy and panic, he allowed Crunch to pull him up, upward, into his arms.
>
> He dared look into Crunch's eyes. Crunch's eyes were wet and deep *deep like a river*, and Arthur found that he was smiling *peace like a river*.[115]

Both of these young men experienced spiritual transformation. This "peace like a river," taken from the song "I've Got Peace Like a River," is typically understood as a peace that only comes when one's heart and mind are saved in the sight of god. However, Baldwin is communicating here that peace and joy, a peace that can only be described as sacred and "salvific," can only be found in the other.

Baldwin reiterates the transformational possibility of Crunch's and Arthur's lovemaking in a description found later in the novel. He posits:

> They were beginning to know each other; the biblical phrase unlocked itself and held them together in a joy as sharp as terror. Crunch lay on his belly for Arthur and pulled Arthur into him, and Arthur lay on his belly for Crunch, and Crunch entered Arthur—it was incredible that it hurt so much, and yet, hurt so little, that so profound an anguish,

thrusting so hard, so deep, accomplished such a transformation, *I looked at my hands and they looked new, I looked at my feet and they did, too!* But that is how they sang, really, something like fifteen minutes later, out of the joy of their surrender and deliverance, out of their secret knowledge that each contained the other.[116]

Again, Baldwin is highlighting the salvific nature of their sex. Arthur feels "new," one could say "born again," which is a direct outgrowth of his willingness to "surrender" himself to his partner, and his partner to him.[117] Douglas Field makes a similar point in arguing that "Baldwin's most radical rewriting of Christian—or at least spiritual identity—can be found in his emphasis on salvation and redemption."[118] That "salvation and redemption," which Field also notes is framed in "the language of religious conversion," comes about through "touch."[119] He states:

Baldwin's emphasis on "touch" is both physical and spiritual, suggesting being moved (to be touched) but also the physical act of reaching out to another. By emphasizing the physicality of touch, Baldwin continues his critique of the way in which American Puritanism prohibits and inhibits both bodily and spiritual contact, what he explicitly refers to as the damage caused by "a fear of anybody touching."[120]

As stated previously, theologian El Kornegay in his book *A Queering of Black Theology: James Baldwin's Blues Project and Gospel Prose,* offers a similar reading of Arthur and Crunch's lovemaking as revealing the significance of sexuality as a religious experience in Baldwin's corpus. It is important to pause now for a brief examination of Kornegay's claims, for he understands Baldwin's life and work as generative for queering the Christian faith broadly (including conversion), and black theological discourse in particular, and highlighting the differences in our interpretations of this scene will provide a helpful means of illuminating what Baldwin is, and is not, communicating in *Just Above My Head.*

In Kornegay's work, he seeks to place Baldwin into conversation with the discourse of black liberation theology,[121] and he argues that Baldwin is, in fact, Christian, seeking to rid the faith of a "puritanism" which has corrupted US American Christianity broadly, and black Christianity in particular, with its anti-black and anti-sexual ethos.[122] According to Kornegay, in order to recover the truth of the Christian tradition for black persons, Baldwin deploys "gospel prose," which is reflective of Baldwin's ability to take the black Christian "vernacular" of the church and "signify on" it toward "the reconciliation of sexuality with faith."[123] Through Baldwin's "gospel prose," Kornegay attempts to offer black theology a "hermeneutic of queer semiotics." In defining this hermeneutic, he claims:

> I define a hermeneutic of queer semiotics as a hermeneutic that is
> used to interpret sexuality, gender, and race as the signs and symbols
> of social constructions through which power is deployed in order to
> maintain nonnormative identities and gives the hermeneut the ability
> to create new interpretation where none is readily apparent. In this
> context, I interpret the blues, emerging from my study of Baldwin, as
> a hermeneutic of queer semiotics that gives new voice and meaning
> to sexualized and racialized bodies (a new hermeneutic) in liberation
> theology.[124]

Thus, Kornegay seeks to offer a new method for queering black theology, a means of providing "new interpretation[s]" of the discourse through a centering of "nonnormative" sexual and racial bodies.

Again, Kornegay's queer semiotics is built on his engagement with Baldwin's "gospel prose." Therefore, in teasing out the meaning of Baldwin's "gospel prose," Kornegay examines the ways in which Baldwin engages Christianity and its god, both "allegorically" and as "a form of Signifyin(g),"[125] drawing a distinction between "metaphor," which "creates permanent likenesses,"[126] and "allegory," which "is extended metaphor: meaning that is not permanently affixed to that which it is being likened."[127] Metaphor, according to Kornegay, has been weaponized against black bodies, particularly through a "heritage"[128] concerning the subhuman nature of black people—i.e., "metaphorical blackness."[129] However, allegory allows Baldwin to reimagine god and Christianity apart from the oppressive images offered by the tradition/metaphors of puritanism. According to Kornegay:

> Baldwin's allegorical consciousness represents a psychological complex
> of race, sex, religion, culture, and politics constituted by the tension
> held between the poles of his dark puritan imagination and his black
> body. His allegorical defense is a psycho-sexual-religious rebellious
> protest against his black inheritance and puritan American heritage.[130]

Thus, Baldwin's "allegorical defense" reveals dominant "metaphors of oppression" as "mere signs"[131] that do not represent the truth of what is being signified—the truth that is blackness, the truth that is god, and the truth that is the Christian faith.

Kornegay's understanding of signification moves along a similar register, defined as "verbal misdirection," a concept borrowed from the work of Charles Long, "rhetorical strategy," taken from the scholarship of Charles I. Nero, or a "closed language of tradition," an understanding of signification put forward by Henry Louis Gates, Jr.[132] Kornegay argues that Baldwin utilizes that "closed language" in an attempt to revise what Christianity means.[133] Kornegay posits:

> Baldwin uses the power of black (religious) vernacular to revise what Christianity means in the context of black (blues) life. Baldwin shifts the power of (black) Christian discourse toward a new meaning: a signification that carries with it the moral authority needed to define blackness and the gospel on its own terms: this is what I call black religious vernacular.[134]

This black religious vernacular is a common language that is "understood by those in the church and in the street,"[135] and it is by means of this signification, this theological revision through black religious vernacular, that Christianity is able to be "reinvested" with its liberatory potential.[136]

In addition, Kornegay offers an intriguing take on "queering conversion." He argues that blackness "is a condition of queerness,"[137] due to "its archetypal Otherness (otherness by way of Christian conversion), which is based on ex- amples of human qualities not to be emulated."[138] In other words, "blackness" functions "as the sign of racial, sexual, social, economic, and religious abnor- mality"[139] and therefore "everything that comes in contact with blackness is itself queered: this includes black theology and conversion."[140] As will be shown later, I am in agreement with Kornegay and others such as Roderick Ferguson, who point out the inherent queerness of blackness. However, what is most important is how Kornegay links this queerness to Christian conversion.

Kornegay goes on to discuss how black Christian conversion, particularly during the period of enslavement, "meant slaves were literally baptized into depravity."[141] In other words, he is pointing to the ways in which, as Clarence Hardy has noted,[142] Christian conversion pulls black people into a "symbolic universe"[143] rooted in "shame, not hope,"[144] or what Kornegay calls "abnormal- ity," or "the colonial abnormalities made opaque by the traditional understand- ing of the Christian experience of conversion."[145] However, according to Kornegay, conversion is "queered" in the literature of James Baldwin. He states:

> In the works of James Baldwin, conversion can be likened to transfor- mation, in that the primary outcome of any cultural-religious en- deavor should transform the person and their god(s) into becoming larger, freer, and more loving. It is therefore a way of signifying on conversion: exposing the gaps between what it means figuratively and what it actually is. As such, Baldwin writes in (queer) ways that incite

the conversion of blues people into something larger, freer, and more loving than a nonqueered understanding of black Christian conversion allows: this is his use of the blues, and at least a partial outcome of black theology when it is queered in this way.[146]

Therefore, Baldwin's "queering conversion liberates black bodies from depravity,"[147] and the "metaphors of oppression" mentioned earlier. In other words, "queering conversion becomes a method or system for normalizing blackness: racially, sexually, religiously, and theologically. In the case of Baldwin, normalization is an act of removing the concept of depravity as an abnormal condition."[148] Kornegay views this as a conversion that understands the "messiness" of black lives, the very thing used to mark them as "depraved" via puritanical "metaphorical blackness," as the source of salvation/the encounter with God.[149]

It should be apparent that my reading of Baldwin's queering of conversion has some similarities with Kornegay's, for I, too, note the ways in which Baldwin reimagines conversion in such a way that centers those typically understood to exist outside the church—i.e., those (to borrow Kornegay's language) deemed "depraved," as showing the true meaning of transformation and the sacred. In addition, this book is in agreement with Kornegay in pointing out the ways in which Baldwin "allegorically defends" against anti-black metaphor[150] and signifies on black religious language and symbols. In fact, disidentification can be read as a type of signification, and signification as at type of disidentification, in that both can entail forms of "misdirection" and allegorical reimagination.[151] However, Kornegay's misstep lies in his thorough baptism of Baldwin's corpus, for he reads Baldwin as a Christian prophet seeking to save both the tradition and its god from the shackles of puritanism. Kornegay argues, "Baldwin is not in tension with or absconding any portion of his religious heritage: he is in tension with puritanism and is using black religious allegory to overcome sublimation of the black body."[152] In other words, Kornegay does not take seriously Baldwin's need to disidentify with Christian language and symbols, for I argue that Baldwin is not deploying the symbols in an attempt to revalorize the tradition, but he is engaging the symbols in creating an *alternative religious vision*, one which riffs on the traditions and common meanings of the symbols, while also creating possibilities for queer "worldmaking" and "survival"[153] through the reimagining of those same symbols.

One example of Kornegay's error, which also reveals the primary difference between my work and his, can be seen in the manner in which he interprets the aforementioned sexual encounter between Crunch and Arthur. As stated previously, Kornegay's interpretation has important similarities with my own, for he, too, makes special mention of how nakedness functions in the narrative, and he discusses the sexual encounter in relation to the theological categories of "conversion," "revelation of the sacred," "confession," and "vow."[154] Kornegay offers:

> In this (homo)sexual encounter nakedness becomes a confession of desire and vow of love. Amidst the "miracle of air, entering, coming out, into your face, mixed with Pepsi-Cola, hamburgers, mustard, whatever, was in the bowels . . ." the revelation of God's creation, God's life-giving divine nature is made evident. . . . Baldwin makes this interaction a sacred act and the body a vessel for the revelation of the sacred. He deftly collapses notions of the sacred and profane when he writes:
>
> > Arthur's tongue licked [Crunch's] sacred balls—*you can't get under him*. Arthur rose, again, to Crunch's lips. *So wide. You can't get around him*.
>
> Baldwin takes what is deemed depraved—the body and sexuality, more pointedly homosexuals *having* sex—frames and pairs it with a Negro spiritual thereby infusing it with spiritual messiness, *the blues*, to expose a spiritual humanness that is a direct reflection of the image of god. *Imago Dei* becomes exposed in the worship, communion, with the "sacred balls" (and/or sacred pussy walls) of another. *The act of fucking is sacramental!* . . . Sexual intercourse becomes the conduit for divine revelation and access to the power of God.[155]

In this same section, Kornegay offers that "Baldwin makes this interaction [between Arthur and Crunch] a sacred act and the body a vessel for the revelation of the sacred," while also stating that "this is the true revelation of the divine whereby that which created us in its own image is reimagined/recreated in the sexual intimacy between bodies."[156] Kornegay is correct in his claim that "fucking" is often sacramental for Baldwin, in addition to his argument that Baldwin is framing the sexual exchange between Crunch and Arthur as a revelatory act that reveals the "sacred." However, Kornegay's reading falls short in his attempt to name Baldwin's praxis, which I argue is a disidentifying praxis, as consistent with and buttressing normative Christian theological constructs such as the "Imago Dei."[157] In other words, "God" in Kornegay's treatment, remains the normative Christian god.[158] Kornegay does not take Baldwin at his word, as reflected in Baldwin's strong rejection of Christianity and its understandings of god. Baldwin is attempting to disrupt normative constructs of the sacred and god, locating the sacred wholly in the flesh. In other words, rather than disidentification, which reimagines a phenomenon, bringing forth something new, Kornegay understands Baldwin as *identifying with* Christianity, framing Baldwin as a reformer committed to the tradition, all while trying to save it.

To put it slightly differently, Kornegay mistakes *what* the sacred *is* in this moment. Crunch, and his balls and shaft are literally divine, holy, and of ultimate worth, and not mere approximations of the sacred. *They are the sacred.* Crunch and Arthur's lovemaking brings about a conversion, a radical change, not because their bodies become a conduit for the salvific work of the Christian god, but because their black flesh, freely given to one another in this moment of erotic vulnerability, mysteriously brings about a life-altering transformation, in and of itself. Capital G "God" is not needed or necessary in this moment, for the love of human beings for one another brings about a transformation that Christian conversion fails to replicate. Again, the decision to trade the love of human beings for the love of god is a trap, a trap which ensnared Margaret in *The Amen Corner*, for it is only the love of the other that can change us.[159]

Yet, this is not the only moment in *Just Above My Head* that highlights the salvific nature of sex. Baldwin also uses this language in relation to an encounter between the characters Crunch and Julia. Julia being the one-time child evangelist who suffered violent sexual abuse at the hands of her father. The description of their sexual encounter is rich with theological meaning:

> She murmured his name again with an unbelievable exultation, he pulled up, thrust down again and again, harder and harder and deeper and deeper, she laughing and crying and calling his name and pulling him always deeper into her—almost as though his lunging body would touch and open and drench and heal her soul. He, as it were, prayed with her, longing to give her all that she needed. . . .[160]

Later, when this moment of "prayer" concludes, Crunch asks Julia how she feels, to which she responds, "Saved."[161] Douglas Field in his work, *All Those Strangers: The Art and Lives of James Baldwin*, argues that for Baldwin, "Julia's true conversion begins with her relationship with Crunch, a sexual act that explicitly heals and transforms her."[162] Julia, who had, at this point in the novel, already walked away from the ministry and the church, was *saved* by this intimate exchange with Crunch, set free to new life, a life which had been violated by her father.

Elsewhere, in *If Beale Street Could Talk*, we see yet another example of Baldwin's disidentification with and queering of "conversion" and "salvation." *Beale Street* recounts the love story of two young black people—Fonny and Tish—who face the impending birth of their child in the midst of seeking justice against a corrupt police officer who framed Fonny for rape. One moment in particular, the first sexual encounter between Fonny and Tish, is especially relevant for this discussion. As Fonny and Tish make love for the first time, Tish states that Fonny's "body became sacred"—his "buttocks," "chest," and "thighs."[163] As their lovemaking intensifies, Tish describes "something absolutely new" beginning in them both, as she "strained to receive it all, all, all of him."[164] When the moment has passed, Tish describes the event using theologically explicit language:

> Well, we were something of a sight. There was blood, quite a lot of it—or it seemed like a lot to me, but it didn't frighten me at all, I felt proud and happy—on him and on the bed and on me; his sperm and my blood were slowly creeping down my body, and his sperm was on him and on me; and, in the dim light and against our dark bodies, the effect was as of some strange anointing. Or, we might have just completed a tribal rite. And Fonny's body was a total mystery to me—the body of one's lover always is, no matter how well one gets to know it: it is the changing envelope which contains the gravest mystery of one's life.[165]

In essence, for Tish, the sexual encounter resulted in a type of sacramental anointing, or what Trudier Harris calls a "sexual conversion," one which sealed their love for one another as a "sacred" event.[166] Harris, in *Black Women in the Fiction of James Baldwin*, states: "[Fonny] guides Tish through sexual initiation, and he is responsible for the change she undergoes, the religious conversion in the creation of their love religion. He initiates the action, calms her fears, baptizes her, and brings her forth anew."[167] In the essay "The Eye as Weapon in *If Beale Street Could Talk*," Harris makes a similar claim: "Fonny and Tish, then, are thus converted into an unbreakable union with each other—to love and to save (figuratively and literally) each other by loving. . . . Fonny and Tish will look to no other source, save a human one, for whatever they may need."[168] The transcendent mystery of this moment was not the mystery sometimes called god, but the material *body* of the other. The rest of their lives will be spent searching out the "mystery" of the other.[169]

What is it about these sexual acts that make them sacramental touchpoints for the sacred? This brings us back to the orienting paradigm of Baldwin's life and work—love. As Field states, ". . . it is love, often sexual, but infused with spirituality, that Baldwin insists upon, what he refers to in *Blues for Mister Charlie* as 'the holy and liberating orgasm.'"[170] For Baldwin sex, in and of itself, is not sacramental, for sex devoid of the acknowledgment of the humanity of the other is utterly empty. Field supports this claim in arguing, "Baldwin's emphasis on the sanctity of spiritual/sexual love is clearly distinguished from sexual gratification."[171] The character Hall Montana, in *Just Above My Head*, in a passage also noted by Field, reflects Baldwin's critique of empty sexual encounters: "I had one girl after another. But if there's no future for you, if fucking doesn't become something more than fucking, then you have to forget it. And then you're worse off than you were before."[172] However, love expressed through the mutual recognition of the humanity and sacredness of the other *is* sacramental in and of itself. This is not sentimentality[173] or "romantic love," nor is it an appeal to a type of "love" language which Roger Sneed argues is deployed for the purposes of "policing" and "normaliz[ing]" queer sex.[174] Baldwin is, by no means, arguing that one has to be "in love" with a person in order to experience sex as ultimately meaningful (for Crunch was not "in love" with Julia), but Baldwin is clear that one must honor the humanity of the other, and that act, in and of itself, is holy. As Baldwin states in *The Devil Finds Work*:

> To encounter oneself is to encounter the other: and this is love. If I know that my soul trembles, I know that yours does, too: and, if I can respect this, both of us can live. Neither of us, truly, can live without the other: a statement which would not sound so banal if one were not endlessly compelled to repeat it, and, further, believe it, and act on that belief.[175]

Therefore, to love another person through the materiality of sexual expression is to experience a conversion, a transformation. Baldwin claims that in loving another person, "the world changes then, and it changes forever."[176] He goes on to say:

> Because you love one human being, you see everyone else very differently than you saw them before—perhaps I only mean to say that you begin to *see*—and you are both stronger and more vulnerable, both free and bound. Free, paradoxically, because, now, you have a home— your lover's arms. And bound: to that mystery, precisely, a bondage that liberates you into something of the glory and suffering of the world.[177]

This change and transformation is not simply personal, but the radical confrontation with the truth and the vulnerability required in the sex act holds a key to larger social transformation. To be converted through the medium of love is to come to the recognition of the sacred humanity of the other, which bears the potential to disrupt "the trap of color,"[178] patriarchy, and cisheterosexism.

Conclusion

What one sees in this chapter is Baldwin's continued concern with the transformational potential of the conversion experience. However, Baldwin reads that transformational possibility as something much larger than what conversion to Christianity could possibly capture, for it comes to symbolize, for Baldwin, the radical confrontation of human beings with themselves, their fears, and the other, making possible the experience of new life and genuine change. In order to reimagine conversion as potentially liberating, Baldwin had to disidentify with the symbol, thoroughly queering its common usage in such a way as to make forbidden modes of being and actions the very spaces out of which conversion is possible (i.e., the blues/jazz and (queer) sexual love).

It is also important to note that queerness, in and of itself, is not salvific for Baldwin. Ashon Crawley is right in pointing out that "he [Baldwin] didn't romanticize nor make heroic the pursuit of blackqueer life, just elaborated as if it were one in many, one in infinite, ways that one could live life. And there's a devastating precision with which he writes."[179] In addition, Field notes that "Baldwin explores the tensions and dynamics between the spiritual and the sexual across multiple sexual identities—something not limited or constrained to a specifically queer sexual identity."[180] However, in Baldwin's choice to narrate and center queer characters, there is an implicit heroism, a certain audacity, being pointed to in queer sexuality. These characters, despite being ridiculed, persecuted, and violently "othered" in the United States, radically embrace the truth of who they are and who they desire, living into the life-transforming possibilities of sex and love. This, I argue, is the reason that queer sexuality features so prominently in Baldwin's literature, for queer sexuality requires courage in its expression and bold truth in its manifestation that other forms of sexual expression do not, a courage and truth that society should embrace if we are to create a more just world.

In addition, one should not discount the role of queerness—even in seemingly heterosexual exchanges in Baldwin's corpus. It would be easy to read the sexual encounters of Crunch and Julia, and Tish and Fonny, as heterosexual and heteronormative encounters, undermining my claim that queer sexuality plays a distinct role in Baldwin's corpus. However, as the scholarship of Roderick Ferguson has made clear (in addition to our previous discussion of Kornegay's understanding of the inherent queerness of blackness), black sexuality in the United States, even that understood to be heterosexual, has existed and continues to exist outside the bounds of heteronormativity, and is in some sense "queer" in and of itself.[181] Ferguson demonstrates that, in the history of the United States, black sexual, gender, and familial constructs have always been deemed "perverse," a troubling violation of the structure of white heteronormativity and the "American family ideal."[182] Ferguson states:

As figures of nonheteronormative perversions, straight African-Americans were . . . heterosexual but never *heteronormative*. This construction of African-American sexuality as wild, unstable, and undomesticated locates African-American sexuality within the irrational and therefore outside the bounds of the citizenship machinery. Though African-American homosexuality, unlike its heterosexual counterpart, symbolized a rejection of heterosexuality, neither could claim heteronormativity.[183]

It is also important to note Ferguson's claim about Baldwin's literature: "As Baldwin's work illustrates, white racial dominance 'others' African-Americans as 'queer' subjects, as people who exist somewhere outside of proper heterosexual interaction."[184] What this should make clear is that black sexuality is queer, and by centering the black sex act as a touchpoint for the sacred, Baldwin brings black queer sexuality to the center of his religious (re)imagination.

2

Jimmy's Communion: Race, Peoplehood, and the Tone of (Black) Community

In 1967, in a letter published in the journal *Freedomways*, Baldwin offered this powerful statement—"I would like us to do something unprecedented: to create ourselves without finding it necessary to create an enemy."[1] This challenge raises profound questions, for what does it mean to *create ourselves?* Why is it *unprecedented* to create ourselves without also creating an *enemy?* This concise, yet profound, statement captures a broader reality so utterly common, yet also unimaginably destructive. *This chapter is an extended examination of Baldwin's analysis of the violence out of which US Americans create their collective identities—their sense of peoplehood—and the ways in which those identities require the simultaneous creation of an enemy, an Other.*[2] What will become apparent is that the *us* to which Baldwin refers extends across racial bounds, for Baldwin recognizes that both white and black communities engage in alterity creation, building both racial and theological understandings of collective identity by means of marking the boundaries between *us* and *them*, those who are *in* and those conceived as existing *outside.*

In this chapter, we will first engage Baldwin's understanding of the creation of white collective identity, which he argues was birthed out of a theo-racial[3] logic that reached maturity in the age of colonialism. To put it slightly differently, what Baldwin clearly recognized was that at the historical "nexus" of encounter, colonization, enslavement, and commercialism,[4] European (and eventually white) Christians discursively, politically, and theologically created themselves, taking on a sense of peoplehood which inextricably linked their growing sense of racial whiteness with *Christianness.*[5] Thus, one of the primary aspects of Baldwin's thought is that whiteness is a theo-political[6] construct, a means of baptizing the power of one community over another.

However, Baldwin never discusses white identity without also showing that whiteness required the simultaneous creation of an Other, a *heathen* Other, a racialized Other, a people marginalized in relation to the body politic. In other words, white people *needed* the black, the Negro, the nigger, to bolster and build up white collective identity. The Negro, in Baldwin's estimate, is *also* a theo-political "creation," a fantastical product of the white "Christian mind."[7] There-fore, long before the rise of scholarship centered on the intersection of race and religion, Baldwin understood that the category / language / identity of the Negro must be radically reexamined and deconstructed, for stalking beneath the sur-face of racial blackness is a theology, one which conflates blackness with "evil . . . sin and suffering."[8] So, this chapter will not only discuss Baldwin's under-standing of whiteness (a signifier of Christianity *par excellence*), but it will also examine the mechanism, the oppositional identity, that made whiteness possi-ble—that of the Negro (which Baldwin shows signifies the heathen—a symbol of sin, evil, and depravity). To engage this topic, Baldwin will be put into con-versation with contemporary discourses on the subject of race and religion, particularly the scholarship of Kathryn Gin Lum and Sylvester Johnson, both of whom home in on the ways in which group identities, particularly racial and religious identities, become a means through which colonial power is exercised. Their work on theological and racial constructs such as "the heathen" and Ham-itic identity will be of particular importance to the project at hand.[9]

As mentioned earlier, the tendency to create group identities through the simultaneous creation of an Other extends across racial bounds. Therefore, the second portion of this chapter engages the alterity-creating practices of black Christian communities, for Baldwin adeptly shows the ways in which black sanctified[10] churches also displayed a potent exclusivism and the inability to accept, embrace, and—most importantly for Baldwin—love, those who dif-fered theologically, and those "sinful" bodies which violated the morality of these sanctified congregations. In other words, within black sanctified spaces, *the experience of salvation and sanctification served as the means by which peo-plehood was established, which, in turn, required the creation of an Other, those conceived as unsaved, unredeemed, in essence "sinful."* Although significant differences will be shown between the alterity-creating practices of white and black expressions of Christianity, both are confronted by Baldwin in his attempt to dismantle the artificial categories of difference rooted in what he understands to be the collective fictions of color, salvation, and "divine peoplehood."[11]

Lastly, after investigating Baldwin's critique of the ways in which groups seek to create themselves and the Other, we will close the chapter by showing how Baldwin disidentifies with the (theo)logic of peoplehood and grounds the meaning of black communal identity in a narrative of suffering and joy—a narrative communicated and cultivated through the medium of black art, and black music in particular. In other words, in conversation with the work of Ed Pavlić and Ashon Crawley, I will show that, rather than rooting notions of black peoplehood in the logics of race or theological notions of "salvation" and "sanctification," Baldwin seeks to show that black communal identity is a matter of *tone*—what Pavlić calls "a tonal narrative"[12] and Crawley a "black tone"[13]—for black music serves as the medium that brings the narrative of black suffering and joy to the surface, while also providing the connective tissue by which black lives are entangled in an authentic sense of communal identity. It will also be shown that this is not simply liberating for black bodies in the world, but in this black communal identity, located in the sound and rhythm of black music, white people are provided the opportunity to face, to borrow Eddie Glaude's language, "the lie"[14] that grounds white communal identity, a confrontation which might contribute to the slow crumbling of the mythos of whiteness and offer a way forward for "white" people to imagine peoplehood "*otherwise*."[15]

Whiteness and the Theology of Negro Identity

We will begin our examination of Baldwin's complex understanding of peoplehood by first discussing his provocative claim that "the Negro" is in fact a theo-political creation of the white Christian imagination.[16] It is important to note that I use the language of "the Negro" as a signifier for the "inferior status"[17] and negative forms of subjectivity that Baldwin critiques as being created by the white Christian mind. This is by no means a definitive claim as to how Baldwin viewed or used the term "Negro" at all times. As Michelle M. Wright points out in her essay "'Alas Poor Richard!' Transatlantic Baldwin, the Politics of Forgetting, and the Project of Modernity," the term Negro, at the beginning of Baldwin's literary career:

> . . . was beginning to acquire poignant political significations informed by (to name just a few) Richard Wright, Ralph Ellison, and the *négritude* writers. By 1948 the term *Negro* conjured up not only centuries of violent oppression and white hatred but active political, cultural, and social resistance to continued racial repression. In both popular and intellectual circles, *Negro* was a term that reclaimed "blackness" from the wholly derogatory attitudes with which it had been infused—quite consciously—by white segregationists and—we will assume, unconsciously—by those who championed integration, both white and black.[18]

However, Wright goes on to say that Baldwin, in "Everybody's Protest Novel," seems to use the term "Negro" as a means to "signify [the] Other," clearly seen in the "protest fiction" of Richard Wright and Harriet Beecher Stowe, a symbol of racial blackness that exists in the white mind.[19] This is similar to my use of "Negro" as a means of analyzing Baldwin's critique of the alterity-creating practices of white people, and throughout the rest of this chapter I will deploy the term to symbolize the oppressive forms of subjectivity (which Baldwin *sometimes* speaks of in terms of "the Negro") in juxtaposition to those reclaimed forms of identity which, Baldwin shows, black people have willingly embraced for the cause of their own liberation (i.e., "I'm black and I'm proud").[20]

In addition, Baldwin is not, by any stretch of the imagination, the first to raise these questions. Black people in the United States have always engaged in critical reassessments of the underlying meanings and histories surrounding the identifiers "black," "colored," "Negro," "Afro-American," etc. For example, Judith Weisenfeld, in her work *New World A-Coming: Black Religion and Racial Identity During the Great Migration*, offers an examination of what she calls "the religio-racial movements" which rose to prominence during the 1920s and 1930s in the United States. Groups such as the Ethiopian Hebrews, the Moorish Science Temple, and Nation of Islam attempted to radically reimagine, not simply the names, but the *meaning* of black racial identity, revalorizing and rerooting black identities in new theological histories/narratives.[21]

Philosopher Robert Birt is correct in positing that "every struggle for human liberation is invariably a struggle for a liberated identity."[22] Baldwin is searching for that liberated identity, for he claims: ". . . the question of color, especially in this country, operates to hide the graver questions of the self."[23] Baldwin's "existential" inclinations[24] inevitably led him to engage in the ongoing task of reimagining, and perhaps re-creating, the meaning of Negro identity in the United States.

In order to engage Baldwin's critique of the racialized identities birthed out of the white imaginary in the United States, we should begin with Baldwin's speech "White Racism or World Community?," delivered to the World Council of Churches in 1968. In this speech, Baldwin brings an "absolutely necessary accusation" against the Christian church, an accusation rooted in the "historical confrontation between nonwhite peoples of the world and the white peoples of the world, between the Christian Church and those people outside the Christian Church."[25] To put it slightly differently, borrowing the language of Anthony Pinn, Baldwin is describing the "terror of dehumanization" which took place in the initial encounter of African peoples with European Christendom via the transatlantic slave trade.[26] Baldwin makes clear that because he was born Christian, his own "freedom" was "frozen or strangled at the root." In this same passage he posits: "Because I was born in a Christian culture, I never considered myself to be totally a free human being. In my own mind, and in fact, I was told by Christians what I could do and what I could become and what my life was worth."[27] Here, Baldwin is articulating that black life in the United States was subject to particular *identity formations* ("what I could become") which were, in fact, determined in part by varying Christian theologies and controlled within the strictures of a white Christian culture.

This claim becomes ever more explicit in his discussion of civil rights activist and black power advocate Kwame Ture (then known as Stokely Carmichael), who Baldwin points out, was deemed by the press to be a "very dangerous, radical, black fanatic racist." Baldwin reminds his audience that Ture was at one point a Christian, "marching up and down highways in my country, in the deep south."[28] Yet, Ture grew tired of doing the work that the church was "supposed to do," i.e., "to walk from door to door, to feed the hungry, to speak to those who are oppressed," and soon realized that "petitioning" was getting black people nowhere, leading to his now (in)famous call for black power.[29] It is here that Baldwin provides further explication of his understanding that certain forms of racialized identity were circumscribed and "created" by white Christians. Baldwin argues that when Ture calls for black power, "He's only insisting that he is present only once on this earth as a man, not as a creation of the Christian conscience, not as a fantasy in the Christian mind.[30] In other words, Ture's call for black power is a direct assault against the Christian church, and a peculiar *theology* that served to "create" an Other, a "fantasy" produced by the Christian "conscience" and "mind." Baldwin even personalizes this identity struggle, referring to himself as "a creation of the Christian Church, as a black creation of the Christian Church."[31] Hence, through this language of "fantasy," "definition," and "creation," it is evident that Baldwin is articulating a potent critique, which is that black people have been subjected to a form of alterity creation, one that sought to mark black people as radically Other, while also *allowing white people to build a sense of peoplehood in relation to this racialized figure.* As Baldwin so famously claimed, white people "needed" the Negro, the nigger, the heathen, the slave, in order to build their own identities.[32] Yet, Baldwin's "White Racism" speech does not go far enough in providing the necessary detail to tease out the content of this Christian "creation" that is a distorted "Negro," and/or racialized, subjectivity. To gain further clarification as to its meaning we will need to move into other fiction and nonfiction works of Baldwin's.

In "Many Thousands Gone," Baldwin adopts the viewpoint of the white US American Christian,[33] stating:

> In the case of the Negro the past was taken from him whether he would or no; yet to forswear it was meaningless and availed him nothing, since

his shameful history was carried, quite literally, on his brow. Shameful;
for he was heathen as well as black and would never have discovered
the healing blood of Christ had not we braved the jungles to bring him
these glad tidings. Shameful; for, since our role as missionary had not
been wholly disinterested, it was necessary to recall the shame from
which we had delivered him in order more easily to escape our own.
As he accepted the alabaster Christ and the bloody cross—in the bearing of which he would find his redemption, as, indeed, to our outraged
astonishment, he sometimes did—he must, henceforth, accept that
image we then gave him of himself: having no other and standing,
moreover, in danger of death should he fail to accept the dazzling light
thus brought into such darkness.[34]

What is Baldwin pointing to here? What he is attempting to show is that white
US Americans viewed black people as having a shameful past, and *that shame
was rooted in the non-Christian "origins" of diasporic Africans—their "heathen"
past*. This quote makes clear that white people believed that, prior to their
encounters with Europeans, African peoples existed in "darkness," the blackness of their skin simply being an outward expression of the state of their souls.
But these Africans were fortunate, for white people offered these dark peoples
a theological gift, "the healing blood of Christ." Yet, Baldwin argues, with
this gift came *an image*. Now, the content of that image is not difficult to
ascertain for it is found, in part, in the quote itself. The image that black
people were forced to bear is the theological narrative undergirding the quote,
which is that the black past is one of shame, that black subjectivity is inextricably linked to "heathenness," and that the Jesus that Africans embraced was
not their own, but an alabaster, white, savior.[35] However, it will become apparent that the symbol upon which the whole of this *image* hangs is that of
"the heathen," so we must spend some time examining the meaning of this
symbol/language.

According to Sylvester Johnson, although the category of heathen "has a
complex etymological history," it "most frequently denoted 'irreligious,' 'un-
cultured,' and 'uncivilized,'" and most importantly, "non-Christian."[36] However,
we would be remiss to think that this language of heathen is an innocent marker
of difference through which Christians could simply establish the borders of
their world in relation to that of the Other. Kathryn Gin Lum, in her work
entitled *Heathen: Religion and Race in American History*, traces the history of
this notion of the heathen. Lum argues:

Classifying people as heathen has long served as a ticket of impunity
to justify taking over their lands, and enslaving and reconstructing

their bodies, in the name of saving their souls. Such classification
has also justified violence against, and state exclusion of, people
deemed heathen who have refused to accept or conform to such
"assistance." Heathenness has never simply been about wrong and
changeable belief. It also has to do with the manifold repercussions
that wrong belief is supposed to wreak on lands and bodies, turning
fertile soil into deserts and hale bodies into sickly ones, corrupted by
idolatry, the oppression of women, and neglect of infants, the sick,
and elderly.[37]

Heathenness, therefore, was not simply a marker of nonbelief—the category of
the heathen became a primary weapon in colonial processes. As Lum makes
clear, to mark a people as heathen was to deem them deficient. To mark a
people as heathen served as a justification for seizing their lands. To mark a
people as heathen provided one of the primary justifications for enslavement,
for if a population's heathen status could be established, their capture could
then be justified as a means through which to Christianize and civilize said
people. As Lum makes clear, the symbol of the heathen undergirds "Americans'
conviction that other people need to be transformed."[38]

Although many peoples have been subjected to the category of the heathen,
diasporic Africans have an extensive history with this symbol. What Baldwin
is pointing to is that black subjectivity in the United States is conflated with
heathenness, a theo-political construct used to mark black life as radically
Other. Historically, the heathen status of black people originates in the early
encounters of Europeans with West African peoples in the fifteenth century.
Sylvester Johnson's groundbreaking text, *African American Religions, 1500–2000:
Colonialism, Democracy, and Freedom,* offers a substantive overview of that
history, and the ways in which heathenness came to mark black subjectivity as
radically Other. According to Johnson, in this moment of encounter, varying
European polities sought to become global empires by means of trade and
commodities exchange, i.e., commercialism.[39] In many ways, West Africa became the center for what would become an international market, driven by
trade in grain, iron, gold, and most importantly human chattel. Europeans—
first the Portuguese and, subsequently, the Dutch, English, French, and others—were on a quest for global dominance, thus they entered West Africa with
an eye toward colonial expansion.[40]

In addition, Johnson also makes clear that this moment of economic exchange was also a time of intense "religious exchange," and colonial expansion
and the spread of Christianity moved in tandem.[41] The Christianity of

Europeans was a Christianity wed to "the philosophical and practical imperatives of empire," and it was a Christianity shaped over the course of centuries through "guerrilla warfare" against non-Christian neighbors, particularly Muslims. This was not a Christianity well-versed in forming relationships based on mutual respect and tolerance, but was a Christendom driven by the logics of "supremacy"—"political and religious."[42] Johnson powerfully captures the mindset driving European Christians during this period. He states:

> The worship of any gods other than the Christian deity was arguably the most incriminating action in the Christian imagination. Its theological importance easily outweighed that of such horrendous acts as murder, pillaging, sexual violence, or genocide. In Christian grammar, it was an exceptional category—idolatry—and it constituted the most direct form of rebellion against the Christian deity.[43]

Thus, religion became a primary site through which European nations marked Africans as different and deficient—as Other—giving rise to notions such as "the fetish," a kind of shorthand for "the religion of the Blacks."[44]

This framing of African religion, i.e., fetish/religion of the blacks, became according to Johnson, the content of the notion of the "heathen," a marker of an "essential type."[45] What might at first seem to simply be a difference of belief/spirituality/religion between Europeans and West Africans, is shown to be much more insidious, for religious difference came to signify "differential essence," which, in turn, functioned as the weapon to justify "differential treatment."[46] Johnson posits:

> As in the earlier colonial orders of domination that shaped polities of the Mediterranean world, religion functioned to constitute colonial meanings of *differential essence*—fundamental ontologies articulated through a plurality of domains such as political dispositions (Blacks do not have states), intellectual capacities (the mind of the Guinea African is delusional and child-like), aesthetic sensitivities, climate-induced sensibilities (Africans are lazy and prone to excessive sexual passions), phenotype, and linguistic bearings—that differentiated human populations into essential, different types (races).[47]

In other words, the African "type" was conceived as religiously, politically, phenotypically, linguistically, and intellectually Other. Thus, as a heathen people, religious and theological difference served as but one marker of a much deeper and all-encompassing difference. This was not simply for the sake of

showing their difference but was a colonial and political act. It became the
means through which to oppress a populace and "mark" them "as perpetually,
ineluctably alien."[48] In fact, this form of othering was a means of racializing
African people. This quote by Johnson illustrates this point:

> Racialization articulates and manages human differences—conceived
> as absolute and fundamental—to rationalize differential treatment.
> This differential is a relation of domination mystically represented
> through the more respectable idiom of absolute, fundamental human
> difference. This power relation, in turn, is fundamental to the political
> order of colonialism.[49]

Racial blackness was never only about phenotype, but to racialize a populace
meant that a people were framed as Other by means of varying markers of
difference, including *religious* difference. This absolutization of difference is
what Baldwin is pointing to in "Many Thousands Gone," for he recognized
that white US American Christians had created a theological image—the
heathen/blackness/the Negro/African, which served as the means of justifying
differential treatment. The heathen is a figment of the white Christian mind.
This is why Baldwin claimed in his speech/essay "A Talk to Teachers" that "I
had to realize when I was very young that I was none of those things I was told
I was. . . . *I had been invented by white people.*"[50]

Moving into the nineteenth century, and the context of the United States,
it is important to note that the heathen status of black people becomes inextricably linked to one particular symbol and biblical narrative, the so-called
myth of Ham, found in Genesis 9:18–27. Turning to yet another text by Sylvester
Johnson, *The Myth of Ham in Nineteenth-Century American Christianity: Race,
Heathens, and the People of God*, Johnson posits that "Ham was a heathen par
excellence,"[51] or to put it slightly differently, "the ultimate representative of the
heathen."[52] In the biblical narrative, Ham's progeny are cursed with perpetual
slavery due to Ham having offended his father Noah by seeing him naked.
According to Johnson, most nineteenth-century Americans, "*both* scientists
and Christian religionists who sought to explain race variation,"[53] "presumed
. . . that the races descended from Noah's three sons"—Ham, Shem, and
Japheth.[54] As white Americans traced their origins to the biblical figure Japheth
(not to mention their assumption that the first humans were, in fact, white),[55]
black people were almost universally understood, by black as well as white
Christians in the United States, to descend from the biblical figure Ham.[56]
Therefore, racial groupings in the United States engaged in a peculiar practice,
one in which they "read [themselves] back" into the biblical text itself.[57]

Therefore, cultural understandings arose which posited "the white race as first peoples who had first knowledge of the one true God"[58] and reinscribed an already pervasive understanding of Negroes as "heathens."[59] Johnson argues:

> Race discourse concerned narrations that associated God with a *people*. Some people were people of God. Others were not; they were heathens. The heathen as a social construct, furthermore, was symbolically associated with Native Americans and Negroes. And this confluence of the religious and racial definitively shaped American religious experience.[60]

This, yet again, points to the ways in which the white Christian imagination inextricably linked black subjectivity with "heathenness." Hamitic rhetoric simply added more content to the alterity-creating narratives weaponized by Europeans in West Africa. Hamitic rhetoric served as a means of further signifying black people's radical otherness. This, too, does not escape Baldwin's attention. In *The Fire Next Time*, he explicitly connects blackness to the mythos of Ham:

> I knew that, according to many Christians, I was a descendant of Ham, who had been cursed, and that I was therefore predestined to be a slave. This had nothing to do with anything I was, or contained, or could become; my fate had been sealed forever, from the beginning of time.[61]

Baldwin, in that one short passage, captured the varying contours of a centuries old idea which had reached a fever pitch in nineteenth-century US America, while continuing to hold influence into the twentieth century, in which Baldwin was born.

Baldwin also makes an allusion to Hamitic rhetoric in his work, *Go Tell It on the Mountain*. In the book's climactic scene, in which the main character John is undergoing a conversion experience, he is confronted by an "ironic voice." The narrator recounts:

> Then the ironic voice, terrified, it seemed, of no depth, no darkness, demanded of John, scornfully, if he believed that he was cursed. All niggers had been cursed, the ironic voice reminded him, all niggers had come from this most undutiful of Noah's sons. . . . Could a curse come down so many ages? Did it live in time, or in the moment? But John found no answer for this voice, for he was in the moment, and out of time.[62]

What this moment gestures toward is that Baldwin is suspicious, which scholars such as Clarence Hardy make clear, that the conversion of black people to Christianity is grounded in "shame, not hope."[63] No matter how "Christian" black people became, in order to live and move within this Christian nation as *Christian*, they would be forced to take on the "image" given to them out of the white Christian imaginary. They would remain, despite their conversion, a heathen people, inextricably linked to a biblical figure who was not only the embodiment of "evil" in the biblical world,[64] but also representative of a lineage understood to be the "extreme antithesis to the people of God."[65]

In Baldwin's engagement of Hamitic rhetoric, supported by Lum's and Johnson's historical work, we see clearly one particular way in which Negro subjectivity was formed out of the white Christian imaginary. Black modes of being in the world were violently tethered to the theo-political construct of the heathen. As this section should make clear, the goal was not simply to mark diasporic Africans as different, but that difference served as the justification for subjecting black people to colonial violence. However, we cannot move too quickly from this subject, for although Baldwin takes special care to point to the ways in which white people have created a fantasy of black existence, they did so in order to, simultaneously, construct their own white identity.

The Delusion of Whiteness

We must remember that the conflation of black/Negro identity with theo-political constructs such as the heathen and the figure of Ham was not simply a means of marking black people as Other, the creation of the Negro is just one part of white European attempts at constructing the meaning of whiteness, of white "divine peoplehood."[66] Kathryn Lum echoes this point, stating that "the heathen world has been constitutive, not incidental, to White Protestant Americans' sense of history and collective identity."[67] This is why Baldwin makes clear throughout the whole of his literary corpus that the problem of race in this country is not, in fact, the problem of "the Negro," but the problem of whiteness.[68]

In an interview with Kenneth B. Clark, Baldwin posits:

> What white people have to do, is to try to find out in their own
> hearts why it was necessary to have a nigger in the first place, because
> I'm not a nigger, I'm a man, but if you think I'm a nigger, it means you
> need it. Why? That's question you have got to ask yourself—the white
> population has got to ask itself—north and south, because it's one

country for a Negro . . . . If I'm not a nigger here and you, the white people invented him, then you've got to find out why. And the future of the country depends on that. Whether or not it's able to ask that question.[69]

What is captured in this statement is Baldwin's belief, which is repeated throughout his corpus, that the creation of the "nigger" and/or "Negro" stems out of an unacknowledged need on the part of white people, a need which Baldwin believes is rooted in the project of constructing a national white identity. That national identity, or white collective self, is understood to be the exemplary image of all that is divine, pure, and most importantly "innocent."[70] The perpetuation of this mythos required the creation of a foil, one which served to amplify the virtues of whiteness by means of embodying all that white people believed themselves *not* to be—evil, uncontrolled, guilty, criminal. The image of the Negro, as discussed in the previous section, served as that necessary fiction in that it functioned to "safeguard [white people's] purity," providing the means by which white people could be protected from recognizing their own history of genocide, theft, and brutality.[71]

Therefore, through a type of racial and theological sleight of hand, white people were no longer guilty of those aforementioned evils—they eased their collective conscience by displacing their crimes onto the figure of the Negro.[72] Baldwin states this explicitly in *The Fire Next Time*, arguing: "The white man's unadmitted—and apparently, to him, unspeakable—private fears and longings are projected onto the Negro."[73] This has required the image of the Negro to function as a proverbial "scapegoat" in the US racial imagination, taking on, and suffering for, the sins of white Americans. Baldwin states:

That the scapegoat pays for the sins of others is well known, but this is only legend, and a revealing one at that. In fact, however the scapegoat may be made to suffer, his suffering cannot purify the sinner; it merely incriminates him more, and it seals his damnation. The scapegoat, eventually, is released, to death: his murderer continues to live. The suffering of the scapegoat has resulted in seas of blood, and yet not one sinner has been saved, or changed, by this despairing ritual.[74]

Elsewhere, speaking as the white US American in "Many Thousands Gone," Baldwin posits: "it is we, who, every hour that we live, reinvest the black face with our guilt; and we do this—by a further paradox, no less ferocious— helplessly, passionately, out of an unrealized need to suffer absolution."[75] Thus, although white Americans sought to displace their guilt onto the Negro, this tactic, in Baldwin's estimate, has and continues to fail. It fails due to the fact that the cycles of violence endure as white persons seek over and again to escape their legacy, hiding their faces from the brutal truths of Euro-American history.

This brings us again to the idea of innocence.[76] Baldwin is clear that whiteness is a collective identity rooted in "a stupendous delusion,"[77] one in which white people have convinced themselves that they are the recipients and continuation of a valiant history of discovery, a divine people blessed with a sacred mission to bring civilization to the globe. Baldwin, in "A Talk to Teachers," states:

> What passes for identity in America is a series of myths about one's heroic ancestors. It's astounding to me, for example, that so many people really appear to believe that the country was founded by a band of heroes who wanted to be free. That happens to not be true.[78]

This delusion might be understood as a kind of Sartrean "bad faith." Lewis Gordon describes "bad faith" as such: "We can tentatively define bad faith as the effort to hide from responsibility for ourselves as freedom. . . . In bad faith, I flee a displeasing truth for a pleasing falsehood. I must convince myself that a falsehood is in fact true."[79] Bringing Gordon's tentative definition into conversation with Baldwin, we might conceive of whiteness as a lie, a falsehood, intentionally told and retold each and every day in an attempt to "hide from responsibility" and hence the possibility of guilt, allowing white people to rest in the safety of their perceived innocence.[80]

Elsewhere, Baldwin makes a similar claim in pointing out the ways in which white people have and continue to wreak destruction all over the world, and yet seem to "not know it." In other words, they claim to be "innocent." In *The Fire Next Time*, Baldwin states:

> . . . and this is the crime of which I accuse my country and my countrymen, and for which neither I nor time nor history will ever forgive them, that they have destroyed and are destroying hundreds of thousands of lives and do not know it and do not want to know it. One can be, indeed one must strive to become, tough and philosophical concerning destruction and death, for this is what most of mankind has been best at since we have heard of man. (But remember: *most* of mankind is not *all* of mankind.) But it is not permissible that the authors of devastation should also be innocent. It is the innocence which constitutes the crime.[81]

What these two quotes highlight is that white people, in Baldwin's estimate, attempt to cling to a false innocence—an innocence rooted in a lie. The white attempt at claiming and maintaining "innocence," in the midst of a historical record soaked in the blood of the nonwhite Other, created and perpetuates "the racial nightmare"[82] now gripping the globe.

This begs the question, what hope is there for a people "still trapped in a history which they do not understand; and until they understand it they cannot be released from it?"[83] Baldwin hints at an answer in *The Fire Next Time*, stating: "White people in this country will have quite enough to do in learning how to accept and love themselves and each other, and when they have achieved this—which will not be tomorrow and may very well be never—the Negro problem will no longer exist, for it will no longer be needed."[84] Later, what was previously only hinted at is now made explicit:

> The only way he [the white person] can be released from the Negro's tyrannical power over him is to consent, in effect, to become black himself, to become a part of that suffering and dancing country that he now watches wistfully from the heights of his lonely power and, armed with spiritual traveller's [sic] checks, visits surreptitiously after dark.[85]

Baldwin is not speaking of white people literally becoming darker in their pigmentation, but he is pointing to the necessity of white people willfully and intentionally standing face-to-face with the truth of their histories, which would lay the groundwork for their deliverance from the shackles of whiteness. However, black artistic expression can lay the groundwork for that confrontation, for black art is, in and of itself, *the experience of blackness*.

However, before addressing this question, we must first move into a brief discussion of the alterity-creating practices of black Christians, found in theologies of salvation and sanctification which serve as a means of marking particular manifestations of black life as deficient in relation to a given Christian norm. Remember, Baldwin envisions the creation of collective selves not dependent upon the creation of an enemy, an Other. Thus, Baldwin also critiques the Christian community out of which he came, for he remained disturbed that black Christians also mark particular people as deficient and heathen. As Lum makes clear, part of the logic that drives this strategic deployment of the symbol of the heathen is the belief that the heathen is a person in need of transformation.[86] Baldwin seeks to radically undermine this logic in white as well as black communities.

Black Sanctified Churches and the Non-Christian Other

In the previous sections, James Baldwin's vehement indictment of white Christianity's role in creating an Other, which sought to construct, in opposition to the image of the Negro, an understanding of peoplehood rooted in whiteness, was examined. Yet, Baldwin's accusation against this form of theo-political group formation is not solely leveled at white Christian churches. Baldwin's work reveals a particular practice and mentality within black sanctified culture that echoes the white Christian desire to create an Other, reflected in sanctified churches' failure to love and embrace those outside of their religious community, whether those of other religious orientations, or those whose lifestyles violate the community's sense of morality. This should not be a surprise, for scholars such as Lum point out that "some Christian converts from missionized groups have also viewed their ancestors and unconverted relatives as heathens and sought to save them."[87]

Before moving into a discussion of Baldwin's critique of the black Christianity of his youth, it is important to note that neither Baldwin or I are attempting to conflate the alterity-creating practices of black and white Christians, nor are we attempting to accuse black Christianity of crimes as violent and egregious as those found in the history of white Christianity. European, and eventually white, Christianity has been inextricably linked to state power, and has functioned through the genocidal machinations of colonialism. This has been death-dealing the world over. Therefore, although black US Christians and denominations have, at various historical moments, participated in state-sponsored colonial incursions, like those found in the settler colony of Liberia which included violence against native African peoples,[88] Baldwin seems to be pointing to a theological mentality and practice of division that is profoundly Christian, while lacking an entanglement with state power in his particular context. However, before moving into a detailed analysis of Baldwin's critique, I will first ground Baldwin's distinct experience with the sanctified church historically, in order to gain a fuller understanding of the particular theological community with which he was contending and in which he came of age.

As stated in Chapter 1, Baldwin converted to the Christian faith within the Harlem ministry of "Mother" Rosa A. Horn,[89] a Pentecostal community within the tradition of the sanctified church.[90] James Baldwin's most explicit treatments of black, sanctified Christianity can be found in *Go Tell It on the Mountain* and *The Fire Next Time*. In *Fire*, Baldwin weaves a narrative which, in part, discusses his personal relationship to, and the public effects of, religion in the United States, including both the sanctified church of his youth and the black Muslim movement. He begins his narrative with events in the summer leading up to his fourteenth birthday, for it was around this time that Baldwin began to experience a sexual awakening, one in which his own sexual attractions (which for Baldwin included same-gender attraction) were beginning to come to the fore.[91] He states, ". . . I became, during my fourteenth year, for the first time in my life, afraid—afraid of the evil within me and afraid of the evil without."[92] This moment of fear for Baldwin was tied to the belief that he, personally, was "depraved,"[93] and that the broader community around him reflected "the wages of sin," "visible everywhere, in every wine-stained and urine splashed hallway, in every clanging ambulance bell . . . [and] in every knife and pistol fight on the Avenue."[94] In Baldwin's adolescent mind, his own "depravity," and that of his community, reflected an unredeemed mode of being, one marked by estrangement from a "salvific" Christian deity.

It is not surprising that a young Baldwin would link "depravity" to sexual desire, for a deeply anti-sex ethos was a hallmark of his Christian community. Kelly Brown Douglas, in her work *What's Faith Got to Do with It?: Black Bodies/Christian Souls*, in a section which explores Baldwin's *Go Tell It on the Mountain*, clearly outlines the ways in which many black Christians have adopted what she calls a "hyper-proper sexuality." She states:

> Offsetting white cultural hyper-sexualization of them, black people adopt a hyper-proper sexuality primarily defined and legitimated by a platonized theology. With a singular commitment to a hyper-proper sexuality, black people can at once affirm their humanity and redeem their souls. Such an approach to sexuality potentially disproves white cultural characterizations and promises a "saved" soul. This hyper-proper sexual attitude is characterized by a determination to engage sexuality in a "proper" manner.[95]

She goes on to say that this demonization of sexuality leads to a type of othering within black Christian communities. She posits:

> This adoption [of a hyper-proper sexuality] has at least two detrimental implications. First, it sets hyper-proper sexual black people apart from those black people who perhaps foster the sexual stereotype by unabashedly finding pleasure in nonprocreative sexual expressions. Such persons become a part of the "unsaved," the "unredeemed," and the "unholy," while those who follow the platonized ethic are part of the "saved," "redeemed," and "holy." Black people potentially fall prey to placing a judgement on one another similar to the way that white culture judges them, only in this instance the defining categories are holy versus nonholy as opposed to white versus black. Such a judgment is hauntingly similar in nature to the judgment white culture places on black people.[96]

Therefore Baldwin, while becoming increasingly aware of his own queer sexual desire, knew that he would have to make a choice—would he choose the church, a bastion of "safety"[97] and holiness, or would he choose to be one of the "unholy," the "unredeemed"? This question reflects Baldwin's very clear real-ization that many young black people, in order to survive, must find "a gim-mick" in which to find purpose.[98] Baldwin's "gimmick" would be black Christian life, for it was there that he found "safety."[99] However, it became evident to Baldwin that this "safety" was a life-denying reality, one that he would be forced to reject.

For the purposes of this chapter, what is most important in Baldwin's nar-rative is the *revelation* which occurred shortly after his conversion to Christi-anity. Baldwin posits that after converting to the Christian faith, he quickly realized that both god and the black religious community of his youth were, in fact, "loveless."[100] This "lovelessness" stemmed out of the "white" Christian god's clear indifference to the plight of black people in the Unites States,[101] and the exclusivist worldview perpetuated by his religious community, one that excluded anyone outside of their Christian way of life.[102] This "lovelessness," a term which serves to encapsulate Baldwin's critique of the sanctified church, is captured in a confrontation between Baldwin and his father, recorded in *The Fire Next Time*. He states:

> My best friend in high school was a Jew. He came to our house once, and afterward my father asked, as he asked about everyone, "Is he a Christian?"—by which he meant "Is he saved?" I really do not know whether my answer came out of innocence or venom, but I said coldly, "No. He's Jewish." My father slammed me across the face with his great palm, and in that moment everything flooded back—all the hatred and all the fear, and the depth of a merciless resolve to kill my father rather than allow my father to kill me—and I knew that all those sermons and tears and all that repentance and rejoicing had changed nothing. I wondered if I was expected to be glad that a friend of mine, or anyone, was to be tormented forever in Hell, and I also thought, suddenly, of the Jews in another Christian nation, Germany. They were not so far from the fiery furnace after all, and my best friend might have been one of them.[103]

It is here that Baldwin is faced with a potent intolerance, captured in his father's question, "Is he saved?" What these words highlight, I argue, is a particular Christian identity formation, one that sets the Christian apart from the non-Christian through a theological identity, often articulated through the language of "salvation," and in the case of Baldwin's community, "salvation" *and* "sanc-tification" before god. Cheryl Sanders explains this *new* sense of identity be-stowed upon believers in sanctified circles, stating:

To be saved means that one has repented, asked forgiveness of sins, and confessed Jesus Christ as Savior and Lord. This experience imparts a basic "entry level" of liturgical identity that distinguishes the saint from the unbeliever. To be sanctified is to receive some second form of blessing that conveys upon the believer a distinctive ethical identity of being set apart for God, literally to be made holy.[104]

We see here a clear distinction taking place, one reflective of a recurring practice by which human groups are distinguished from one another through the marking of a populace as Other—a people in need of transformation. Hence, in light of this new "set-apart" identity, one which marks the point of distinction between the "saint" and "the unbeliever," what Baldwin deems "lovelessness," is in fact another means of highlighting a particular alterity-creating behavior.

In some expressions of Christian soteriology, "the saved," and for some "the sanctified," are understood to occupy a new ontology, a new mode of being, one that places their identity over and against those who do not share their beliefs, and those who do not hold to their moral code. This inability to love, as Baldwin frames it, is in fact an inability to embrace alternative modes of being, religious or otherwise, outside of the sanctified Christian norms represented by his father. In *The Fire Next Time*, Baldwin states: "When we were told to love everybody, I had thought that that meant *everybody*."[105] Later, he continues:

In the same way that we, for white people, were the descendants of Ham, and were cursed forever, white people were, for us, the descendants of Cain. And the passion with which we loved the Lord was a measure of how deeply we feared and distrusted and, in the end, *hated almost all strangers*, always, and avoided and despised ourselves.[106]

Although black suspicion of white people is more than understandable in light of the legacy of white supremacy in the West (referring to Baldwin's claim that black people identified white people with the biblical figure Cain),[107] Baldwin's critique goes further than simply highlighting the exclusion and lack of love displayed toward white people by his black Christian community. What is particularly striking is that Baldwin argues that his community's exclusive practices came to include "*all strangers*," all those who did not hold to their Christian way of life.

Baldwin's critique is not only found in *The Fire Next Time*, but it is a theme that can also be seen in his fiction works, particularly his novel *If Beale Street*

Could Talk. This book highlights the struggle of two black youths (Fonny and Tish), who fall in love only to find their relationship shattered by Fonny's arrest and Tish's subsequent discovery of her pregnancy with Fonny's child. In one passage in particular, Tish and Fonny visit the church that Fonny's zealously religious mother (Mrs. Hunt) and sisters attend. At the height of the passionate worship experience, Tish recounts: "The church began to rock. And rocked me and Fonny, too, though they didn't know it, and in a very different way. Now, we knew that nobody loved us: or, now, we knew who did. Whoever loved us was not here."[108] Tish's feeling of "lovelessness" in the midst of this group of Christians, I argue, stems from her and Fonny's presumed "unsaved" status in the eyes of the church members. This claim is supported by the narrator of the novel, who posits that "Mrs. Hunt . . . from the moment we walked through the church doors, became filled with a stern love for her two little *heathens* and marched us before her to the mercy seat."[109] Through his strategic deployment of the language of "heathen" yet again, Baldwin is highlighting the ways in which Fonny's mother, and in turn her community, understood the subjectivity of the "unsaved," which was a deficient mode of being, a type of subjectivity in need of correction and "redemption."

Take, for instance, another moment in *Beale Street,* in which Mrs. Hunt goes so far as to claim that her son's unjust arrest and incarceration might have been the work of god. She declares:

> The *Lord* holds *me* up. I just pray and pray and pray that the Lord will bring my boy to the light. That's all I pray for, every day and every night. And then, sometimes I think that maybe this is the *Lord's* way of making my boy think on his sins and surrender his soul to Jesus.[110]

What initially might strike the reader as a seemingly cold, and possibly absurd, theoretical leap, is simply the reflection of a theological worldview in which being "surrendered to Jesus" marks the apex of identity to which all should aspire.[111] To fall outside of this status, whether through a rejection of the Christian faith, or through violation of the community's standards of morality, was to be marked by a deficient ontology, a deficient way of being in the world. This is, again, consistent with our ongoing discussion of theo-political forms of alterity creation.

One of the most profound examples of Baldwin's indictment of the Christian community of his youth comes in one of his final works, *The Evidence of Things Not Seen.* In this text, Baldwin recounts the story of a teenage boy named Buddy, who "backslid" in the eyes of the community, going back to the "sinful" life he was supposed to reject. Baldwin recounts:

I remember seeing him, for the last time, on the avenue, in the day-time. I was coming home from school. He looked very sad and weary, with a cigarette between his heavy lips.

I remember the cigarette because the cigarette signaled, proved, his sinful state. He had been a member of the church, sanctified, holy, but had "backslid," had "gone back into the world," and we were forbidden to speak to him. By speaking to Buddy, I risked a reprimand and might have been forced to undertake a purifying fast.[112]

Despite his being forbidden to do so, Baldwin did speak to Buddy, which would be for the last time, for Buddy soon died of tuberculosis.[113] Baldwin claimed that he was "haunted" by his final moments with Buddy, for he believed that "he died because he had been rejected by the only community he knew, that we had had it in our power to bring the light back to his eyes. He was a sinner and he died, therefore, in sin."[114]

Baldwin is explicit in his indictment of the Christian community for Buddy's death.[115] Not only did they reject Buddy, but in that rejection they *made* Buddy a "sinner," a "transgressor," a person of a deficient ontology who existed in relation to the community as Other.[116] Baldwin is aware that this practice of creating an Other was necessary for the perpetuation of the black sanctified community of which he was a part. He posits, "The way of the transgressor is hard, indeed, but it is hard *because the community produces the transgressor in order to renew itself.*"[117] Therefore, in Baldwin's estimate, the black sanctified communities of his youth had to be rejected, had to be abandoned, for they failed to live into the reality of "community," which for Baldwin "means our endless connection with, and responsibility for, each other."[118]

To be "unsaved" in Baldwin's community was to exist in a deficient mode of being. The only remedy for that deficiency was conversion, and submission to the sanctifying work of a Christian god. Baldwin rejected this alterity-creating exclusivism, rebelling against the "lovelessness" of a community, and its god, who refused to embrace the non-Christian Other. In the final section of this chapter, I will examine Baldwin's response to this recurring practice of creating collective identity by means of creating an enemy, rooted in his reimagined and artistically constituted understanding of peoplehood.

Suffering and Joy: Black Music and the Tonal Roots of Black Community

As Chapter 1 made clear, throughout his literature Baldwin often seeks to engage and reimagine Christian theological symbols through a method of disidentification, and in the case of this chapter, he is disidentifying with the form/logic of peoplehood. What this final section makes clear is that Baldwin continues to work with and through a notion of peoplehood, but rather than rooting communal identity in what he understands to be the fiction of race or theology (i.e., salvation and sanctification), Baldwin disidentifies with peoplehood and grounds the meaning of black communal identity in black sound and song. To put it slightly differently, Baldwin understands blackness to be a matter of *tone*, what Ed Pavlić calls "a tonal narrative"[119] and Ashon Crawley calls a "black tone."[120] Therefore, black music/tone not only serves as the vehicle through which the narrative of black life in this country is shared, but black music/tone, mysteriously, is *constitutive of* black communal identity.[121] However, black song/tone is not simply liberating for black people. If white people pause and truly hear the narrative carried in black sound, they *might* be forced into a confrontation with the lie that serves as the bedrock of their identity, a confrontation which might contribute to the deconstruction of the mythos of whiteness.

For Baldwin, black art comes to signify what religion *could* and perhaps *should* be, for it can, in fact, contribute to the "salvation," or as Clarence Hardy claims, the "redemption," of others.[122] That redemption is found in black art's ability to both reveal the realities of suffering and struggle in human lives and create what Pavlić calls the "links between (as well as within) human interiors,"[123] which connect human beings together in community.[124] Baldwin speaks to this in a conversation with Nikki Giovanni, stating:

> Look, the very first thing a writer has to face is that he cannot be told what to write. . . . But in any case, the one thing you have to do is try to tell the truth. And what everyone overlooks is that in order to do it— when the book comes out it may hurt *you*—but in order for me to do it, it had to hurt *me* first. I can only tell *you* about yourself as much as I can face about myself. . . . You go through life for a long time thinking, No one has ever suffered the way I've suffered, my God, my God. And then you realize—You read something or you hear something, and you realize that your suffering does not isolate you; your suffering is your bridge. Many people have suffered before you . . . and all you can do is bring hopefully, a little light into that suffering. Enough light so that the person who is suffering can begin to comprehend his suffering and begin to live with it and begin to change it, change the situation. We don't change anything; all we can do is invest people with the morale to change it for themselves.[125]

In other words, artistic expression is not a form of Christian "salvation" for the soul, but it provides a lens by which people might be equipped to change, and perhaps "save" themselves in the midst of their suffering. However, this deeply spiritual work is not done in an isolated and individualistic sense, as evangelical notions of "personal salvation" often are, but it takes place through the realization that human communities are often bound and knit together through their experiences of suffering and struggle. Thus, we see here the two primary ways in which the artist, and artistic creation contribute to the building and sustaining of human community. First, the artist, through their own suffering, captures the struggles of life and communicates that experience to the world. Second, in that communication, those who are suffering discover the ties that bind, or "link,"[126] human beings to one another (i.e., the grounds of an authentic peoplehood). Ironically, the artistic expression that is examined most extensively in Baldwin's own work is not literature but music—both the gospel music of the church and the genres of blues and jazz. However, it would be a mistake to draw a stark juxtaposition between the two, between black literature and black music. For Baldwin, it is black music which most powerfully expresses black literature. He states, "What we call black literature is really summed up for me by the whole career, let's say, of Bessie Smith, Ray Charles, Aretha Franklin, because that's how it's been handed down, since we couldn't read or write, as far as they knew."[127]

In "Many Thousands Gone," Baldwin brings the centrality of black music in lives of black US Americans to the fore, stating: "It is only in his music, which [white] Americans are able to admire because a protective sentimentality limits their understanding of it, that the Negro in America has been able to tell his story. It is a story which otherwise has yet to be told and which no American is prepared to hear."[128] What Baldwin is communicating here is that black music carries *"the narrative"* of black life, or what Saadi Simawe calls "a narrative for a story that language cannot grasp."[129] This early nod to music's ability to communicate the story of black life in the United States matures over the years, and eventually the language of the blues becomes one of the key "metaphor[s]"[130] by which Baldwin articulates the catastrophe and beauty of black existence in the United States. Baldwin builds on this idea in his 1964 essay "The Uses of the Blues," in which he argues that when he speaks of the blues, he is not speaking simply of a musical genre, but of a "state of being, out of which the blues comes." He goes on to say: "Consider some of the things the blues are about. They're about work, love, death, floods, lynchings; in fact, a series of disasters which can be summed up under the arbitrary heading 'Facts of Life.'"[131] In other words, the blues speaks to a texture and substance of black

US American experience, an experience marked significantly, although not completely, by the reality of suffering—that certain "series of disasters."

This idea recurs again in his last published novel, *Just Above My Head*. Hall Montana, the narrator and one of the main protagonists in the novel, reflects:

> Niggers can sing gospel as no other people can because they aren't singing gospel—if you see what I mean. When a nigger quotes the Gospel, he is not quoting: he is telling you what happened to him today, and what is certainly going to happen to you tomorrow: it may be that it has already happened to you, and that you, poor soul, don't know it. In which case, *Lord, have mercy!* Our suffering is our bridge to one another. Everyone must cross this bridge, or die while he still lives—but this is not a political, still less, a popular apprehension.[132]

We see yet again that black music, birthed out of a shared history of suffering,[133] serves as a "bridge," the medium out of which black communal experience is shared. However, that experience found in black music also makes black communal identity *possible*, for in the experience of the performance, in listening to the rhythm, beat, and lyric of the song, comes the realization that we are not singular, isolated selves in the world, but a community knit together through a shared story of "love, death, floods, lynchings," the "Facts of [black] life."[134]

Ed Pavlić, in his groundbreaking work on the role of music in the literature of James Baldwin entitled, *Who Can Afford to Improvise? James Baldwin and Black Music, the Lyric, and the Listeners,* also points out the ways in which Baldwin links blackness to sound throughout his literary corpus. In discussing Baldwin's relationship to the rise of the "Black Power" slogan and subsequent movement, Pavlić shows that Baldwin sought to articulate a notion of "Black Power" which rejected "the blindnesses, pitfalls, and paucities of white power—principal among them, the concept of color itself."[135] In other words, Pavlić is calling attention to the fact that Baldwin offers an understanding of black power, and blackness in general, which is more than the "mirror image"/reflection of whiteness. Pavlić claims, "For him, predictably, a crucial key to reflecting black lay in sound not sight. If heard for what they were almost saying, the voices in the music could liberate the face of black power from its white mask in the mirror."[136] Pavlić continues on:

> Based upon a tonal narrative—a kind of code, he heard deeply embedded in the sound, structure, and origins of black music— Baldwin advocated a black power freed from the schisms at the core of the Western myth, immune to the blindness staring back from the

bottom of the whiteness of the Western well, and refashioned as the determination of a self back in touch (or black and in touch) "with its selfless tonality."[137]

A "black power" freed from the logic of race/color? This notion, which might on first reading seem oxymoronic, is exactly what Baldwin sought to "create." Baldwin, in his search for a reimagined peoplehood, sought a blackness birthed out of aesthetic soil. He is explicit in naming this in his essay, "Anti-Semitism and Black Power," stating: "Black arts has nothing to with color, either. It is an attempt to create a black self-image which the white Republic could never allow. It is an attempt to tell the truth about black people *to* black people because the American Republic has told us nothing but lies."[138] Black art is about *creation*, the creation of a *black* sense of self, decoupled from the logic of race/color. Black art gives birth to this reality.

This notion of blackness as a matter of "sound not sight"[139] is also articulated by Ashon Crawley in his work *Blackpentecostal Breath*. Crawley argues that "the blues ain't just the lyric. The blues is enfleshment; the blues is material."[140] In other words, Crawley makes clear that blackness is carried in sound, blackness is the blues "enfleshed." Crawley solidifies this claim by hearkening to James Baldwin and his 1961 interview with Studs Terkel.[141] In this interview, Baldwin claims that in order to write his first novel, he had to contend with being "ashamed of where I came from and where I had been," his shame in relation to blackness.[142] To reconcile himself to that history, Baldwin returned to black music, specifically Bessie Smith. He recounts:

> I had to find out what I had been like in the beginning, in order, just technically as a writer, to re-create Negro speech. I realized it was a cadence; it was not a question of dropping s's or n's or g's, but a question of the *beat*. Bessie had the beat. . . .
>
> And I played Bessie every day. A lot of the book is in dialogue, you know, and I corrected things according to what I was able to hear when Bessie sang, and when James P. Johnson plays. It's that *tone*, that sound, which is in me.[143]

This is what Crawley calls "black tone," and he goes on to say that Baldwin's "writing is not antithetical to the material force of the form that speech, song, takes but must be materialized *through* the materiality, the texture and weight, the thickness and intensity, of vibration, of sound, of sonic force."[144] In other words, for Baldwin to write, and in essence to recover his blackness, required his reclaiming a tone, a sound, a song, *a beat* which is the materiality of blackness, and blackness the materiality of sound.[145]

However, one does not simply experience blackness, but as the music plays and one sits and listens to the performance, collective identity is being brought to the fore and knit together. As Crawley makes clear, "the materiality of blackness," "the animating breath" that undergirds "shouting," "whooping," and black song, is the means by which black social life is established.[146] In other words, these "performative practices," which include sound and song, "constitute a disruptive force, generative for imagining otherwise modes of social organization and mobilization."[147] Crawley frames these practices in relation to "Blackpentecostalism," which should not be confused with the tradition which bears that name. He posits:

> Blackpentecostalism does not belong to those Saints called Blackpentecostal, those Saints that attend traditionally considered Pentecostal church spaces. Rather, Blackpentecostalism belongs to all who would so live into the fact of the flesh, live into this fact as a critique of the violence of modernity, the violence of the Middle Passage and enslavement, the violence of enslavement and its ongoing afterlife, live into the flesh as a critique of the ongoing attempt to interdict the capacity to breathe. The aesthetic practices cannot be owned but only *collectively produced*, cannot be property but must be given away in order to *constitute community*.[148]

Thus, black breath, undergirding black sound, is that which "must be common and used by all, for vitality, for life. This sharing in and as commons enacts violence against any form of marginalization or oppression."[149] Black sound serves as the medium out of which modes of black life are constituted.

In a similar fashion, Baldwin argues, "No one knows precisely how identities are forged, but it is safe to say that identities are not invented: an identity would seem to be *arrived at* by the way in which the person faces and uses his experience."[150] Therefore, music provides the medium by which a person can "face and use" experience, and out of the experience of black music a black identity is birthed and perpetuated. In this moment of exchange, one in which black life produces music and, in turn, black life is produced by music, we find Baldwin's unique, tonally informed understanding of black communal identity.

It is important to note that the ability of black music to both communicate the black experience and create black community is a reflection of what Baldwin calls "true religion."[151] This again points to the fact that Baldwin is disidentifying with understandings of peoplehood rooted in religious identity. Despite his criticisms of the black church, Baldwin first encountered the potential for the sharing and overcoming of suffering in community in black

church spaces, black Pentecostal spaces. In *The Fire Next Time*, Baldwin rem-
inisced about his time as a preacher, stating:

> Nothing that has happened to me since equals the power and the
> glory that I sometimes felt when, in the middle of a sermon, I knew
> that I was somehow, by some miracle, really carrying, as they said,
> "the Word"—when the church and I were one. Their pain and their
> joy were mine, and mine were theirs—they surrendered their pain
> and joy to me, I surrendered mine to them—and their cries of
> "Amen!" and "Hallelujah!" and "Yes, Lord!" and "Praise His name!"
> and "Preach it, brother!" sustained and whipped on my solos until we
> all became equal, wringing wet, singing and dancing, in anguish and
> rejoicing, at the foot of the altar.[152]

In other words, Baldwin is pointing to the fact that black Christian churches
can and have served as hubs for this exchange of suffering and communal
belonging, being described in richly religious terms such as "power" and "glory."
However, as discussed in Chapter 1 many, if not all churches in Baldwin's estimate, fail to carry the weight of this religious exchange, due to their repressive
structures and commitment to "the principles" of "Blindness, Loneliness, and
Terror."[153] For this reason, Clarence Hardy argues that, for Baldwin, "it is music
that sanctifies religion and not religion that sanctifies music."[154]

Therefore, it is in music that one finds the power of this community-building
exchange most powerfully expressed. Baldwin's conversation with Nikki
Giovanni captures this point:

> Baldwin: . . . you were talking before about the church you went to
>   visit. I thought about the Apollo Theater. The last time I saw Are-
>   tha, what did she do at the Apollo Theater but turn it into a gospel
>   church service—!
> Giovanni: Everybody testified.
> Baldwin: And that's true religion. A black writer comes out of that.[155]

In other words, what marks *true religion* for Baldwin is the possibility of bringing human beings into the experience of exchange, which he and Giovanni
understand through the language of "testimony."[156] In African American
churches, the testimony period, or testifying, is a particular moment in which
persons express the unvarnished truth of what they have "been through" in
regard to life's struggles, reflecting on the pain and adversity they have faced,
either in particular instances or in regard to the larger narrative of their lives.
This is often followed by an expression of how those moments of adversity were
overcome, often with the help of god or the religious community. What is

important for Baldwin is music's ability to serve as a medium of unvarnished testimony, a means of telling the story of black life while also revealing the ways in which we overcame, together, as a community. This is what writers and musicians do for the community.

However, to lean too heavily on the narrative of "suffering" and struggle misses an equally significant facet of Baldwin's understanding of black communal identity—which is the reality of joy. In "The Uses of the Blues," Baldwin comments:

> . . . I want to talk about the blues not only because they speak of this particular experience of life and this state of being, but because they contain the toughness that manages to make this experience articulate. I am engaged, then, in a discussion of craft or, to use a very dangerous word, art. And I want to suggest that the acceptance of this anguish one finds in the blues, and the expression of it, creates also, however odd this may sound, a kind of joy.[157]

As stated previously, black art and music provide a means of contending with suffering, and it is in facing one's suffering that the possibility of joy comes to the fore. Pavlić, also referencing "The Uses of the Blues," argues that for Baldwin, "joy becomes possible through a lyrical relationship with basic intensities of life."[158] Therefore, blackness, as an artistically constituted, communal identity "is a tremendous spiritual condition,"[159] for out of the fires of suffering and struggle an identity marked by an unprecedented joy is revealed. Baldwin posits:

> The blacks have now taken over this once pejorative term and made of it a rallying cry and a badge of honor and are teaching their children to be proud that they are black. It is true that the children are as vari-colored—tea, coffee, chocolate, mocha, honey, eggplant coated with red pepper, red pepper dipped in eggplant—as it is possible for a people to be; black people, here, are no more uniformly black than white people are physically white; but the shades of color, which have been used for so long to distress and corrupt our minds and set us against each other, now count, at least in principle, for nothing.[160]

This is not a type of "chauvinism in reverse," for as mentioned above, Baldwin's understanding of blackness has little to do with the delusion of color.[161] But to *be* black is to exist in the joy of life bursting forth from the trauma of suffering. Color ceases to have meaning, and yet the color black becomes a metaphor for an experience rooted in suffering and joy.

This raises the question, what has all of this to do with white communal identity, or the othering which produces lines of division within black religious spaces? Baldwin, in an interview with Studs Terkel, states: ". . . if you can examine and face your life, you can discover the terms with which you are connected to other lives, and they can discover, too, the terms with which they are connected to other people. . . . This is a very great liberation."[162] Elsewhere, Baldwin states, ". . . in re-creating ourselves, in saving ourselves, we can re-create and save many others: whosoever will."[163] In other words, for Baldwin, one must radically assess one's life, a kind of re-creation, and one medium for re-creation is found in black music, which offers the opportunity for an encounter both with oneself and with the Other. This confrontation provides the means by which people come to see the ways in which their lives intersect and connect with other lives. Whiteness requires the belief that black life is radically Other, radically different from whiteness, and black art provides the hammer by which to shatter this illusion.

As previously articulated, white racial identity requires the continued lie of innocence, one in which the white collective history of destruction, rape, and pillage is obfuscated and denied. This is the reason that white people cannot "comprehend the force of such a woman as Mahalia Jackson, who does not sound like anyone in Canterbury Cathedral" and are "unable to accept the depth of sorrow, out of which a Ray Charles comes."[164] In *Just Above My Head*, Baldwin builds on this point through the main character Hall, commenting:

> If this sound always makes me think of a black cat, it is because the
> sound is black. It is black because the people who have betrayed them-
> selves into being white dare not believe that a sound so rude and horri-
> ble, so majestic and universal, can possibly issue from them—though it
> has, and it does; that is how they recognize it, and why they flee from
> it: and they will hear it in themselves again, when the present delusion
> is shattered from the earth.[165]

Blackness, as found in black music, has the potential to shatter the illusions of whiteness which, in turn, bears the possibility of liberating white persons *from* whiteness. In the music, white people are forced to engage the question and reality of the mythos they have created, birthed in an attempt to escape what they have done and what they continue to do.[166] Baldwin argues that "I feel very strongly, though, that this amorphous people [white Americans] are in desperate search for something which will help them to re-establish their connection with themselves, and with one another. This can only begin to happen as the truth begins to be told."[167] In this confrontation with the truth of who they are, which happens through black art, whites will no longer need the Negro, nor will they need "whiteness." This is one possible meaning for Baldwin's enigmatic statement in *Fire* that white people will need to "become black" themselves in order to find deliverance. However, what forms of life might come out of the corpse of whiteness, if in fact white US Americans are able to face the truth of who they are, is yet to be seen.[168]

In reference to the theological othering of the black church, for Baldwin the theological markers of difference, like that of sanctification, fail to offer black people a true glimpse of blackness and authentic life, for the Christian faith only serves to initiate black believers into a world of "Blindness, Loneliness, and Terror."[169] Christianity seeks to keep persons "safe" from the world, allowing them to hide behind "totems, taboos, crosses, blood sacrifices, steeples, mosques, races, armies, flags, nations, in order to deny the fact of death, which is the only fact we have."[170] However, within artistically based understandings of blackness, one finds a mode of being rooted in the confrontation of the community with the visceral "Facts of Life."[171] This confrontation tears down the myth of safety, rooted in Christian narratives of salvation, that would seek to shield the human being, forcing the community to radically "confront with passion the conundrum of life."[172] Baldwin roots community not in color, nor theological difference, which for him are problematic sides of the same coin, but in the common story that has created a people, a history which contains in it the anguish and triumph of the black community on this continent.

Conclusion

In this chapter, Baldwin's contentious relationship with the Christian church was examined, with a special emphasis being paid to Baldwin's resistance to the alterity-creating practices of both white and black Christian communities in the United States. What we see in this resistance is Baldwin's attempt at undermining what he understands to be the lies which bind human communities together, those of race/color and the myths of theological peoplehood which provide the fuel for the engine of alterity creation.

However, what was also shown was the way in which Baldwin roots a reimagined blackness not in color or "divine peoplehood," but in the aesthetic beauty of black art. This is an understanding of blackness retold and reimagined with every song, note, and lyric. In an interview with Studs Terkel, Baldwin states:

> Obviously I wasn't white—it wasn't so much a question of wanting to
> be white—but I didn't quite know anymore what being *black* meant.
> I couldn't accept what I had been told.

All you are ever told in this country about being black is that it is a terrible, terrible thing to be. Now, in order to survive this, you have to really dig down into yourself and re-create yourself, really, according to no image which yet exists in America. You have to impose, in fact— this may sound very strange—you have to *decide* who you are, and force the world to deal with you, not with its *idea* of you.[173]

Baldwin is not, necessarily, seeking to theorize blackness throughout his corpus, nor is he attempting to essentialize blackness as the flipside to the delusion of whiteness, but he is prophetically calling attention to blackness' constitution in music, literature, poetry, and diverse artistic mediums. Blackness cannot be intellectually grasped, it must be experienced, it must be heard, and it must be sung.

3
Jimmy's Eschaton:
Hope in "the New Jerusalem"

In 1987, Mavis Nicholson questioned Baldwin on his view of the state of the world:

> Nicholson: Are you still in despair about the world?
> Baldwin: I never have been in despair about the world. I'm enraged by it. But I don't think I'm in despair, I can't afford despair. I can't tell my nephew, my niece, you can't tell the children there's no hope.[1]

What is fascinating about this exchange is that Nicholson, who seemingly had some grasp of Baldwin's literature and public work, understood Baldwin to be *in despair* about the world. Now, one could easily point out that Nicholson is quite off base in reducing Baldwin's positionality, whether in his published works or public discourse, to "despair." However, Nicholson's question does indicate something present in Baldwin's work, for despite Baldwin's perhaps too hasty response that he has "never . . . been in despair about the world," in his literature his "optimism" is always haunted by the ever-encroaching possibility of black despair, birthed in the confrontation of the black person with an anti-black world.

The threat of despair and the possibility of hope will be the focus of this chapter. We will begin by showing that the threat/reality of despair is always and already present in Baldwin's work, which he once framed as the possibility for "suicide, or death, or madness."[2] I believe that these three realities serve as a kind of metaphor in Baldwin's literature for one aspect of the state of black existence, or what he calls the "Facts of Life"—more accurately the facts of *black* life.[3] To get at Baldwin's understanding of despair, we will explore his 1964 piece, "The Uses of the Blues," an essay in which the blues metaphorically

74

symbolizes the "pain" and "anguish" that marks black existence in an anti-black world.[4] In addition, we will spend some time discussing Baldwin's father—David Baldwin—for he embodied, in Baldwin's view, the toll that white supremacy takes on the black mind and body. In essence, the life of David Baldwin materialized the outcome of despair.

After engaging the theme of despair, we will explore Baldwin's vision of hope, framed in the language of "the New Jerusalem."[5] In articulating his message of hope through the language of "the New Jerusalem," Baldwin is disidentifying[6] with Christian eschatological motifs, reimagining the Christian theological notions of "promise" and hope for a future rooted in justice. In order to understand Baldwin's hope, this chapter must examine the meaning of the symbol of "the New Jerusalem" in Christian scripture, in addition to Jürgen Moltmann's understanding of eschatology as being rooted in notions of "hope" and "promise."[7]

Lastly, this chapter will explore Baldwin's framing of hope in relation to the "metaphor" of "the kid" or "the child."[8] Baldwin's corpus reveals that black children serve as the primary symbols for hope in both his personal life and literature. In conversation with Josiah Ulysses Young's work, *James Baldwin's Understanding of God*, which was essential in pointing out "the hopes [Baldwin] had for the next generation,"[9] the hopes Baldwin had in relation to children, I will build on and extend Young's argument in noting that black children, in Baldwin's estimate, carry the promise that a new world can be constructed.[10] Not only is this readily apparent in Baldwin's essays, but it is given fictional representation in his novels such as *Tell Me How Long the Train's Been Gone*, and to a greater degree *If Beale Street Could Talk*. In *Beale Street*, an unborn child stands as the symbol of black hope in the midst of one family's struggle against an unjust criminal justice system, represented by police violence and the prison industrial complex. As Young claims in relation to *Beale Street*, "[the baby] is the reason for Baldwin's hope that we can make the world better than it is."[11] The survival of the family hinges on the survival of the child, a notion that serves as a powerful allegory for Baldwin's understanding of black children as being both the bearers of hope and the builders of a new and just society.

Baldwin's Despair

In his essays and novels, Baldwin seeks to offer a visceral portrait of the state of black life in the United States. In his essay, "The Uses of the Blues," he utilizes the "metaphor" of "the blues" as a means of highlighting "the state of being, out of which the blues come," for "they're about work, love, death, floods, lynchings; in fact, a series of disasters which can be summed up under the arbitrary heading 'Facts of Life.'"[12] In other words, "the blues" are Baldwin's means of discussing the everyday struggles of black people against the on-slaught of white supremacist oppression. That is why Baldwin aptly claims that he could just as easily call the essay "'The Uses of Anguish' or 'The Uses of Pain,'" for the blues capture the anguish, pain, and struggle of black life in this country.[13]

It is important to note that Baldwin does not claim that black life is *only* a struggle against pain and hardship, but this particular essay, in part, seeks to shed light on the weight of oppression bearing down on the black community. Baldwin posits:

> I want to make clear that when I talk about Negroes in this context I am not talking about race; I don't know what race means. I am talking about a social fact. When I say "Negro," it is a digression; it is import-ant to remember that I am not talking about a people, but a person. I am talking about a man who, let's say, was once seventeen and who is now, let's say, forty, who has four children and can't feed them. I am talking about what happens to that man in this time and during this effort. I'm talking about what happens to you if, having barely escaped suicide, or death, or madness, or yourself, you watch your children growing up and no matter what you do, no matter *what* you do, you are powerless, you are really powerless, against the force of the world that is out to tell your child that he has no right to be alive. And no amount of liberal jargon, and no amount of talk about how well and how far we have progressed, does anything to soften or to point out any solution to this dilemma. In every generation, ever since Negroes have been here, every Negro mother and father has had to face that child and try to create in that child some way of surviving this particular world, some way to make the child who will be despised not despise himself. I don't know what "the Negro problem" means to white people, but this is what it means to Negroes.[14]

In this passage, Baldwin frames "the Negro problem," the so-called "Facts of [black] Life," as a struggle against the conditions—the unrelenting and violent "force"—of an anti-black US American culture, which creates the possibility for black despair. He first seeks to pull the discussion out of the realm of the abstract, rooted in theoretical notions of "race" and "people," and place it in relation to black families, specifically parents and their children.[15] For Baldwin, the struggle of black parents, in particular, gets to the root of the problem of black life, for black parents, due to the machinations of white supremacy, find themselves "powerless" to provide materially for their children, while also being "powerless" in creating the means for their children's survival in a world that seeks to kill them at every turn, a world which communicates to black children that they are "despised" and have "no right to be alive."[16] This struggle is exacerbated as black parents attempt to stave off the threat of "suicide, or death, or madness"—realities that they too "barely escaped"—in addition to fighting against internalized self-hatred, leading some black children to despise their black selves.[17] It is this state of black life in the United States, according to Baldwin, that pushes black persons to the edge, and some tumble over the proverbial side into despair—i.e., "suicide, or death, or madness."[18]

The possibility of "suicide, or death, or madness" was profoundly personal for Baldwin. Baldwin himself, as pointed out by his biographer David Leeming, had numerous suicide attempts throughout his life.[19] One of the earliest took place in 1949 after being arrested in Paris "as a receiver of stolen goods"—the aforementioned "goods" being a bedsheet which had, in fact, been stolen, but not by Baldwin. This led to his incarceration for eight days.[20] This incident, the subject of his essay "Equal in Paris," contributed to Baldwin's failed attempt to hang himself upon his release from prison.[21] According to Leeming:

> The hanging had been a desperate act of solidarity with all those literally and metaphorically imprisoned "blacks" of all races who must bear the agony of not being recognized as human beings. . . .
>
> Baldwin was obsessed by what had happened to him. The sheet case brought home to him the precariousness of his expatriation as well as the universal pain of the "wretched." In reworking the incident in "Equal in Paris," he made full use of the method that would always mark his essays, that of taking an event from his own life and using it and himself as metaphors for the larger issues that concerned him.[22]

Again, Baldwin was "obsessed" with this incident, which he understood as highlighting the social and economic state of countless "wretched" throughout the world,[23] expendable and oppressed people with little recourse in the face of state power, people with little hope of being recognized as human. This incident caused a despair that contributed to a suicide attempt; thus, Baldwin must have asked himself how many more of the "wretched" are forced to live in this type of despair, how many more die as a direct result of this unjust system?[24]

However, as Leeming mentioned, Baldwin often utilized his own personal history, including his relationships, as a means through which to analyze larger social phenomena. Arguably, the life of his father, David Baldwin, becomes one of the primary metaphors for the dangers of despair, the possibility of "suicide, or death, or madness." In his essay, "Notes of a Native Son," published in the famous collection of the same name, Baldwin describes in intricate detail the circumstances surrounding the death and funeral of his violently abusive father, a father who suffered from a severe mental illness which eventually contributed to his death.[25] For Baldwin, his father's death was not simply the byproduct of having been institutionalized due to a mental illness,[26] nor was his father's tuberculosis solely to blame,[27] but Baldwin posits that his father's "madness" and death were also the result of white supremacy— "the weight of white people in the world."[28] Baldwin claims, "I saw that this had been for my ancestors and now would be for me an awful thing to live with and that the bitterness which had helped to kill my father could also kill me."[29]

The weight that killed Baldwin's father was not simply represented by the white world in general, but also specific institutions which act as channels for anti-blackness, such as the Christian church. In his speech "White Racism or World Community," Baldwin speaks of the ways in which both the Christian church and white supremacy coalesced in "destroying" his father's mind. He states:

> . . . I watched what the Christian Church did to my father, who was in the pulpit all the years of his life, I watched the kind of poverty, the kind of hopeless poverty, which was not an act of God, but an act of the State, against which he and his children struggled, I watched above all, and this is what is crucial, the ways in which white power can destroy black minds, and what black people are now fighting against, precisely that.[30]

Elsewhere, Baldwin offers a similar analysis of his father's plight, positing:

> I mean, I had to watch my father and what my father had to endure to raise nine children on twenty-seven dollars and fifty cents a week— when he was working. Now, when I was a kid I didn't know at all what the man was going through; I didn't know why he as always in a rage; I didn't know why he was impossible to live with. But I had not yet had to go through his working day. And he couldn't quit his twenty-seven-dollars-and-fifty-cents-a-week job *because* he had nine kids to feed. . . .
>
> My father finally went mad, and when I became a man I understood how that could happen. It wasn't that he didn't love us; he loved his wife and his children, but he couldn't take, day after day, hour after hour, being treated like a nigger on that job and in the streets and on the subways—everywhere he went.[31]

What these two quotes make clear is that Baldwin believed that his father suffered and died from a life consistently under siege by anti-blackness. Baldwin claims that as a child, he did not know or understand what his father went through daily, as he left home to work an incredibly low paying job in an attempt to feed his large family. However, as an adult, Baldwin came to see that much of his father's rage, violence, and despair stemmed from the poverty and humiliation he suffered under the yoke of white supremacy, subjecting him to "being treated like a nigger on that job and in the streets and on the subways— everywhere he went."[32] Thus, the life of Baldwin's father, like the struggles of other black parents, becomes for Baldwin, a means of glimpsing the larger "dilemma"[33] facing the black community, which is the fight to stave off the tentacles of despair in a world of anti-black violence.

James Cone, in his 1969 work *Black Theology and Black Power*, discussed the possibility of black despair through the philosophical category of "the absurd," originally offered by Albert Camus.[34] Cone's use of Camus is profoundly relevant, for Cone links the absurd and despair to white supremacy, and to the question of how black people might respond to the absurdity that is black existence in an anti-black world. He claims:

> When he [the black person] first awakens to his place in America and feels sharply the absolute contradiction between *what is* and *what ought to be* or recognizes the inconsistency between his view of himself as a man and America's description of him as a thing, his immediate reaction is a feeling of absurdity.[35]

Cone continues, stating:

> . . . absurdity arises as man confronts the world and looks for meaning. The same is true in regard to my analysis of the black man in a white society. It is not that the black man is absurd or that the white society as such is absurd. Absurdity arises as the black man seeks to understand his place in the white world. The black man does not view himself as absurd; he views himself as human. But as he meets with the white world and its values, he is confronted with an almighty No and is defined as a thing. This produces the absurdity.
>
> The crucial question, then, for the black man is, "How should I respond to a world which defines me as a nonperson?"[36]

What Cone powerfully captures in these descriptions of the absurd is a reality not at all dissimilar to Baldwin's "blues" or "Facts of Life,"[37] for Cone is making clear that black persons in the United States face a particular type of absurdity in the world, one which arises as black people seek to reconcile *"what is"*—an anti-black world that seeks to reduce black humans to "nonpersons," and *"what ought to be"*—a world in which black families can provide for their children and feel fully affirmed in their personhood. The absurd is what is being signified by Baldwin when he speaks of "the force of the world," a force that reminds the black child "that he has no right to be alive"—it is the wellspring of black despair.[38] The absurd is also clearly visible in Baldwin's assessment of his father's violence and "madness." David Baldwin only sought *"what ought to be,"* which was the means to provide basic necessities for his family, but was tragically faced with *"what is,"* a world of unrelenting white supremacy that economically starved both his family and the black community at large. This is why Cornel West claims, "in fact, the major enemy of black survival in America has been and is neither oppression nor exploitation but rather the nihilistic threat—that is, loss of hope and absence of meaning."[39] In other words, the danger, for Baldwin, Cone, and West is the possible response to the absurd in an anti-black world, which is the ever-present possibility for hopelessness and despair.

To borrow the language of philosopher Lewis Gordon, one might ask, "why go on?"[40] in the face of the absurd, a question haunted by the specter of despair. This chapter is concerned with Baldwin's response to this question, which is as relevant today as it was in Baldwin's time. For one might ask if there is hope for contemporary movements for black lives, movements which seek to counter both the continued proliferation of anti-black violence at the hands of law enforcement and the judicial and legislative assaults on black flourishing, stemming from reentrenched, radical right-wing state governments and a deeply conservative supreme court which has served to intensify white supremacy in the highest echelons of US American politics. What is one to do if, as contemporary Afropessimists would argue, the world *is* anti-black?[41] For Baldwin, there seems to be an implicit recognition that the current order of things—the world—will indeed have to end. Or, as Fred Moten so eloquently states in his essay "Blackness and Nothingness": "The promise of another world, or of the end of this one, is given in the general critique of the world."[42] The remainder of this chapter will discuss Baldwin's "promise of another world," which is rooted in a theological category that bears in it the presumption of the end of this world and the arrival of another—"the New Jerusalem."

Baldwin's Eschatology

In reading Baldwin's assessment of black life in the United States as offered in the previous section, one might be tempted to accuse him of pessimism, as James Mossman did in his 1965 interview with Baldwin.[43] However, in addition to Baldwin's assessment of the depth and breadth of struggle that marks black life, one also finds in his work what Clarence Hardy calls Baldwin's "stubborn hopes for a New Jerusalem."[44] Baldwin's metaphor of "the New Jerusalem," I argue, might be the best paradigm for framing his understanding of hope, a hope that Baldwin never surrendered, even in the face of intractable white supremacist resistance to black movements for liberation.

Baldwin speaks of "the New Jerusalem" in a few key places throughout his corpus. One of those instances can be heard in the final scene of the documentary *The Price of the Ticket*, in which he offers:

> A day will come when you will trust you more than you do now. And you will trust me more than you do now. We can trust each other. I do believe, I really do believe in the New Jerusalem. I really do believe that we can all become better than we are. I know we can. But the price is enormous, and people are not yet willing to pay it.[45]

A similar take on this idea is also found in Baldwin's final interview with Richard Goldstein, who asks Baldwin: "Do you have good fantasies about the future?" To which Baldwin responds: "Oh, that I am working toward 'the New Jerusalem.' That's true, I'm not joking. I won't live to see it but I do believe in it. I think we're going to be better than we are."[46] In these two quotes a few key themes arise, for although Baldwin does not offer a substantive definition of what is meant by "the New Jerusalem," he makes clear that "the New Jerusalem" is an object of future-oriented belief, one inextricably bound to the idea that human beings can "be better than we are." Thus, Baldwin seeks to point toward a different world, a better world, one that he himself is working to construct alongside other people of goodwill.

This raises the question: What is the meaning and significance of "the New Jerusalem"? In speaking of the necessity of building a "New Jerusalem," Baldwin is pulling from early Christian imagery, particularly that imagery found in the book of Revelation, chapter 21. Christopher Z. Hobson, in his work *James Baldwin and the Heavenly City*, convincingly shows that "the most important biblical book for Baldwin, by far, is Revelation, to which he alludes or refers directly in most of his novels."[47] In Revelation, a work of apocalyptic literature which, according to Wes Howard-Brook and Anthony Gwyther, serves as a radical "critique of empire,"[48] one finds a juxtaposition of two cities, Babylon and "the New Jerusalem."[49] Howard-Brook and Gwyther point out that conflict between these two symbolic cities serves as "the master metaphor of the book,"[50] and it is Babylon which signifies the violence,[51] "imperial arrogance,"[52] and economic injustice[53] of the first-century Roman Empire. The book of Revelation is calling on Christians "to persevere in their resistance to empire and embrace God's alternative way."[54] New Testament scholar Brian K. Blount, in his work *Can I Get a Witness? Reading Revelation Through African American Culture*, makes a similar claim, arguing: "John asked his hearers and readers to live a life of . . . resistance. He demanded that they refuse any opportunity, no matter how seemingly inconsequential, to acknowledge Roman imperial or pagan lordship."[55] Later Blount states, ". . . John was essentially asking his people to pick a social and religious fight. He was asking them to witness."[56]

That "alternative way," a "life of . . . resistance," the "polar [opposite]" of Babylon,[57] is represented by the symbol of "the New Jerusalem," which, according to Howard-Brook and Gwyther, "is found wherever human community resists the ways of empire and places God at the center of its shared life."[58] Revelation 21:1–4 records:

> 1 And I saw a new heaven and a new earth; for the first heaven and the first earth passed away, and there is no longer *any* sea. 2 And I saw the holy city, new Jerusalem, coming down out of heaven from God, made ready as a bride adorned for her husband. 3 And I heard a loud voice from the throne, saying, "Behold, the tabernacle of God is among men, and He shall dwell among them, and they shall be His people, and God Himself shall be among them, 4 and He shall wipe away every tear from their eyes; and there shall no longer be *any* death; there shall no longer be *any* mourning, or crying, or pain; the first things have passed away (NASB).[59]

Clearly, the heavenly city is a vision of a hope, one in which god's dwelling with humanity brings about the flourishing of human life. In interpreting this passage, Howard-Brook and Gwyther posit:

> Revelation envisioned life in New Jerusalem not as a grim contrariness to Babylon but as a joyous alternative to empire, which constituted "real" living. Authentic community is a place where life can be celebrated, songs can be sung, and human relationships can flourish.[60]

In other words, "the New Jerusalem" is a vision of what is to come, marking a period in which "cycle[s] of violence," "death," "empire's economic exploitation," and human division are vanquished once and for all.[61] Again, "the New Jerusalem" serves as the radical "alternative" to Babylon, thus it can signify the ultimate beacon of hope while at the same time serve as a symbol of "resistance" to the machinations of empire and injustice.

It should be apparent that Baldwin is attempting to articulate a future-oriented vision of hope through his engagement with this biblical symbol. Baldwinian hope in "the New Jerusalem" is rooted in the possibility that empire can end, and that the machinations of white supremacy can be destroyed. Josiah Ulysses Young, III, in *James Baldwin's Understanding of God*, highlights Baldwin's essay "Notes on the House of Bondage," arguing that it "explains what [Baldwin] means by 'Jerusalem.'"[62] Young quotes this passage as capturing Baldwin's sense of Jerusalem: ". . . the earth's populations can be fed if—or, rather, when—we alter our priorities. We can irrigate deserts and feed the entire earth for the price we are paying to build bombs that we will be able to use, in any event, only once."[63] However, I believe a separate quote from this same essay better captures Baldwin's sense of "the New Jerusalem." Baldwin claims:

> I am speaking of the breakup—the end—of the so-overextended Western empire. I am thinking of the black and nonwhite peoples who are shattering, redefining and re-creating history—making all things new—simply by declaring their presence, by delivering their testimony. The empire never intended that this testimony should be heard, but, *if I hold my peace, the very stones will cry out.*
>
> One can speak, then, of the fall of an empire at that moment when, though all of the paraphernalia of power remain intact and visible and seem to function, neither the citizen-subject within the gates nor the indescribable hordes outside it believe in the morality or the reality of the kingdom anymore—when no one, any longer, anywhere, aspires to the empire's standards.[64]

Therefore, Baldwin, too, is seeking the end of a "Western empire." That empire for Baldwin is represented by a history of conquest, genocide, and theft by white US Americans, placing all of us within a literal "house of bondage."[65] However, Baldwin remains hopeful, and draws yet again from Revelation 21 in claiming that the work of "making all things new," is being enacted by "black and non-white people."[66] To "make all things new," signifies an "alternative" reality, a "New Jerusalem," constructed by the oppressed who are "shattering, redefining, and re-creating history."

I would go so far as to say that Baldwin, in pointing to "the New Jerusalem," is articulating a kind of "critical utopianism" as put forth by José Esteban Muñoz in his work *Cruising Utopia: The Then and There of Queer Futurity.*[67] In this work, building primarily, though not exclusively, on the philosophy of Ernst Bloch, Muñoz puts forth a vision of a "concrete utopia" as opposed to a kind of "abstract" utopianism—again, two concepts borrowed from Bloch, a utopianism "relational to historically situated struggles," and a utopia that captures the "hopes of a collective."[68] That historically situated struggle, and the collective to which he refers, is the queer community in all of its multifaceted expressions. Therefore, against what he views as "the antirelational turn in queer studies"[69] and the "pragmatic gay agenda" and its obsession with a liberal "politics of the here and now,"[70] Muñoz articulates his "critical" and "queer utopianism."[71] He states:

> QUEERNESS IS NOT yet here. Queerness is an ideality. Put another way, we are not yet queer. We may never touch queerness, but we can feel it as the warm illumination of a horizon imbued with potentiality. We have never been queer, yet queerness exists for us as an ideality that can be distilled from the past and used to imagine a future. The future is queerness's domain.[72]

He continues on:

> Queerness is a longing that propels us onward, beyond romances of the negative and toiling in the present. Queerness is that thing that lets us feel that this world is not enough, that indeed something is missing. Often we can glimpse the worlds proposed and promised by queerness in the realm of the aesthetic. The aesthetic, especially the queer aesthetic, frequently contains blueprints and schemata of a forward-dawning futurity.[73]

What makes this relevant for the project at hand is that Baldwin, too, is challenging us to see that "this world is not enough, that indeed something is missing"; and in recognizing that deficit, that inherent wrongness in the present, we must continually look to, and work toward, that "forward-dawning futurity," a world that does not yet exist. Muñoz believes that queerness specifically serves as a sign of that futurity, it is (and Muñoz borrows here from Giorgio Agamben) a "potentiality."[74] Baldwin, pulling from his "inner vocabulary"[75]—that interior language made up of black Christian symbols and theological tropes—points toward "the New Jerusalem" as the reality that captures that future "potentiality." However, queerness also factors into Baldwin's futurity, even if not as centrally as one finds in Muñoz, for "queer relationality"[76] does, for Baldwin, signify the coming of "the New Jerusalem."

"The New Jerusalem" and Eschatological "Hope" and "Promise"

Again, it is important to highlight that for Baldwin, "the New Jerusalem" is a future-oriented possibility, for he cannot point to definitive evidence that the empire will fall, which is why he argues that "all of the paraphernalia of power remain intact and visible and seem to function."[77] However, in pointing toward a future reality in which "the New Jerusalem" might be fully realized, using the apocalyptic language and symbols of the book of Revelation, Baldwin is engaging in a type of eschatological theorizing, which according to Jürgen Moltmann in his work *Theology of Hope*, is rooted in "hope" and the "promise" of what is to come, the promise of god to make "all things new."

According to Moltmann, "eschatology," as traditionally conceived:

> . . . was long called the "doctrine of last things" or the "doctrine of the end." By these last things were meant events which will one day break upon man, history and the world at the end of time. . . . These end events were to break into this world from somewhere beyond history, and to put an end to the history in which all things here live and move.[78]

For many, eschatology was, and continues to be, understood as an apocalyptic inbreaking of God, and God's Christ, into the world from outside of human history at a particular, and singular, moment in the future. The eschaton is often conceived as an extrahistorical event, wholly supernatural in its expression.

However, Moltmann offers another understanding of eschatology that he argues is more in line with the Christian tradition. He posits:

> In actual fact, however, eschatology means the doctrine of the Christian hope, which embraces both the object hoped for and also the hope inspired by it. From first to last, and not merely in epilogue, Christianity is eschatology, is hope, forward looking and forward moving, and therefore also revolutionizing and transforming the present. The eschatological is not one element *of* Christianity, but it is the medium of Christian faith as such, the key in which everything in it is set, the glow that suffuses everything here in the dawn of an expected new day.[79]

In other words, eschatology, Christian eschatology, is a matter of "hope," a hope in a future reality that energizes and "revolutionizes" the present.

Connected with Moltmann's "theology of hope" is the notion of "promise." According to Moltmann, the god of the Hebrew and Christian scriptures is a god whose "appearances" are always and already accompanied by "a word of divine promise."[80] That promise is the declaration of a "as yet unrealized future."[81] Christopher Z. Hobson, in his work *James Baldwin and the Heavenly City*, brings our attention to Hebrews 11:13–16, which, for our purposes, reveals how the notion of "promise" is inextricably linked to "the city" "to come," a symbol that resonates deeply with the idea of a "New Jerusalem."[82] The passage states:

> 13 All these died in faith, without receiving the promises, but having seen them and having welcomed them from a distance, and having

confessed that they were strangers and exiles on the earth. 14 For those
who say such things make it clear that they are seeking a country of
their own. 15 And indeed if they had been thinking of that country
from which they went out, they would have had opportunity to return.
16 But as it is, they desire a better country, that is a heavenly one.
Therefore God is not ashamed to be called their God; for He has
prepared a city for them (NASB).

This passage makes clear that those faithful who have passed on did not receive
their promise, but they recognized, even "from a distance," the promise to
come. It is a promise rooted in the idea that God will prepare a new country,
a city in which they will dwell. Hobson states:

> If we secularize the passage, a crucial but partial step, we can say
> those it refers to seek not a better country among those in their time,
> but a new one that may exist someday. This secularization is vital but
> insufficient, since in Hebrews the country is not simply "better" but
> "heavenly," and, at the end of the eschatological history already re-
> ferred to, is to come "down out of heaven" to exist on earth, in the
> city Hebrews says God has prepared (Rev. 21:2). The Hebrews writer,
> then, has defined the heavenly city that may exist on earth one day if
> the "promises" seen by faith are true.[83]

As this passage makes clear, Hobson directly links this Hebrews passage about a
promised future to "the New Jerusalem" found in Revelation 21. Therefore, returning to Moltmann, Christian eschatological belief is not grounded in "existing
reality which we can all experience,"[84] but "hope's statement of promise, however,
must stand in contradiction to the reality which can at present be experienced."[85]
In other words, Moltmann's understanding of Christian eschatology is not a type
of otherworldly logic, but it speaks to a historic reality that cannot yet be imag-
ined, one in which "the possibility of new experiences" comes to the fore.[86]

In showing that Baldwin is drawing from this tradition of Christian eschatology, rooted in the symbol of "the New Jerusalem," it is apparent that Baldwin
seeks to offer an understanding of *hope* rooted in the *promise* of not-yet-realized
future, one in which death and disruption are displaced and black life is renewed. This promise is not based in anything that can yet be seen in a definitive
sense, but functions in a similar fashion to faith as being "the substance of
things hoped for, the evidence of things not seen."[87]

However, it is necessary to note at this point that Baldwin's hope in "the
New Jerusalem" is dependent on the work of humanity. In other words, it is
always articulated in relation to Baldwin's belief that humans can "be better

than we are,"[88] and thus human beings are responsible for constructing that new future. As Clarence Hardy states in *James Baldwin's God:* "perhaps this new city would be made with human hands and not supernatural ones, but Baldwin . . . believed in the possibility of a new sacred reality."[89] This should give pause to anyone who would too easily claim that Baldwin is full-on embracing/"identifying"[90] with the tradition of Christian eschatology in a definitive sense, but consistent with Baldwin's practice concerning religious imagery, he is, in fact, *disidentifying* with eschatological hope. Unlike Moltmann, whose understanding of "promise" is rooted in god's "faithfulness" in bringing that promise to fruition,[91] Baldwin decouples the promise of a "New Jerusalem" from any theistic molding, making it clear that human beings must "build the New Jerusalem" themselves. One moment in *The Fire Next Time* captures this powerfully. Baldwin states:

> Everything now, we must assume, is in our hands; we have no right to assume otherwise. If we—and now I mean the relatively conscious whites and the relatively conscious blacks, who must, like lovers, insist on, or create, the consciousness of the others—do not falter in our duty now, we may be able, handful that we are, to end the racial nightmare, and achieve our country, and change the history of world.[92]

This language of "everything" being "in our hands," supported by the claim made elsewhere by Baldwin that "we must save each other[,] I don't depend on anyone else to do it,"[93] makes it clear that Baldwin parts ways with Moltmann's understanding of eschatological hope and promise as being rooted in Christian understandings of god. For although some Christian eschatologies offer the possibility of human beings working *with* god in building a new world, Baldwin believes that the responsibility for building that world is *solely* our own.

Although it is now clear that human beings must create and "re-create" the world through the work of their own hands, Baldwin has specific hands in mind which will be responsible for carrying the promise of a new world— these are the hands of children. The following sections will examine the particular role of children in Baldwin's corpus, for it is the children who serve as the inspiration for Baldwin's hope and are also the builders of "the New Jerusalem."

A Future Built by Children's Hands

In examining Baldwin's understanding of hope, one must engage what Baldwin calls "a useful metaphor," which is the metaphor of "the kid."[94] Baldwin understands children to be the raison d'être for pursuing and promoting the idea of hope, but also the means by which hope will be realized in the world. In other words, to borrow Moltmann's language, children for Baldwin, are "both the object hoped for" and the "inspiration" for hope.[95] However, although Baldwin calls the symbol of the child "a useful metaphor," he also understands the importance of the child in a quite literal sense, for his personal relationships to both his own nieces and nephews and his godchildren serve as the real-world touchpoint for his eschatological vision, his critical utopianism.[96]

Baldwin's commitment to hope stems from his commitment to building a different world for those closest to him, particularly his nieces and nephews. To surrender to despair, according to Baldwin, would be to surrender those children's futures. Let us return briefly to the exchange between Baldwin and Mavis Nicholson that opened this chapter, for it vividly captures this point. When asked if he was "in despair about the world," Baldwin responds: "I never have been in despair about the world. I'm enraged by it. But I don't think I'm in despair, I can't afford despair. I can't tell my nephew, my niece, you can't tell the children there's no hope."[97] In this quote, Baldwin claims that one can be angered at the state of the world as it exists for black human beings and other oppressed groups living under the yoke of a white supremacist empire, but one "can't afford despair," for to despair in the face of the absurdity that marks black existence in an anti-black world would be to surrender the future of black children to hopelessness. Therefore, Baldwin chooses to embrace a vision of hope, not (only) for one's own sake, but "for the sake of those who are coming after us,"[98] for those who will be left with the world as it currently exists.

A similar sentiment can be seen in Baldwin's dialogue with Nikki Giovanni. At one point in the conversation, Baldwin foretells that a "holocaust," a racial holocaust, "will come eventually,"[99] and in thinking of this moment, Baldwin's mind returns to the future of black children. He states:

> I will also be able to ride out the storm, but what is more important is not so much riding out the storm for you, Nikki, and me, Jimmy. In my mind's eye there's always that kid. He's going to be here when you're gone. And when I am long gone. So my point of view is that it is about the children. It is about the children. We have to give the children something which in a way was, after all, given to us, though we had to learn how to translate it. Your kid will be moving in a very different world than the one in which I grew up, which he won't know anything about at all. Or the world in which you grew up, which will be remote for him. And yet he comes out of it and has got to carry it much further than you or I will be able to carry it.[100]

What one sees in this exchange is that Baldwin understands the importance of surviving the struggle as being not for his own sake, or for the sake of Nikki

Giovanni, but for the sake of the child. To give the children "something," speaks to the tools that older generations must give the children in order to survive. Perhaps, one could say that what the older generations give the children is a "critical utopianism," a discontent with how the world currently operates. It is the children who must "carry" the world, and "carry it much further than you or I will be able to carry it." Baldwin is claiming here that his work, his struggle to create a new world out of the ruins of the old, always and already has "that kid" as his central paradigm.

However, it is important to note that it is not simply for the sake of children that Baldwin hopes, but in a related, although different fashion, Baldwin understands children as the purveyors and bringers of hope to the world. What will become apparent is that children, in Baldwin's corpus, are often framed as harbingers of hope in a way that bears starkly Christological underpinnings.[101] Those Christological influences can be seen in Baldwin's understanding of the sacred nature of children, but also in the ways in which the coming of those sacred children creates the world anew. In speaking of the "sanctity" of children in *The Devil Finds Work*, Baldwin claims:

> The children of the despised and rejected are menaced from the moment they stir in the womb, and are therefore sacred in a way that the children of the saved are not. And the children know it, which is how they manage to raise their children, and why they will not be persuaded—by their children's murderers, after all—to cease having children.[102]

This quote is particularly astute, for Baldwin argues that the children of the oppressed, even after being brought into the world, are sacred, especially those from the black community. Baldwin is not at all claiming that the children of white people, the so-called "saved," are not also sacred, but the children of the "despised" are sacred because they face death even in the womb, and therefore their coming into the world is that much more of a miracle, a sacred act. The sacred nature of the black child, Baldwin claims, is an idea shared within the whole of the black community, which serves as the reason that black children grow up and choose to have and raise more black children, and on and on into future generations. What this clearly shows is that Baldwin is framing the births of black children as one of the more radical acts of rebellion against black despair. In choosing to create black life, generation after generation, black communities continue to engage in a revolutionary act of defiance, for despite the pressures offered by the white world, black adults cannot be convinced to stop having children. Children, for Baldwin, are indeed sacred, for they stand both as a symbol of hope and are the bringers of hope for the "despised."

This theme of children being the bringers of hope is repeated again and again throughout Baldwin's corpus. Josiah Ulysses Young notes that Baldwin's 1973 interview with *The Black Scholar*, "indicates the hopes [Baldwin] had for the next generation."[103] When asked, "what closing words would you like to leave with *The Black Scholar* readers,"[104] Baldwin speaks of his godchildren, stating:

> I think the revolution begins first of all in the most private chamber of somebody's heart, in your consciousness. I think that what is happening now is that a new vision of the world which has always been there, but a new vision of the world, is beginning to be born. And if that is so, then the little boys that I am talking about will be the architects of that world.[105]

Baldwin claims that the new world being constructed will be one made by the hands of the children, who will shape its contours, values, and "vision." Young also draws attention to Baldwin's description of how the world used to exist—a society "without policemen, without torture, without rape, where gold was an ornament, not the summit of human desire"—as an indication of how Baldwin imagines the world to come.[106] Baldwin states, "it has happened before and it can happen again." Therefore, Baldwin is indicating that his vision of the new world is one free of policing, sexual violence, and intractable greed.[107] "Civilization," i.e., western civilization according to Baldwin, "is on its death bed," and "those three little boys who are living in California, my godchildren, will not be doomed."[108] Again, this is a "critical" and "concrete" utopia, a means of pointing to a world that does not yet exist. It is important to note that Young explicitly connects Baldwin's centering of hope in children to Baldwin's portrayal of the child in *If Beale Street Could Talk*.[109] More will be said about this below.

This understanding of children as being the bearers of the new world is also seen in Baldwin's novel *Tell Me How Long the Train's Been Gone*. In one particular scene, the book's protagonist Leo Proudhammer, who at this moment in the novel is a world-famous actor and entertainer, is preparing to speak at a large protest rally.[110] Accompanying Leo at the rally is Black Christopher, a young, black radical who is also Leo's lover. Just before Leo stands to deliver his speech, a young black girl stands up to sing:

> There was a little black girl on the platform, she was part of a junior choir from a Brooklyn church. They were singing. . . . They were singing a song about deliverance; she had a heavy, black, huge voice. She was the leader of the song, and her voice, in all that open air, rang

against the sky and the trees and the stone walls of the office buildings
and the faces of the open-mouthed people and the closed faces of the
cops, as though she were singing in a cave. *Deliverance will come*, she
sang, *I know it will come, He said it would come.* And, again, *Deliver-*
ance will come. He said it would come. I know it will come.[111]

As Leo stands listening, he reflects on the lyrics of the song, asking "Would
it?" Would deliverance indeed come for black people in this country? Leo is
fully aware of the fact that the very reason they were protesting that day was
"because deliverance had *not* come."[112] He continues to ponder:

> Deliverance will come: it had not come for my mother and father, it
> had not come for Caleb, it had not come for me, it had not come for
> Christopher, it had not come for this nameless little girl, and it had not
> come for all these thousands who were listening to her song.[113]

In pointing out the untold masses for whom deliverance "had not come," Leo
is raising an existential question, rooted in the reality of the continued violent
onslaught on black existence in an anti-black world. What could deliverance
possibly mean for a community who has consistently seen those hopes dashed?

As Leo's mind continues to reflect on the little girl, his lover Christopher,
and his brother Caleb, he posits:

> Whatever had happened to me could have no meaning unless it
> could help to deliver them. But the price for this deliverance, this
> most ambitious of transactions, could only be found in a wallet which
> I had always claimed was not mine. I began to sweat. The little girl's
> voice rang out. Caleb's face hung steadily in the center of my mind.
> *Deliverance will come.* Well, if she believed it, then it had to be made
> possible; though only she, after all, plain, stocky, beautiful, black girl,
> could really make it true.[114]

It is here that we see the sacred nature of black children, and their sacred task
of bearing hope for a new world. Despite Leo's doubts, the young girl's procla-
mation, offered through song, that deliverance was in fact possible, produced
in Leo a belief in the possibility of deliverance. Leo is now allowing himself to
hope in the face of hundreds of years of history, and his own personal narrative,
which offers myriad pieces of evidence against the possibility that justice for
black lives will arise. However, Leo knows that "deliverance, however, was not
in my hands," it was in the hands of the children.[115] The power of this moment
is captured as the little girl approaches him at the end of his speech asking for
an autograph, and Leo "signed it . . . above my name, *Deliverance will come.*"[116]

However, Baldwin is not always quite so explicit in his work, for sometimes one must read beneath the surface of a narrative to see the "forward-dawning futurity"[117] which Baldwin is gesturing toward. As Muñoz discusses in *Cruising Utopia*, building again on Bloch's philosophy, "art" has a "utopian function," and "the utopian function is enacted by a certain surplus in the work that promises a futurity, something that is not quite here."[118] Returning to Baldwin's final novel *Just Above My Head*, and the queer characters Arthur and Crunch, we see the manner in which Baldwin, in a much more subtle way, is highlighting how young people gesture toward a future, a potential utopia.

Arthur and Crunch belong to a vocal quartet, and while on tour Arthur and Crunch begin their love affair which brings a transformation that affects the rest of their lives. However, immediately following the passage in which their lovemaking is narrated as a type of conversion experience (as discussed in Chapter 1 of this book), Arthur and Crunch now have to face the world, and the gaze of their forty-seven-year-old "impresario" Clarence Webster[119] who questions, "what's going on between you two?"[120] Baldwin narrates the morning after their initial sexual encounter, stating:

> Nothing can be hidden; secrets do not exist. They were on the road for ten more days. They were called the "lovebirds," they were called "Romeo and Romeo." They laughed, with their arms around each other sometimes, far too happy to be afraid. For one thing, they were far too young to be afraid. As far as they knew, and as far as they cared, what was happening between them had never before happened in the entire history of the world. Other people had words for whatever it was, too bad, too sad—they were not to be found in that dictionary. They walked in the light of each other's eyes, absolutely unaware of white people or black people, waking up, sometimes, in each other's arms, not knowing what town it was, and not caring: they were called "love-birds" and "Romeo and Romeo" because they were alone, they were far from other people, they were in danger.[121]

Muñoz's claim in his analysis of one of Frank O'Hara's poems is relevant in our examination of *Just Above My Head*, for the passage describing Crunch's and Arthur's love "signifies a vast lifeworld of queer relationality, an encrypted sociality, and a utopian potentiality."[122] Arthur and Crunch, who were touring the deep south in the mid-twentieth century, were living in radical contradiction to their world. "Their arms around each other," their public displays of love and affection, are to borrow yet again Moten's language, a "critique of the world," that bears in it "the promise of another world, or of the end of this one."[123] For Muñoz, the "quotidian act[s]" contain the possibility for signifying utopia,[124] and Arthur and Crunch, with these simple gestures, are signifying a world that could one day exist, one in which black queer young people can move through the world, openly displaying their love and desire without the fear of danger and violence. That world had not yet come, yet their love offers a glimmer of its possibility.

Their bold choice to live into a reality that in many ways did not yet exist, captured the attention of others—it put them in danger. Webster, their adult impresario who was responsible for booking their gigs and safely guiding them through the South, (mis)recognized something in Arthur and Crunch's relationship. He wanted to know, "what's going on between you two?" and then said, "I might want to do it, too."[125] Webster, through threats and cajoling, attempted to participate in their sexual activities, but he wanted to do so in secret, through conniving and predatory behavior. He (mis)recognized what was truly taking place between them. Crunch and Arthur were living into a queer future that had not yet come, a reality that queer men such as Baldwin still looked for. They were living into a reality in which their queer selves would be free to desire and love in whatever ways they deemed necessary. Webster wanted release, he wanted to take advantage of these two young people. This is why Crunch claims, "you *can't* do what we do, brother. You can't sing."[126] For the song, the sound created by Arthur and Crunch together, was yet another manifestation of their queer love. The "miracle" of their music reflected the "miracle" of their connection, both of which gestured toward utopia.[127]

As has been made clear, children serve as the reason for maintaining the promise of hope, but also as the vehicles in which hope will be offered to the world. Baldwin is by no means naively optimistic about the state of the world, for he is fully aware of the possibility of despair in the black community. Yet, as Baldwin claims in his interview with Kenneth B. Clark: "I can't be a pessimist because I'm alive. To be a pessimist means that you have agreed that human life is an academic matter, so I'm forced to be an optimist; I'm forced to believe that we can survive whatever we must survive."[128] Baldwin seeks to offer the world a vision of hope, yet he knows, like Leo Proudhammer, that hope is not in his hands, but in the hands of children.

The following section will be dedicated to parsing out the whole of this chapter's argument through a close reading of Baldwin's novel *If Beale Street Could Talk*, for this novel in particular captures, in literary fashion, both the reality of despair which stems from black people's confrontation with white supremacy, and the hope for a new world offered in the figure of the black child.

Despair and Hope in *If Beale Street Could Talk*

In the epilogue of *No Name in the Street*, Baldwin offers a theologically rich passage about despair, a new world, and the salvific role of black children who are birthed by the Holy Spirit:

> This book has been much delayed by trials, assassinations, funerals, and despair. Nor is the American crisis, which is part of a global, historical crisis, likely to resolve itself soon. An old world is dying, and a new one, kicking in the belly of its mother, time, announces that it is ready to be born. This birth will not be easy, and many of us are doomed to discover that we are exceedingly clumsy midwives. No matter, so long as we accept that our responsibility is to the newborn. . .
>
> Now, it is the Virgin, the alabaster Mary, who must embrace the despised black mother whose children are also the issue of the Holy Ghost.[129]

According to Josiah Ulysses Young, this language of "a new world" about to be birthed out of its mother, in addition to the image of "the despised black mother" giving birth to the black progeny of the Holy Ghost, profoundly captures Baldwin's centering of hope in both the metaphorical and literal image of the child.[130] Young goes on to claim that *If Beale Street Could Talk* is Baldwin's fictional portrait of the aforementioned "despised black mother and the promise of her children."[131] This section will expand upon Young's profound claim that "the baby. . . . is the reason for Baldwin's hope that we can make the world better than it is,"[132] for not only does *Beale Street* capture the promise of hope rooted in black children, but the novel powerfully frames this hope against the backdrop of the ever-present threat of despair.

If Beale Street Could Talk centers on the romance of Fonny and Tish, a young black couple who suddenly find their lives and relationship shattered when Fonny is framed by a cop with a personal vendetta and arrested for rape. In addition, immediately following Fonny's arrest, Tish, who Young explicitly claims is "the despised black mother whose children are also the issue of the Holy Ghost,"[133] discovers that she is pregnant with Fonny's child. Throughout the novel, Tish and Fonny's unborn child serves as a beacon of hope and the inspiration for Tish's family's battle to free Fonny from prison. Hope in this novel is consistently framed against the backdrop of the ever-encroaching threat of despair, which in *Beale Street* is expressed through the trauma that black people face as they contend with a racist criminal justice system broadly, and the prison industrial complex in particular.

Fonny spends the whole of the novel imprisoned, with Baldwin offering flashbacks which allow the reader to glimpse his former life. As the novel progresses, Fonny's hope for release continues to dwindle. He states, "What we going to do about that fucking lawyer? He don't give a shit about me, he don't give a shit about *nobody!* You want me to die in here? You know what's going on in here? You know what's happening to me, to *me, to me,* in *here?*"[134] Fonny is trapped, struggling daily to maintain his sanity and cling to the hope that Tish, her family, and his father might achieve the impossible in having him released. But as time progresses, Fonny is subjected to the violence of the prison, "he loses a tooth, again, and almost loses an eye" for fighting back against an attempted rape.[135] Prison life works to systematically crush Fonny's spirit, and despair haunts his every moment.

This threat of despair in relation to the criminal justice system is also shown through the character Daniel, a friend of Fonny's who served two years in prison after being falsely accused of stealing a car.[136] Upon his release, Daniel reconnects with Fonny and Tish before Fonny's imprisonment. Daniel, in many ways, offers a snapshot into the trauma and brokenness that awaits Fonny if Tish and her family fail to secure his release. Daniel, while describing his imprisonment to Fonny, states:

> Man, it was bad. Very bad. And it's bad now. Maybe I'd feel different if I had done something and got caught. But I didn't do nothing. They were just playing with me, man, because they could. And I'm lucky it was only two years, you dig? Because they can do with you whatever they want. *Whatever they want.* And they dogs, man. I really found out, in the slammer, what Malcolm and them cats was talking about. The white man's *got* to be the devil. He sure ain't a man. Some of the things I saw, baby, I'll be dreaming about until the day I die.[137]

Later, Daniel discloses those "things" that he "saw," for not only did he witness a man being raped by nine others in the prison, but he too was the victim of rape.[138] Baldwin closes the scene with Fonny and Daniel with a pertinent quote, one which haunts both this novel and the whole of Baldwin's corpus: *"Didn't my Lord Deliver Daniel? And why not every man?* The song is old, the question unanswered."[139]

Baldwin's framing of black despair in relation to the US American criminal justice system was inspired, in part, by the arrest and imprisonment of Baldwin's friend and former bodyguard Tony Maynard, who was charged with murder.[140] Upon his first visit to Maynard in prison, Baldwin expressed a deep fear for the emotional and physical state of his friend, stating:

. . . I was afraid of what might have happened to him—in him—the way
one feels when about to see a loved one who has encountered great mis-
fortune. One does not know what is left of the person. Human help
often arrives too late, and if the person has really turned his face to the
wall, no human being can help.[141]

In other words, Baldwin was afraid that Maynard might have surrendered to
despair, turning "his face to the wall" and plunging into a well of hopelessness
outside of the reach of one's friends and community. Although Baldwin's fears
were not realized that day, for he "saw that he hadn't turned his face to the
wall,"[142] in a later visit, Baldwin finds Maynard utterly devastated:

Tony had been beaten, and beaten very hard; his cheekbones had dis-
appeared and one of his eyes was crooked; he looked swollen above
the neck, and he took down his shirt collar, presently, to show us the
swelling on his shoulders. And he was weeping, trying not to—I had
seen him with tears in his eyes, but I had never seen him weeping.[143]

Baldwin later learns that Maynard had been beaten by fifteen men.[144] Although
Maynard would eventually gain his freedom years after his imprisonment,
upon his release Baldwin found Maynard to be a "broken" and "uncommuni-
cative" man.[145]

The question remained for Baldwin, both in relation to Maynard and all
black men and women facing the prison system: *Didn't my Lord deliver Daniel?
And why not every man?*"[146] Baldwin does not answer that question in any definitive sense in *Beale Street*, yet hope remains, rooted in the figure of Fonny
and Tish's unborn child. It would not be exaggeration to claim that Baldwin
frames the narrative of *Beale Street* as a type of nativity story.[147] In it, you find
a mother, father, and child menaced by the world, and all must be done the
save that child, for the child is as Baldwin states above, "the issue of the Holy
Ghost."[148] The child is sacred, bearing the possibility of new life. Again, Young
is correct in stating that Fonny and Tish's child "is the reason for Baldwin's
hope that we can make the world better than it is"[149]

One scene, in particular, captures the sacramentality and hope found in
the possibility of new life, taking place on the night Tish informs her family
of her pregnancy. After hearing the news, her mother Sharon states:

"Tish," she said, "when we was first brought here, the white man he
didn't give us no preachers to say words over us before we had our ba-
bies. And you and Fonny be together right now, married or not, wasn't
for that same damn white man. So, let me tell you what you got to do.
You got to think about that baby. You got to hold on to that baby, don't

care what else happens or don't happen. *You* got to do that. Can't nobody else do that for you. And the rest of us, well, we going to hold on to you. And we going to get Fonny out. Don't you worry. I know it's hard—but don't you worry. And that baby be the best thing that ever happened to Fonny. He needs that baby. It going to give him a whole lot of courage.[150]

Standing in the place of the "preacher," Sharon speaks words of life over the child, and over Tish. She connects the child's impending birth, and the necessity of keeping the child alive at all costs, to the promise that Fonny will be released. In fact, Sharon claims that the child itself will be the anchor that keeps Fonny from drifting into the sea of despair. Not long after, Sharon continues to speak words of blessing as Tish's family drinks to the new baby's arrival, stating: "'This is a sacrament,' she said, 'and, no, I ain't gone crazy. We're drinking to new life. Tish is going to have Fonny's baby.'"[151] As the family communes together, Ernestine, Tish's sister, gives Tish a drink and states: "Save the children," as she "drained her glass."[152]

Despite the struggles that surround the family, Tish's baby bears within it the promise of new life, the promise that things can, and perhaps will, get better. Young points to this passage as highlighting that "the unborn child . . . compels Tish to keep faith," reminding her that "now is not the time to give up. A *change is going to come.*"[153] Tish reflects:

Well. We are certainly in it now, and it may get worse. It will, certainly— and now something almost as hard to catch as a whisper in a crowded place, as light and as definite as a spider's web, strikes below my ribs, stunning and astonishing my heart—get worse. But that light tap, that kick, that signal, announces to me that what can get worse can get better. Yes. It will get worse. But the baby, turning for the first time in its incredible veil of water, announces its presence and claims me; tells me, in that instant, that what can get worse can get better; and that what can get better can get worse. In the meantime—forever—it is entirely up to me. The baby cannot get here without me. And, while I may have known this, in one way, a little while ago, now the baby knows it, and tells me that while it will certainly be worse, once it leaves the water, what gets worse can also get better. It will be in the water for a while yet: but it is preparing itself for a transformation. And so must I.[154]

And things do indeed get worse as the novel draws to a close, as Baldwin brings despair into a radical collision with the possibility of hope. The family learns that the woman who accused Fonny of rape (at the prompting of the racist

police officer), miscarried and subsequently suffered a mental breakdown. This
tragic turn of events now means that Fonny could face even more serious
charges. Upon hearing the news, Fonny's father, Frank, gives into despair.[155]
The novel ends as the family is informed that Frank's body has been found in
his car after dying by suicide.[156]

Yet, at one of the novel's most tragic moments, as Tish is informed of the
news of Frank's death, the child arrives:

> When I opened my mouth, I couldn't catch my breath. Everything
> disappeared, except my mother's eyes. An incredible intelligence
> charged the air between us. Then, all I could see was Fonny. And then
> I screamed, and my time had come.
>   Fonny is working on the wood, on the stone, whistling, smiling.
> And, from far away, but coming nearer, the baby cries and cries and
> cries and cries and cries and cries and cries, cries like it
> means to wake the dead.[157]

The cries of the child, who "cries and cries and cries," carries the weight of
both despair and hope. In those cries, the child bears the cries of the black
community, a community struggling in the throes of white supremacist violence and death. Some people do not survive, and find themselves sinking into
the depths, the victims of an unjust world that drives some to "suicide, or death,
or madness" (as Frank's tragedy makes clear). But the baby's cry is not singular,
for the child's breathy cry bears in it the possibility of hope. As Tish struggles
to "catch her breath," in the face of tragedy, the baby exudes new life through
its breath, life which might succeed in "waking the dead."[158]

Ashon Crawley speaks to the power of black breath in his work *Blackpentecostal Breath: The Aesthetics of Possibility*. In this text, Crawley posits that the
western "world" is a space in which "black flesh cannot easily breathe,"[159] a fact
tragically glimpsed in Eric Garner's murder at the hands of police, his life
expiring as he stated over and again, "I can't breathe."[160] In Crawley's estimate,
black breath, rooted in "Blackpentecostalism [as] an intellectual practice
grounded in the fact of the flesh"[161] which is much broader than the tradition
that bears its name,[162] produces "otherwise possibilities."[163] He goes on to state:
"I do not say new. I say otherwise. Using otherwise, I seek to underscore the
ways alternative modes, alternative strategies, alternative ways of life *already*
exist, indeed are violently acted upon in order to produce the coherence of the
state."[164] In other words:

> To breathe, within this western theological-philosophical epistemol-
> ogy, from within the zone of blackness, from within the zone of

Blackpentecostalism, is to offer a critical performative intervention into the western juridical apparatus of violent control, repression, and yes, premature death.[165]

Therefore, with Crawley, I argue that it is black breath, captured powerfully in the image of the black child breathing new life through its cries, which makes "the New Jerusalem," a world *otherwise* than what is, possible.

Lewis Gordon, in asking the question, "why go on?"[166] in relation to black life, articulates an additional existential question that adds a layer of meaning to Crawley's understanding of breath. Gordon states:

This question of continuing to live on is connected to a controversial theme of all existential thought. It goes like this: There is a sense in which none of us has ever chosen to be born into this world and possibly any possible world. Yet, in our decision to live on, we live a choice that requires our having been born—in a word, our *existence*. In the context of blacks, the implication is obvious. No one chooses to have been born under racial designations, but the choice to go on living, and especially choices that involve recognizing one's racial situation, has implications on the meaning of one's birth.[167]

What this quote powerfully highlights is that the choice to live, which in Crawley's estimate is the choice to breathe, and in Baldwin's work is the choice to live and bring children into the world, in an anti-black world, is in and of itself a choice against despair. Again, for Baldwin, to choose to continue to live, breathe, exist, is to choose black life, to choose hope. This is what Baldwin means in claiming "I can't be a pessimist because I'm alive."[168] To live is to make an existential choice. To live is to hope.

Conclusion

Clearly, Baldwin's attempt to root a type of futurity in the symbol of the child is subject to critique. For instance, I would be remiss to not mention Lee Edelman's powerful polemic against the symbol of the "the Child" in his work *No Future: Queer Theory and the Death Drive*. I am in agreement with Edelman that "the Child," reflective of what he calls a "reproductive futurism,"[169] "remains the perpetual horizon of every acknowledged politics, the fantasmatic beneficiary of every political intervention."[170] However, what Edelman does not acknowledge is that "the Child," which undergirds the organization of our politics in the United States, is not and cannot be a black child. If "the Child" represents the "presupposition that the body politic must survive,"[171] what should be apparent is that the body politic is a white body, and "the Child" whose "fantasmatic" future drives the whole of our politics is a white "Child."[172] This is what makes Baldwin's claim that much more powerful, for Baldwin, utilizing the theo-political symbol of a white Virgin Mary, is seemingly aware that "the Child" driving our politics is in fact white. However, he *disidentifies* with the symbol in making clear that any just future to be had is not located in the white "Child," but in black children. One could say that the survival of the black child marks, not the perpetuation of the body politic, but its inevitable doom and possible rebirth.

In addition, Baldwin's tendency to root hope and futurity in "the New Jerusalem" is also not without its problems. As New Testament scholar Eric Thomas rightly points out, the imagery of "the New Jerusalem" in Revelation has been "used as a means to make outsiders of queer people."[173] According to the New American Standard translation of Revelation 22:14–15, "outside" of "the gates into the city" are found "the dogs and the sorcerers and the immoral persons," with Thomas making clear that some conflate these aforementioned "dogs" with queer persons (biblical scholars included).[174] Therefore, Thomas argues that perhaps "the New Jerusalem that John envisions is not a place Africana queers should ascribe to."[175] This is an important critique that we would do well to keep in mind. Yet, Thomas and Baldwin are engaging in a profoundly similar undertaking. In fact, Thomas himself names that his project seeks to disidentify, in the Muñoz sense,[176] with Revelation. He argues:

> By foregrounding Africana queer lived experience in rereading Revelation, I disidentify with those external and internalized messages and use my own loud voice to proclaim that Revelation's apocalyptic epilogue can be an Africana queer prologue in which to think, feel, and take actions toward alternative futures that can begin now.[177]

Again, Thomas and Baldwin are *both* disidentifying with the text, and both seek, to borrow Thomas's language, to "read" the text "alternatively,"[178] bringing forth "alternative visions of the future."[179] Baldwin's use of "the New Jerusalem" troubles any attempt at keeping the sexual other "outside" "the gates into the city." In fact, by showing future possibility through black queer young people (thinking here of Arthur and Crunch), Baldwin inevitably moves the sexual outsider to the center of the city itself. Or, to put it slightly differently, perhaps Baldwin's city is built by black queer hands.

By no means was Baldwin's optimism reflective of an uncritical naiveté, for Baldwin always kept in his mind's eye, and in his literature, the tragedy and pain of black life. He was fully aware that many of the world's Fonnys and Daniels may never be free, and many Franks and David Baldwins would continue to tumble into the depths of a life-crushing despair. However, despite the ever-present weight of despair, for Baldwin, hope is, also, ever present. What can be gleaned from Baldwin's vision of "the New Jerusalem" is that the continued presence of black lives in these United States is, in and of itself, the definitive blow to pessimistic despair. For black persons to choose life, to breathe, to birth children, to build communities, and to love, is to choose a life in radical opposition to hopelessness. "The evidence of things not seen,"[180] for Baldwin, is carried in the cry of the child, a cry which bears in it the hope for "the New Jerusalem."

4

Jimmy's "Man": The Problem of Sexism in Baldwin's Literature

This chapter explores Baldwin's disidentification with the category "Man"/the human being. The human, in Baldwin's literature, serves as the center of his critical reflections. For Baldwin, larger social struggles, whether those pertaining to race, gender, or sexuality, are mere reflections of a deeper human problem, the problem of human identity. According to Baldwin, "the question of color, especially in this country, operates to hide the graver questions of the self. That is precisely why what we like to call 'the Negro problem' is so tenacious in American life, and so dangerous."[1] However, Baldwin does not simply locate "the problem" of social division with the human being, he also understands the human as the only source of salvation for a culture divided, arguing: "I believe we can save each other. In fact I think we must save each other. I don't depend on anyone else to do it."[2] Thus, Baldwin spends substantial energy exploring who and what the human being *is*, all while troubling the categories that divide human groups from one another.

However, Baldwin's understanding of the human is deeply troubled, for unlike the previous three chapters' explorations of Baldwin's praxis of disidentification, this chapter will primarily examine the ways in which Baldwin *fails* to disidentify with western understandings of "Man."[3] It will become apparent that Baldwin capitulates to dominant understandings of "Man"/the human as signifying cisgender men who are normatively masculine and explicitly nonfeminine.[4] This chapter will first explore "Baldwin's universalizing impulse"[5] in relation to his understanding of the human being, one which frames human difference as secondary to a kind of quintessential humanness shared by all.[6] This section engages the work of queer theorist Matt Brim in displaying how Baldwin's universal human is, possibly, "nothing" and "meaningless," a category that serves to undermine the value of varying sites of identity.[7] However, in conversation with the work of Sylvia Wynter, it will become apparent that Baldwin's human being is not simply "nothing," and hence a kind of empty category, but is reflective of the "descriptive statement" of "Man" found in the west, one which presumes the binary distinction between "men and women."[8]

After establishing that Baldwin's human being is not an innocent category but bears in it normative understandings of "Man" and masculinity, this chapter will then proceed to explore Baldwin's troubling ideas concerning masculinity, women, and the feminine in his nonfiction and fiction writings. According to Baldwin, the most damaging outgrowth of white supremacist oppression in the black community is the denial of black men's ability to live into normative masculine roles. Thus, femininity is always framed as a dangerous reality, one which black men must escape and reject. This section will close with an examination of black feminists' checks on Baldwin's sexism, clearly seen in his public dialogues with Nikki Giovanni and Audre Lorde.

The chapter will conclude by raising the question of whether Baldwin, in fact, heard and heeded the critiques of black feminists late in his life. Although Baldwin's sexism seems deeply entrenched, his late essay "Freaks and the American Ideal of Manhood" offers a profoundly queer glimmer of hope in his attempts to disidentify with masculinity, as he calls for a reclamation of a type of queer gender identity/expression—the "androgynous."[9]

The Failure of Baldwin's Universal "Man"

In a 1963 interview for the BBC program *Bookshelf*, Baldwin emphatically states the fundamental place, and ultimate importance, of the human being in his life and literature. He posits:

> . . . if I'm a novelist with a message, it's only one, and probably, I suspect, every novelist has just one message. In all three of those books it seems to me that the preoccupation is almost exactly the same, and that would be the effort that one has got to make . . . to deal with other people as though they were simply human beings. To remember that no matter what the details of their lives may be like, or how much they may seem to be different from you superficially, or what the social pressures are outside or what the psychological pressures are within, to deal with this other human being precisely as though . . . he or she was here for the first time and the only time. To deal with them in . . . the way you want them to deal with you. And no matter what price. *From*

my point of view, no label, and no slogan, and no party, and no skin
color, and indeed no religion, is more important than the human being.[10]

This quote will serve as the starting point from which to understand the importance of the human being for Baldwin, in addition to providing a glimpse into what the human *is* in Baldwin's corpus. As the above quote clearly shows, for Baldwin, the human being serves as the "center"[11] of his literary endeavors. In other words, the human being occupies a space of immeasurable importance for him. In addition, the above quote makes clear that varying markers of identity—whether political affiliation, race, or religion—are of lesser importance to Baldwin's understanding of the human being. In other words, human identity constructs cannot define the human, for underneath the layers of these constructs lie what Baldwin calls in this same interview, echoing the interviewer, "the human core."[12] However, this begs the question, what *is* this "human core?" In asking what the human being is, this chapter turns to Baldwin's early essay "Everybody's Protest Novel."[13]

In his 1949 essay, "Everybody's Protest Novel," Baldwin offered his now (in)famous critique of the literature of Harriet Beecher Stowe and Richard Wright, arguing that Stowe and Wright, for the sake of making a political point, surrendered the "complexity"[14] of the human being and fell into "pamphleteer[ing]."[15] In other words, Baldwin posits that in Stowe's and Wright's works, the human is reduced to the level of symbol, "a time-saving invention,"[16] being thoroughly emptied of the "complexity" and unruly nature of who and what the human actually is. What is important for our purposes is that it is here that Baldwin introduces his understanding of the human being. He posits:

> We have, as it seems to me, in this most mechanical and interlocking of
> civilizations, attempted to lop this creature down to the status of a time-
> saving invention. He is not, after all, merely a member of a Society or a
> Group or a deplorable conundrum to be explained by Science. He is—
> and how old-fashioned the words sound!—something more than that,
> something resolutely indefinable, unpredictable. In overlooking, deny-
> ing, evading his complexity—which is nothing more than the disquiet-
> ing complexity of ourselves—we are diminished and we perish; only
> within this web of ambiguity, paradox, this hunger, danger, darkness,
> can we find at once ourselves and the power that will free us from
> ourselves.[17]

In essence, Baldwin paradoxically defines the human as that which is "indefinable." However, he does, in fact, offer a tentative definition, one which understands the human being as an "unpredictable" creature marked by "complexity" and "paradox." That is what the human *is*. Yet, because Baldwin believes that varying markers of identity are secondary to the "human core," he argues that society seeks to obfuscate the unruly nature of the human through varying "categorization[s]" that seek to "trap" the human being in a "cage of reality bequeathed us at our birth."[18] These cages, for Baldwin, are the realities of race, sexuality, and to some extent, gender. It is within these cages, these categorizations, that "we" as human beings "take our shape."[19] We see again that the problem of the human, for Baldwin, arises as society attempts to place layers of meaning over one's "human core," not unlike layers of clothing draped over the body. In *The Devil Finds Work*, Baldwin states:

> Identity would seem to be the garment with which one covers the nakedness of the self: in which case, it is best that the garment be loose, a little like the robes of the desert, through which robes one's nakedness can always be felt, and, sometimes, discerned. This trust in one's nakedness is all that gives one the power to change one's robes.[20]

Thus, in Baldwin's estimate, human beings adopt labels, not unlike physical adornment. However, in the end, the unruly and complex nature of the human makes those labels secondary, tentative, and sometimes subject to change, and yet the "human core" remains.

With this in mind, the problem of race in the United States, in one sense, is a problem of the inability of white Americans to accept black Americans as human beings. According to Baldwin, "The black man insists, by whatever means he finds at his disposal, that the white man cease to regard him as an exotic rarity and recognize him as a human being."[21] What one sees in Baldwin's work is an attempt to peel back the layers of identities that only serve to obfuscate our "core" humanity.

It is at this point that one can begin to see a problem arise which is rooted in Baldwin's commitment to, and obsession with, human similarity and "sameness."[22] As shown above, markers of difference are, on some level, a distraction for Baldwin, obscuring that which binds humans together. Matt Brim, in his work *James Baldwin and the Queer Imagination*, supports this claim in pointing out: ". . . Baldwin's insistence time and again that prescribed identity categories invariably betray the complexity of the individual and, by isolating him in their 'cells,' belie his inescapable state of dependence on the other."[23] Brim also highlights a passage from Baldwin's 1949 essay "Preservation of Innocence" while discussing Baldwin's "category-busting . . . vision."[24] In that essay, Baldwin claims:

A novel insistently demands the presence and passion of human beings, who cannot ever be labeled. Once the novelist has created a human being he has shattered the label and, in transcending the subject matter, is able, for the first time, to tell us something about it and to reveal how profoundly all things involving human beings interlock.[25]

This quote is important, for it shows that the role of the novelist, and hence Baldwin's personal work, is to portray human beings in their label-shattering complexity. Once those labels are thoroughly shattered, and the particularity of the subject "transcended," one can see the commonality between humans—the "human core." In fact, Brim states that "in essence, Baldwin denies that representation of the oppressed and representation of the dominant are significantly different endeavors."[26] Inspired by Brim, the question arises—what does it mean to be a black human or queer human within this "label shattering" worldview? Can one find meaning in one's blackness or queerness within the framework of Baldwin's humanism?[27] Or is human difference always and only a distraction?

Matt Brim makes the problem of "universalizing" the human being explicit in *James Baldwin and the Queer Imagination*. In chapter 2 of that text, which offers "queer/gay/trans" readings of Baldwin's *Giovanni's Room*,[28] Brim masterfully examines the ways in which Baldwin's attempt at "transcending homosexual specificity"[29] for the sake of a "common humanity"[30] actually leaves the reader with "nothing,"[31] as the specificity that grounds and makes humanity possible is erased.[32] In beginning his examination, Brim calls attention to Baldwin's final interview with Richard Goldstein in which Baldwin states:

Anyway, *Giovanni's Room* is not really about homosexuality. It's the vehicle through which the book moves. *Go Tell It on the Mountain*, for example, is not about a church, and *Giovanni* is not really about homosexuality. It's about what happens to you if you're afraid to love anybody. Which is much more interesting than the question of homosexuality.[33]

This quote is reflective of Baldwin's desire to highlight the dangers that humans face when they refuse or fail to love. According to Brim, Baldwin deploys the "heterosexual/homosexual distinction" as a means of making a larger point about love. Brim goes on to state:

Giovanni's Room asks us to understand the universal (love) through the particular and "perverse" (love between men), transposing the terms of the usual integrationist analogy "we (homosexuals) are like them (heterosexuals)" so that it reads "they (heterosexuals) are like us (homosexuals)."[34]

Although this might seem like a noble cause, Brim makes clear that in framing gay identity as that which needs to be surpassed in order to *"achieve* full humanity,"[35] Baldwin, perhaps inadvertently, communicates:

> . . . in both his fiction and his essays, he imagines that the homosexual can *achieve* full humanity only by transcending homosexual specificity. Fully human beings cannot only or primarily be gay, as though one's humanity must be staked somewhere other than and evidently beyond homosexuality, lest the stakes pull up and one's humanity floats away, free of the mere homosexual.[36]

In other words, Baldwin's push for a universal human serves to render gay identity as a "limiting element."[37] Brim goes on to state:

> I think Baldwin's universalizing impulse, which degrades the importance of sexual identity in order to privilege our shared humanity, moves in a dangerous direction. The fundamental problem is that humanity, as anyone who has ever needed to argue for theirs knows, is itself the most banal and meaningless of categories. To be forced to insist on one's humanity, as queers are constantly forced to do—to need to fall back on this most obvious and inarguable of claims and to treat that claim as profound—is the incomparably degrading position. To argue that we are all complex human beings is to argue, literally, nothing.[38]

The power in Brim's critique lies in the fact that he troubles Baldwin's primary theoretical assumption, which is that the category of "the human" stands apart as something meaningful in and of itself. Brim believes that the construct of "the human" is literally "nothing"—one could say empty—and his remedy for this is to understand that humanity can only be understood and engaged at human persons' "privileged levels of specificity (sexual and otherwise)."[39] Thus, our "specificity" is reflective of "fully complex, fully human subjectivity."[40] Black humanity, queer humanity, and trans humanity is *human* "by virtue of, rather than despite, the specificity of" peoples' distinct ways of existing in the world.[41]

Brim's claim is correct on one level, for rather than humanizing queer persons, Baldwin succeeds at framing queerness, and thus other markers of difference including race and gender, as superficial to a type of idealized humanity (In the next section, I will demonstrate that Baldwin's striving for a universal human caused him to trivialize the distinct plight faced by black women in the United States). However, this problem is much deeper than Brim indicates. The problem is not simply that Baldwin's ideal human means "nothing," but that the idealized human which he presupposes is always and already content-full,[42] bearing within it centuries of struggle concerning the definition of the human being. In order to examine the unexamined content of Baldwin's "human," we turn now to the work of Sylvia Wynter.

Sylvia Wynter, in her now classic essay "Unsettling the Coloniality of Being/Power/Truth/Freedom: Towards the Human, After Man, Its Overrepresentation—An Argument," powerfully shows the ways in which our modern construction of the human is the product of historical shifts in which "theocentric" understandings of Christian identity came to be "re-invented" in varying historical moments, through the machinations of the "colonizer/colonized relation," into our current cultural understanding of "Man."[43] In other words, what was previously a "religious" understanding of the human and human difference, eventually became a "matrix slot" in which "degodded"/increasingly "secular" understandings of both "Man" and "Other" came to be constituted.[44] The first major shift in understanding the human arose during the period of "the Renaissance to the eighteenth century" (giving rise to understandings of the human rooted in "the physical sciences") and the second from the eighteenth century to the present (marked by the advent of "the biological sciences").[45]

What is important to note in Wynter's formulation is her claim that definitions of the human are determined through what she calls "descriptive statements."[46] Wynter posits that, not unlike "what Foucault has identified as a specific 'regime' and/or 'politics of truth,'(Foucault 1980, 1981)" "descriptive statements" represent a baseline knowledge, "whether at the microlevel of the individual or at the macrolevel of society,"[47] "in whose terms humans inscript and institute themselves/ourselves as this or that genre of being human."[48] In other words, cultures as a whole, and the individuals within those cultures, acquire knowledge through particular "regimes" of knowledge production, which determine the meaning of phenomena like "the human," which "give rise to their varying respective modalities of adaptive truths-for, or epistemes, up to and including our contemporary own."[49]

However, "descriptive statements" are particularly insidious in that they are produced by the culture itself, yet deceptively masquerade as though they stem from some outside source or authority. For instance, Wynter argues that all societies have "mapped their 'descriptive statements' or governing master codes on the heavens, on their stable periodicities and regular recurring movements (Krupp 1997)."[50] Wynter continues on:

> . . . in doing so, they had thereby mapped their specific criterion of being human, of what it was "to be a good man and woman of one's kind, (Davis 1992)" onto the physical cosmos, thereby absolutizing each such criterion; and with this enabling them to be experienced by

each order's subjects as if they had been supernaturally (and, as such, extrahumanly) determined criteria, their respective truths had necessarily come to function as an "objective set of facts" for the people of that society—seeing that such truths were now the indispensable condition of their existence as such a society, as such people, as such a mode of being human.[51]

Later, this "supernatural causation" would be replaced by a "natural" one, as the "Imaginary extrahuman Being" would now be understood as "Nature,"[52] and later the "purely secular" notion of "Evolution."[53] Therefore, the truth of what the human *is*, in any given society, is always and already "determined."[54] However, not only is it "determined," but its source of authority is understood as coming from outside of the human.

Again, varying shifts in the understanding of the human would challenge and morph the "descriptive statement" that began with "the original Judeo-Christian conception of the human" into the distinction between "rationality/irrationality,"[55] and later the distinction between those "selected by Evolution/dysselected by Evolution."[56] According to Wynter, "the code of selected by Evolution/dysselected by Evolution," became a "new master code," and this "master code" was "anchored" in "phenotypical differences," i.e., "the Color Line."[57] That "Color Line," according to Wynter, found its ultimate expression in the distinction "between the Caucasoid physiognomy (as symbolic life, the name of what is good, the idea that some humans can be selected by Evolution) and the Negroid physiognomy (as symbolic death, the 'name of what is evil,' the idea that some humans can be dysselected by Evolution)."[58] However, this "Color Line" transcended the realm of phenotypic difference, but became a "master code" upon which other forms of human division and hierarchy could be established and bolstered.[59] Wynter argues:

> . . . the new extrahuman line, or projection of genetic nonhomogeneity that would now be made to function, analogically, as the status-ordering principle based upon ostensibly differential degrees of evolutionary selectedness/eugenicity and/or dysselectedness/dysgenicity. *Differential degrees, as between the classes (middle and lower and, by extrapolation, between capital and labor) as well as between men and women, and between the heterosexual and homosexual erotic preference—and, even more centrally, as between Breadwinner (job-holding middle and working classes) and the jobless and criminalized Poor, with this rearticulated at the global level as between Sartre's "Men" and Natives (see his guide-quote), before the end of politico-military colonialism, then postcolonially as between the "developed"*

First World, on the one hand, and the "underdeveloped" Third and Fourth Worlds on the other.[60]

To put it slightly differently, Wynter later states:

> It is this new master code, one that would now come to function at all levels of the social order—including that of class, gender, sexual orientation, superior/inferior ethnicities, and that of the Investor/Breadwinners versus the criminalized jobless Poor (Nas's "black and latino faces") and Welfare Moms antithesis, and most totally between the represented-to-be superior and inferior races and cultures—that would come to function as the dually status-organizing and integrating principle of U.S. society.[61]

What Wynter is claiming here is that the new "master code" of racial difference became the template through which other forms of difference are ordered and categorized within culture, including that between men/women, straight/queer, and breadwinner/jobless.

This brings us back to Baldwin. The problem of the human, for Baldwin, as now made apparent by Wynter, is that Baldwin's understanding of the human is not an innocent or empty category, and although he radically calls into question the role of whiteness within culture and in relation to the human being, Baldwin *presupposes other aspects of the underlying "descriptive statement" of "Man," particularly the binary distinction separating men/woman.* Brim is incorrect in stating that Baldwin's argument for the human is, in fact, an argument for "nothing," because by making the human being *central* in his life and literature, Baldwin inextricably capitulates to a definition of the human already established by US American culture's "descriptive statement" which, I argue, is that the human being is most clearly represented in the cisgender, masculine, nonfeminine, "Man."

In a similar fashion to Wynter, Lewis Gordon also points out the problematic nature of "universality" as it pertains to the human. He highlights:

> Since the "racially neutral" in antiblack societies is *white,* all efforts toward purely human significations—that is, "universality"—appear to be problematic: "A man," "a woman," "a child," "one," all of these often signify "a white man," "a white woman," "a white child," "a white person."[62]

I posit that, based on Wynter, one can expand this, arguing that the category "human"/"Man" also presupposes the cisgender man as the center of meaning and value. Again, Baldwin might seek to trouble "whiteness" as it pertains to the "descriptive statement" of the human in the West, but he problematically presupposes the binary logic of man/woman, masculine/feminine, and bread-winner/jobless, all of which are also clearly rooted in the cultural understanding of the human. This erasure of human difference, to which Baldwin seems (at times) committed, without also troubling the category of the human in and of itself, only serves to bolster this problematic rendering of the human, and gives birth to his deeply troubling sexism, reflected in his portrayal of women and his general disdain toward the inability of black men to live into normatively masculine (i.e., patriarchal) roles.

The Problem of Masculinity in Baldwin's Nonfiction

Baldwin's failure to critically assess the content of his universal human, I argue, caused him to dismiss human difference as superficial, allowing troubling aspects of the "descriptive statement" of the human as "Man" to undergird his life and work. Baldwin's problem with women and femininity, and his almost unshakeable commitment to normative constructs of masculinity, can be observed throughout the entirety of his corpus, and the following sections explore this problem in key works of his fiction and nonfiction.[63] In addition, the following sections also examine black feminists' "checks" on Baldwin, powerfully seen in Baldwin's dialogues with Nikki Giovanni and Audre Lorde. Both Lorde and Giovanni challenge Baldwin's normative understanding of the human and his deeply sexist understanding of the feminine.

Masculinity plays a troubling role in Baldwin's corpus, for although he rightly claims that white supremacy is inextricably linked to white toxic masculinity,[64] he falls short in arguing that the problem of white masculinity is its "denial of the masculinity of the blacks."[65] In other words, white supremacy denies black men appropriate *access* to normative masculinity, subjecting the black man to an emasculated and feminized mode of being. In fleshing out this claim, we turn to Baldwin's 1972 work, *No Name in the Street*, in which he uses a personal moment of sexual violation as the means through which to discuss the problem of the emasculation of the black man.[66]

In *No Name*, Baldwin recounts an occurrence in which he "was being groped by one of most powerful men in one of the states I visited," and he frames this moment of violation by harkening back to the violation of black bodies during slavery.[67] Baldwin claims, "The slave knows, however his master may be deluded on this point, that he is called a slave because his manhood has been, or can be, or will be taken from him. To be a slave means that one's manhood is engaged in a dubious battle indeed."[68] If one is tempted to view Baldwin's language of "manhood" as an outmoded attempt at signifying the shared experience of black men and black women, Baldwin makes clear that slavery was especially insidious in its violation of the black man, specifically. He continues with this point, stating: "In the case of American slavery, the black man's right to his women, as well as to his children, was simply taken from him."[69] In other words, the loss of black masculinity is a matter of black men having lost their "rights" to both "their" women and children, which reflects Baldwin's capitulation to an understanding of masculinity that presumes men's responsibility *over* women and children. This loss of the so-called "right" of men to their women and children is a recurring trope in Baldwin's corpus and public discourse. Clarence Hardy supports this claim in his examination of Baldwin's sexism, stating that Baldwin in his essay *No Name in the Street*, "continues again and again . . . to depict the problems and effects of white supremacy around the rights of the black patriarch to the exclusion of other members of the black community. As Baldwin would emphasize: 'the black man's right to his women, as well as to his children, was simply taken from him.'"[70]

One sees this same logic at play in the *The Fire Next Time*, as Baldwin expounds on the inability of black men to "protect [their] women" as being reflective of white supremacy's attempts at emasculating the black man. He states:

> *Protect your women:* a difficult thing to do in a civilization sexually so pathetic that a white man's masculinity depends on a denial of the masculinity of the blacks. *Protect your women:* in a civilization that emasculates male and abuses female, and in which, moreover, the male is forced to depend on the female's bread-winning power.[71]

Yet again, Baldwin's acquiescence to the logic of western/white masculinity undergirds his lamentation that black men cannot "protect" black women, a role Baldwin presumes is "natural" to the relationship between black men and women. This is highlighted by Baldwin's adjacent claim that black men are "forced" to depend on black women's income which, in his estimate, and will be discussed below, is not simply an emasculation of the black man, but is reflective of a troubling gender reversal, one in which the black woman is "out of place" as the primary source of income for the black family.

This negative assessment of black women as "breadwinners" in the family is also found in Baldwin's 1961 interview with Studs Terkel. When discussing the difficulty of black men to find work, Baldwin claims:

> One has got to consider . . . the rage and the anguish of a Negro man, who, in the first place, is forced to accept all kinds of humiliation in his working day, whose power in the world is so slight he can not really protect his home, his wife, his children, when he finds himself out of work.[72]

Baldwin then adds an additional layer to the issue, arguing that "Negroes are raised in a kind of matriarchy, since, after all, the wife can go out and wash the white ladies' clothes and steal from the kitchen. . . . This creates another social and psychological problem."[73] In other words, Baldwin understands the problem to be one of disordered gender roles, reflected in the presence of black matriarchs who are now the chief breadwinners in the family. Baldwin continues to discuss the emasculated and feminized black man after Terkel, the interviewer, mentions Richard Wright's short story, "Man of All Work," which Terkel points out features a black man who must masquerade as a woman to gain employment. Baldwin states, "A beautiful, terrifying story. It really gets something which has been hidden for all these generations, which is the ways in which . . . it really suggests, more forceably than anything I've ever read, the humiliation the Negro male endures."[74] It is important to note that Baldwin is not incorrect in pointing out the humiliation suffered by black *persons* at the hands of white supremacy, reflected in black unemployment and the trauma inflicted on black families. However, Baldwin's problem lies in the fact that he frames black *men's* "humiliation" over and against that of the black woman, whose presumed power is understood to be a direct threat to black masculinity.

However, an assessment of Baldwin's understanding of masculinity would be incomplete without briefly mentioning the recurring trope in his literature of white masculinity's obsession with the black penis. Hardy supports this point in stating: "Baldwin . . . in *No Name in the Street* declares white supremacy as most directly a problem of the black phallus."[75] So, returning now to *No Name in the Street*, Baldwin uses the story of his sexual assault to discuss the common desire that men have to humiliate other men. Baldwin argues:

> That men have an enormous need to debase other men—and only because they are *men*—is a truth which history forbids us to labor. And it is absolutely certain that white men, who invented the nigger's big black prick, are still at the mercy of this nightmare, and are still, for the most part, doomed, in one way or another, to attempt to make this prick their own.[76]

Baldwin then ends with a troubling statement:

> . . . a man's balance depends on the weight he carries between his legs. All men, however they may face or fail to face it, however they may handle, or be handled by it, know something about each other, which is simply that a man without balls is not a man; that the word *genesis* describes the male, involves the phallus, and refers to the seed which gives life. When one man can no longer honor this in another man—and

this remains true even if that man is his lover—he has abdicated from
a man's estate, and, hard upon the heels of that abdication, chaos
arrives.[77]

Yet again, what these two quotes clearly show is that Baldwin frames the problem of white supremacy as centered explicitly on undermining black masculinity, as white men have failed to acknowledge "the weight [the black man]
carries between his legs." For Baldwin, "chaos arrives" when men do not acknowledge one another *as men*, the bearers of "the seed which gives life," a
role that Baldwin believes should be "honored" and respected. Hardy, in his
reflection on this passage, is correct in pointing out that "with his celebration
of the male's capacity for creation and reproduction, Baldwin erases women's
central place in reproduction and replaces it with an all-too-familiar fixation
on male prowess."[78] Although the white obsession with black sexuality in general, and the black penis in particular, is a phenomenon readily seen in cultural
discourses/stereotypes around black sexuality, Baldwin goes too far in overstating
the problem of racism as primarily a problem of the misrecognition of black
"manhood." This masculine focus ignores the particularity of black women's
experiences of white supremacy.[79]

The Problem of Women and Femininity in Baldwin's Fiction

As the previous section made apparent, Baldwin's understanding of black masculinity is rooted in his belief that black men are being denied access to what
is entitled to them, which is a particular role of masculine responsibility over
the lives of women, children, and property. Baldwin often frames the humiliation of the black man in relation to both white men *and* black women, lament-
ing the feminization of black men[80] in the face of black matriarchs who have
now become the source of income in black homes. This troubling relationship
to black women/femininity is clearly seen in Baldwin's works of fiction, both
in the ways in which he frames women characters, as Trudier Harris makes
clear, as only having meaning in relation to black male characters, and in his
disdain for "matriarchs." Harris's 1985 work, *Black Women in the Fiction of
James Baldwin*, is a helpful text with which to begin this discussion, for she
teases out the recurring and troubling themes through which Baldwin narrates
his black women characters. This section will substantively engage Harris's
work and extend her argument.

Harris posits that many of the black women in Baldwin's novels are either
"guilty of some crime or condition of existence that demands their doing pen-
ance," or they "are spiritual outcasts, psychological ghetto dwellers in a familial,

sexual, or religious world where their suffering does not lead to redemption."[81] In other words, according to Harris, black women in Baldwin's corpus are subjected to a life of perpetual unhappiness, and they undergo suffering, and willingly suffer, as the byproduct of their guilt.[82] The entirety of Harris's text seeks to explore "the sources" and "manifestations" of that guilt and suffering for Baldwin's black women characters, and the means "through which the few women who do so manage to escape their guilt."[83]

It is also important to note that Harris understands most of the women in Baldwin's fiction as occupying "traditional" women's roles: "mothers, sisters, lovers, wives—and almost all of them are roles of support for the male characters."[84] In addition, within these traditional roles, women are often expected "to sacrifice for their men" and "almost invariably allow the men to determine their paths in life."[85] All and all, Harris finds Baldwin's women as always secondary and "servile" to the male characters.[86] She states:

> . . . no woman is ultimately so acceptable to Baldwin that she is to be viewed as equal to the prominent male characters. It is a function of their guilt as well as of their creation that most of the black female characters in Baldwin's fiction have been subordinated to the males; they are in a supportive, *serving* position in relation to the males and the male images in their lives. They serve their neighbors; they serve their children and their husbands; and they serve God. The serving position reflects the central fact of their existence: they are incomplete without men or male images in their lives because wholeness without males is not a concept the majority of them have internalized.[87]

One could say that "wholeness without males is not a concept" that *Baldwin* has "internalized." In essence, Harris is pointing out that the problem of Baldwin's narration of black women is rooted in the fact that he cannot escape his own troubling relationship to masculinity, framing women characters as valuable only in relation to the ways in which they bolster and support the lives and masculinity of his more robust male characters. In order to further explore this problem, Harris's primary themes—women as guilt ridden, suffering, and subordinated/servile to men—will be explored in relation to two women characters in Baldwin's corpus—Margaret of *The Amen Corner* and Tish in *If Beale Street Could Talk.*

Although Harris does not examine the women of *The Amen Corner*, I argue that Margaret's character powerfully captures many of the themes offered above. Baldwin, in the introductory notes to the text, makes clear that Margaret is a "tyrannical matriarch" who has lost herself in a life-denying church.[88] As one of Baldwin's black women characters, Margaret indeed suffers, as Harris claims Baldwin's black women characters always do, for throughout the play she feels her power slipping—her power to control her son from leaving the safety of the church, her power in leading her congregation, and her power to stifle her love for her husband Luke. Most importantly, that suffering, I argue, stems from Margaret's "sin" of taking on an improper/matriarchal identity, losing her femininity to the masculine role of pastor. It is the latter that will be given special exploration in this section, for in deeming Margaret a "matriarch," it is apparent that Baldwin is highlighting what he views as a problematic gender reversal of feminine power. Margaret, in Baldwin's estimate, must return to her proper place, which is her role as "Luke's woman" and David's mother.

Throughout the play, Baldwin frames Margaret's role as pastor as always being in tension with her femininity. Before becoming a pastor, Margaret was, as Luke describes, a "funny, fast-talking, fiery" woman.[89] However, Margaret claims that her old life, and her life as the wife and lover of Luke, has now been "burned out . . . by the power of the Holy Ghost," as she has taken on the mantle of a sanctified believer and pastor.[90] Baldwin seeks to make plain that Margaret's authority lay in the fact that although she is a woman, she no longer functions as a woman in her role as pastor, which is clearly shown when her authority over the congregation is troubled by the church elders. In one scene, Sister Boxer calls Margaret's leadership into question due to her still being "a woman." She states:

> Odessa, a church can't have no woman for a pastor who done been married once and then decided it didn't suit her and then jump up and run off from her husband and take a seat in the pulpit and *act like she ain't no woman no more.* That ain't no kind of example to the young. The Word says the marriage bed is holy.[91]

Later, as Margaret faces being removed as pastor by the church elders, her sister states: "You's got to pull yourself together and think how you can *win*. You always been the winner. Ain't no time to be a woman *now*."[92] Again, we see that Margaret's being "a woman" is placed in opposition to her pastoral role and ministry. As she begins to feel her authority slipping, her sister reminds her that she cannot "be a woman *now*," she must fight for her place in the church.

In addition, a conversation with the elder Brother Boxer illuminates this point:

> Margaret: Brother Boxer, even if you don't want me for your pastor no more, please remember I'm a woman. Don't talk to me this way.
> Brother Boxer: A woman? Is *that* where all your fervor done gone to? You trying to get back into that man's arms, Sister Margaret? What

you want him to do for you—you want him to take off that long white robe?[93]

He goes on to say, "I never thought I'd live long enough to find out that Sister Margaret weren't nothing but a woman who run off from her husband and then started ruling other people's lives because she didn't have no man to control her."[94] It is important to note that Baldwin is not in any way portraying the elders of the church in a positive light, but what Baldwin seeks to make clear is that it is Margaret's lost womanhood that she needs to recover, not her role as pastor.

Again, Baldwin understands Margaret's role as pastor as being dependent on her abandonment of femininity. Magdalena J. Zaborowska in her work *Me and My House: James Baldwin's Last Decade in France,* makes a similar claim: "Before, [Margaret] created herself into a powerful and often unforgiving pastor—a patriarch in a woman's body and hence a performative gendered persona modeled on male preachers in black churches."[95] Therefore, Margaret is suffering due to her inability to be both a powerful pastor who leads a congregation of men and women, and a woman, who, in Baldwin's estimate, needs the help of the two men in her life to properly live into her womanhood. Margaret's trouble stems from her having "gotten out of place," for she has forgotten how to properly be a woman, and in turn "how to treat her husband and her son as men," as Baldwin states in the introduction to the play.[96] Baldwin understands Margaret's matriarchal and out of place femininity to be an impediment to David's masculinity, reflected in his need to leave home in order to be free of her domineering style of parenting, and a failure to Luke who "needed" her love. For Baldwin, Margaret's life belonged to the men in her life. She states, "I'm thinking how I throwed away my life . . . I'm thinking now—maybe Luke needed it more. Maybe David could of used it better. I know. I got to go upstairs and face them people. Ain't nothing else left for me to do. I'd like to talk to Luke."[97]

Although Chapter 1 of this book framed Margaret's salvation as being rooted in her love for Luke, which is accurate, that salvation also requires that Margaret return to her proper place of womanhood. Margaret's conversion only comes through a man—Luke. She states, "Maybe it's not possible to stop loving anybody you ever really loved. I never stopped loving you, Luke. I tried. But I never stopped loving you."[98] Baldwin states:

Her triumph, which is also, if I may say so, the historical triumph of the Negro people in this country, is that she sees this finally and accepts it, and, although she has lost everything, also gains the keys to the kingdom. The kingdom is love, and love is selfless, although only the self can lead one there. She gains herself.[99]

That self, in a troubling manner, is rooted in the necessity of Margaret to know her proper place in relation to men, abandon being a matriarch, and rediscover proper womanhood through the only character capable of bringing about that transformation, her husband.

However, this troubling portrait of black womanhood is not limited to Baldwin's early representations of women, for a brief examination of the character Tish in his later work *If Beale Street Could Talk* also shows that Baldwin had not moved beyond his problematic framing of women characters. Tish is a unique figure, for according to Harris, "Tish is the first black woman Baldwin allows to tell her own story."[100] However, as Harris clearly shows, it becomes apparent that Tish only functions as a mechanism through which to frame and tell Fonny's story.

As Harris makes clear in her examination of *Beale Street*, Tish has "very little" identity in the novel apart from Fonny, her lover and the father of her unborn child, for he is "her raison d'être."[101] To put it slightly differently, according to Harris: "Tish and Fonny are one; or rather, Fonny is the center of the circle and Tish revolves around him."[102] In addition, while Tish works in a department store, Fonny is portrayed as a gifted artist. Harris is correct in noting that Tish seems to have "no ambition beyond being wife to Fonny and mother to his children. She works at a perfume counter in a department store, and no mention is ever made of her wanting to go to school or otherwise change her status."[103] Fonny, however, views Tish as always occupying "a second place position" in relation to his art.[104] It is also worth noting that Baldwin frames Fonny's love of art as his "salvation" in the midst of the death-dealing realities of Harlem. Baldwin, through Tish's narration, states:

> Fonny had found something he could do, that he wanted to do, and this saved him from the death that was waiting to overtake the children of our age. Though the death took many forms, though people died early in many different ways, the death itself was very simple and the cause was simple, too: as simple as a plague: the kids had been told that they weren't worth shit and everything they saw around them proved it.[105]

Yet, despite this beautiful imagery of art providing a means out of which black youth find life and purpose, Baldwin does not offer Tish that "something" to enrich her character, that "something" to save her from potential death. Again, Tish's life and purpose are only found in relation to Fonny.[106]

A few lines later, after expressing Fonny's salvation through his art, Tish posits: "And perhaps I clung to Fonny, perhaps Fonny saved *me* because he was just about the only boy I knew who wasn't fooling around with the needles or drinking cheap wine or mugging people or holding up stores."[107] Fonny is the source of Tish's salvation.[108] In Baldwin's estimate, it appears as though women need nothing besides the love offered by men; that is enough for them.[109] Harris comments in reference to Tish:

> In her relationship to Fonny, she is a very traditional black woman character. Her raison d'être comes from her man; she is very little without him. Her attitudes toward sex, the baby, and general male/female relationships have been shaped by Fonny. It is Fonny who makes the story what it is; Tish is only alive, as suffering, as in pain as Fonny's predicament demands that she be. From their earliest encounters, Tish's reality is shaped by Fonny's reality.[110]

As Harris makes clear, Tish's "attitudes toward sex" (her belief that she is "still a child" until she has sex with Fonny)[111] and her sense of self (that she is ugly[112] and "not very bright,"[113] are based on Fonny's "evaluation[s]."[114] This limitation on Tish's character appears purposeful, for Baldwin, through Tish's narration, makes clear that woman are, in fact, shaped by the male imagination. He believes that:

> This is a mystery which can terrify and immobilize a woman, and it is always the key to her deepest distress. She must watch and guide, but he must lead. . . . I suppose that the root of the resentment—a resentment which hides a bottomless terror—has to do with the fact that a woman is tremendously controlled by what the man's imagination makes of her—literally, hour by hour, day by day; so she becomes a woman. But a man exists in his own imagination, and can never be at the mercy of a woman's.[115]

Although Baldwin might be offering a critique of the ways in which women are subject to the male imagination, the bitter irony is, as Harris's work makes clear, that Tish is "not free of the creator who continues to draw in [her] potential for growth on the short rein of possibility," she is beholden to the imagination of Baldwin, who proceeds to subject her to a flat existence wholly dependent on her relationship to Fonny.[116]

Lorde and Giovanni: Black Feminists' Check on Baldwin

After exploring Baldwin's troubling ideas as it pertains to masculinity, we will now examine black feminists' pushback on Baldwin's claims, which are clearly seen in his 1971 conversation with Nikki Giovanni (recorded for the television program "Soul!" and later published as A Dialogue in 1973) and his 1984 conversation with Audre Lorde.[117] In both of these exchanges, one sees again Baldwin's inclination to reduce the problem of white supremacy to the emasculation of the black man, in addition to his tendency to ignore difference for the sake of universality. Baldwin is thoroughly challenged by both Giovanni and Lorde, who bring to the forefront of the conversation the distinct experience of black women in relation to both a white supremacist and misogynistic/misogynoiristic US culture.

In Baldwin's conversation with Nikki Giovanni, he introduces into a dialogue that spans a variety of topics—including black literature, music, and religion—one of his commonly offered claims, which is that white supremacy emasculates black men. He states:

> The price of being a black man in America—the price the black male has had to pay, is expected to pay, and which he has to outwit—is his sex. You know, a black man is forbidden by definition, since he's black, to assume the roles, burdens, duties and joys of being a man. In the same way that my child produced from your body did not belong to me but to the master and could be sold at any moment. This erodes a man's sexuality, and when you erode a man's sexuality you destroy his ability to love anyone, despite the fact that sex and love are not the same thing. When a man's sexuality is gone, his possibility, his hope, of loving is also gone.[118]

So again, we see here Baldwin's return to the belief that black men are unable to live into normative masculinity, taking on the "roles" owed to men. What might be viewed as a slight variation in language reveals Baldwin's troubling sexism, for he refers to the black child "produced" during slavery as "my child" (read: the black man's child) which is "produced from" the "body" of the black woman. In other words, the child is not equally the responsibility of the black man and black woman, but primarily belongs to the black man, whose natural rights as a man are being undermined by the white enslaver. The black woman is reduced to being the site of production, not an equal steward of the life of the black child. Therefore, we see Baldwin falling back, yet again, on this normative trope of male responsibility over, and right to, the lives of both women and children.

However, Baldwin also takes it a step further, arguing that this disruption of the black man's masculinity also makes it impossible for him to love another. It is out of that place of dehumanization that black men act out in their homes—subjecting their partners and children to the dehumanizing violence that they receive from white supremacist culture.[119] Baldwin admits that this behavior is "wrong,"[120] yet the wrongness of it is always framed as being the byproduct of white supremacy, and the black emasculation which is the outgrowth of that oppression.[121] It is at this point that Giovanni pushes back, beginning her masterful challenge to Baldwin's normative understandings of men and masculinity. She states, "I don't understand how a black man . . . can be brutalized by some white person somewhere and then come home and treat me or Mother the same way that he was being treated."[122] Shortly thereafter, she states:

> I have seen how the community . . . And even today, in the seventies, even today there are divisions based on those same kinds of problems, so that black men say, In order for me to be a man, you walk ten paces behind me. Which means nothing. I can walk ten paces behind a dog. It means nothing to me, but if that's what the black man needs, I'll never get far enough behind him for him to be a man, I'll never walk that slowly.[123]

What Giovanni's comments highlight is that Baldwin is correct in arguing that many black men desire to live into a particular type of masculine performance, a masculinity that they believe is being denied to them. However, Giovanni makes clear that black women are paying the price for black men's attempts at living into normative masculinity. Black men are literally building their "masculine" sense of self on the backs of the black woman.

Giovanni continues on, setting her sights on Baldwin's normative understanding of the man as provider. She argues:

> Let's say a guy's going with a girl. You're going with Maybelle and Maybelle gets pregnant, and all of a sudden you can't speak to Maybelle because you don't have the money for a crib, right? Maybelle doesn't need a crib. The baby's going to sleep someplace. The baby's going to eat something. But what Maybelle needs at that moment is a man. You see, if the man functions as a man he is not necessarily a provider of all that stuff. . . . Maybelle understands there is no job. But what she needs is a man to come by and say, Hey baby, you look good. And black men refuse to function like that because they say, I want to bring the crib when I come. You're never going to get the crib.[124]

What Giovanni names here is that many black women do not expect or desire black men to live into normative masculine roles as sole "breadwinners," for rather than offering the love and care needed in a partnership, black men are lost chasing a standard, one which only serves to disrupt their partnerships and families. Giovanni goes on to claim, ". . . I've seen so many people get so hung up in such crappy, superficial kinds of things that, for lack of being able to bring a steak in the house, they won't come. I can get my own damn steak. . . . I need you."[125]

Throughout this portion of the conversation, Baldwin is able to admit that men live into normative understandings of masculinity, due to the fact that "the standards of the civilization into which you are born are first outside you, and by the time you get to be a man they're inside of you . . . . And in this civilization a man who cannot support his wife and child is not a man."[126] This is a fascinating admission on Baldwin's part, for although he is able to see, at least in a theoretical sense, that the "standards" of masculinity to which black men are beholden arise "outside" of the black man, he continues to promote and abide by those "standards," as this chapter has made clear. Giovanni is attempting to show Baldwin that black "men build their standards on false rationales," and rather than acquiescing to those rationales, she argues that we must build new ones.[127]

According to Giovanni, black women will no longer allow the black man to establish their skewed sense of manhood at the expense of the black woman. This exchange makes this "demand" clear:

> Giovanni: Yes, but black men—to me, as a woman, which is all I can say—have to say, Okay, I can't go that route; it doesn't work. And it's so illogical to continue to fight that, to continue to try to be little white men. Which is what you're still trying to be. We have our dashikis and your hair is growing, but you're still trying to be little white men. It doesn't work.
> Baldwin: I agree with you, and I even agree with what you're saying about black women and what you're demanding of black men. I agree with you, but—
> Giovanni: I demand that you be the man and still not pay the rent. Try it that way.
> Baldwin: All right.
> Giovanni: Try it because it's going to be harder.[128]

Later, the exchange intensifies:

> Baldwin: Yeah, but be careful as a woman what you demand of a man.
> Giovanni: I demand that he be a man.
> Baldwin: But you can't say you demand it; you have to suggest it.
> Giovanni: Well, that's your ego that *demands*. No, I demand it. Now, you deal with that.
> Baldwin: All right, okay.[129]

Giovanni is making a "demand" on black men in general, and James Baldwin in particular, and it is this demand that he must contend with in order to trouble his deeply entrenched sexism, a sexism which undergirds his understanding of black masculinity and his portrayals of black women. Giovanni is issuing a challenge to reject "standards" laid down by the white world, the temptation to try and "be little white men," calling on Baldwin and black men to imagine new ways of being "men" in the world, new ways of expressing and living into masculinity. However, despite the impassioned demand leveled by Giovanni, it will become apparent that Baldwin is not yet able to truly listen to black women, as is made clear in his conversation with Audre Lorde thirteen years later.

In Lorde's exchange with Baldwin, she stresses the importance of understanding and acknowledging "difference," which serves as means of troubling Baldwin's tendency to erase difference for the sake of his universal "Man."[130] In response to the common refrain that to be black in the United States is to be "America's nightmare," Lorde states, "Even worse than the nightmare is the blank. And Black women are the blank." Lorde is attempting to highlight for Baldwin that the experiences of black women and men are indeed different, and that difference serves as the root of the troubled relations, what she calls "the deep bitterness," between black men and black women. However, Lorde argues that in order to deal with "the deep bitterness," then difference must be faced. She continues on, stating, "Well, in the same way when we look at our differences and not allow ourselves to be divided, when we own them and are not divided by them, that is when we will be able to move on. But we haven't reached square one yet."

Interestingly, Baldwin disagrees with her on this point, positing that black men and black women are "much more sophisticated" on matters of sex and gender "than the western idea." Baldwin then attempts to trouble Lorde's understanding of difference, saying that we must deal with "differences and samenesses." Remember, Baldwin operates with an understanding of the human being in which difference is always secondary to his understanding of the universal human / a shared "human core," which serves to trivialize difference. However, Lorde immediately counters Baldwin in a way similar to that of Nikki Giovanni, disrupting his universal human. She states:

> Differences and samenesses. But in a crunch, when all our asses are in the sling, it looks like it is easier to deal with the samenesses. When we deal with sameness only, we develop weapons that we use against each other when the differences become apparent.

Lorde continues on, arguing that we must "acknowledge" the "power differences between" black men and black women, for black women are literally dying because those power differences are not recognized. Lorde insists, "I'm talking about Black women's blood flowing in the streets—and how do we get a 14-year-old boy to know I am not the legitimate target of his fury?" In this moving rebuttal, Lorde is exposing the cracks in Baldwin's universal "Man," for in his attempt to situate "sameness" at the expense of difference, the distinct ways in which black women experience racial and sexual violence is pushed aside.

However, even in the midst of this impassioned plea, Baldwin falls back on his familiar ideas concerning masculinity, the same offered to Nikki Giovanni. Baldwin claims that "for generations men have come into the world, either instinctively knowing or believing or being taught that since they were men they in one way or another had to be responsible for the women and children." As was made apparent in the previous conversation with Giovanni, Baldwin clearly believes that gender roles are entrenched, and rather than troubling these ideas, he capitulates to those roles, speaking as though they are incapable of change. Thus, even thirteen years after the conversation with Giovanni, Baldwin has not heeded her advice; he has not allowed himself to thoroughly disrupt the category "Man," nor has he begun to imagine masculinity differently.

Baldwin's failure to reimagine "Man" is clearly seen as the conversation progresses. In a particularly problematic moment, Baldwin yet again, claims that white racism is primarily concerned with emasculating the black male. He states:

> But you don't realize that in this republic the only real crime is to be a Black man? . . . A Black man has a prick, they hack it off. A Black man is a ****** when he tries to be a model for his children and he tries to protect his women.

By returning yet again to normative understandings of men's responsibility for and over black women and children, Baldwin makes clear that he is still incapable of analyzing white supremacy and anti-black racism in any way apart from viewing it as a threat to black masculinity. He even accuses Lorde of being "sentimental," frustrated by what he believes is Lorde's unfairness in "blaming" the black man for enacting violence that is not his (the black man's) "fault." Thus, in a similar fashion to his conversation with Giovanni, Baldwin struggles, and perhaps fails, to truly hear black women.

Lorde's challenge is clear. She insists that:

I can't tell you what I wished you would be doing. I can't redefine masculinity. I can't redefine Black masculinity certainly. I am in the business of redefining Black womanness. You are in the business of redefining Black masculinity.

Lorde, in a fashion similar to Giovanni, makes a demand on Baldwin, stating that it is his, and hence all black men's, responsibility to redefine masculinity outside of the bounds of toxic understandings of white masculinity. She is calling on Baldwin to engage in "a new act of creation,"[131] deconstructing the mythos of white masculinity that is literally killing all black people. It should now be apparent that despite Baldwin's precision in assessing the depths and struggles of black life in the United States and the "stupendous delusion"[132] that is white identity, he alone cannot serve as a theoretical basis for understanding the intersecting realities of gender and racial oppression, for his perspective is always and already skewed by sexism. However, the question becomes, does Baldwin eventually heed the demands of Giovanni and Lorde? Is Baldwin capable of imagining the human being outside of normative constructs of masculinity? The final section of this chapter will raise the possibility that Baldwin did in fact, in a limited way, hear the voices of black women/black feminists, for toward the end of his life he began to trouble the meaning of "Man" and masculinity through his notion of "androgyny."

Baldwin's Queer Possibility

Although Baldwin's framing of masculinity and femininity is deeply troubling, I argue that he does, in fact, offer a glimmer of hope for disrupting "Man," that symbol which bears within it the weight of white cisheteronormativity. As Sylvia Wynter makes plain, ". . . one cannot 'unsettle' the 'coloniality of power' without a *redescription of the human outside the terms of our present descriptive statement of the human, Man, and its overrepresentation*."[133] In other words, one cannot "unsettle" the category "Man" within the same logic that birthed the "descriptive statement," and I believe that Baldwin begins to trouble both his and the wider culture's understanding of the human, and thus "Man" and masculinity, in the final years of his life. In fact, Joseph Vogel, in his work *James Baldwin and the 1980s: Witnessing the Reagan Era*, argues that Lorde's challenge to Baldwin to do the work of "redefining black masculinity" "seems to be the direct inspiration for" Baldwin's essay "Freaks and the American Ideal of Manhood," which Vogel notes was written not long after the exchange with

Lorde.[134] In this essay, Baldwin offers a queer glimpse toward reimagining "Man," through his troubling of the binary logic of man/woman, and his deconstruction of the "ideal" of white masculinity.

In "Freaks and the American Ideal of Manhood," Baldwin theorizes about human sexuality and gender through the idea of "androgyny." He begins the essay stating, "To be androgynous, *Webster's* informs us, is to have both male and female characteristics. This means that there is a man in every woman and a woman in every man."[135] It is important to note that Baldwin distinguishes this more general human androgyny from persons deemed "hermaphrodite[s]," a derogatory and offensive term for contemporary readers that sometimes signifies intersex persons. For Baldwin, "hermaphrodite[s]" are those persons born with "both male and female sexual equipment,"[136] but in arguing for the androgynous nature of all humans, Baldwin is acknowledging that the gender/sexual binary is a troubling deception, a deception embedded in "the American ideal of masculinity," or better, white masculinity.[137]

Vogel notes that "Freaks and the American Ideal of Manhood" was written in the midst of the "Reagan Revolution," which according to Vogel "wasn't just about policies; it was about images and narratives of strength, individualism, patriotic militarism, and unambiguous machismo."[138] Vogel states, "By the end of the Carter presidency, the American ideal of manhood was perceived to be in trouble. Men had gone soft, the narrative went, and the nation, as a result, was weaker, more vulnerable, and uncertain."[139] The Reagan presidency, as Vogel outlines, came on the scene in the midst of this general cultural uneasiness concerning the loss and need to revive notions of masculinity, and Reagan himself came to embody the masculinity that many in the US American public sought to recover.[140]

Baldwin was able to recognize the danger of this brand of masculinity, and he makes clear that American masculinity, which I read as white masculinity, is established in "violence," "a romance . . . of genocide and slavery" that "has created cowboys and Indians, good guys and bad guys, punks and studs, tough guys and softies, butch and faggot, black and white."[141] In other words, Baldwin claims that the ideal of masculinity is rooted in both fear and a false sense of the self, a bifurcated existence that roots masculinity in the rejection of that which is feared or disruptive to the ideal—femininity, blackness, queer desire, etc. Later, Baldwin restates this point, arguing: "Freaks are called freaks and are treated as they are treated—in the main, abominably—because they are human beings who cause to echo, deep within us, our most profound terrors and desires."[142]

It is out of these fear-rooted understandings of masculinity that gender and sexual performance are policed and regimented. Those bodies which violate the line of separation between masculine and Other are subject to social stigmatization and violence. Take for instance, Baldwin's reflection on his perceived "effeminate" nature. He states:

> It wasn't only that I didn't wish to seem or sound like a woman, for it was this detail that most harshly first struck my eye and ear. I am sure that I was afraid that I already seemed and sounded too much like a woman. In my childhood, at least until my adolescence, my playmates had called me a sissy. It seemed to me that many of the people I met were making fun of women, and I didn't see why. *I* certainly needed all the friends I could get, male *or* female, and women had nothing to do with whatever my trouble might prove to be.[143]

Baldwin is keenly aware that his *queerness* in the eyes of the other children stemmed from his inability to properly perform masculinity. They recognized something, something that failed to approximate "Man." Therefore, Baldwin admits that to avoid the ire of his friends, he in fact did *not* want to be perceived as a woman. However, Baldwin, in this essay, seems to overestimate his own perceived progressive attitudes on gender. He states, "For what this really means is that all of the American categories of male and female, straight or not, black or white, were shattered, thank heaven, very early in my life."[144] Clearly, this is a questionable statement given this chapter's examination of Baldwin's views of women and femininity. However, what is important here is that Baldwin, in 1985, is in fact beginning to trouble the binary, trying to imagine humanity "otherwise."[145]

It is important to note that for Baldwin, this radical questioning of the gender/sexual binary was deeply personal, in addition to being theoretical. Baldwin biographer David Leeming argues that late in his life, Baldwin began to "[give] a great deal of thought to the idea of gender identity,"[146] and that the idea of "the female within the male had long fascinated Baldwin."[147] With this questioning came Baldwin's personal experimentation with his gender expression, for Leeming claims:

> . . . Baldwin not only enjoyed female company, there was a part of him that envied their style, their clothes, their gestures. For much of his life Baldwin avoided flamboyant clothes because he believed it was important to not "signify" a particular sexual stereotype. Yet by the 1980s he had long since given in to a love of silk, of the recklessly thrown scarf,

the overcoat draped stole-like over the shoulders, the large and exotic ring, bracelet, or neckpiece. Even his movements assumed a more feminine character.[148]

Leeming goes so far as to say that Baldwin "dreamed of novels he could write about women who would convert the Jimmy Baldwin he still sadly thought of as an ugly little man into someone tall, confident, beautiful, and, to use a favorite word of his, 'impeccably' dressed in silks and satins and bold colors."[149] So, what one sees in both Baldwin's later work and personal life is the potential troubling of the binary, the disruption of masculinity.

According to Baldwin, writing in 1985, he understood the United States to be in the midst of what he called an "androgynous 'craze,'"[150] one in which gender was being disrupted with renewed energy. That androgynous upheaval was most clearly seen in a number of music artists of the time. Vogel posits:

> From [Michael] Jackson and Boy George, to Prince, David Bowie, George Michael, and Freddie Mercury, the 1980s was a time of unprecedented mainstream "gender bending." Female artists such as Madonna, Annie Lennox, Grace Jones, Pat Benatar, and Janet Jackson also openly experimented with and transgressed gender expectations. For a wave of 1980s artists, the androgynous "look" and performance was a way of signifying a rejection of traditional roles and scripts. In "Freaks and the American Ideal of Manhood," Baldwin describes this new "androgynous craze" in positive terms. It was, he felt, an "attempt to be honest concerning one's nature."[151]

Baldwin is claiming that the movement toward gender fluidity, gender disruption, gender questioning is, in fact, a means of being honest with oneself, honest about the artificial reality of the gender binary. It is true, as Leeming states, that "in the idea of androgyny . . . Baldwin found still another metaphor to contain his gospel."[152]

Conclusion

Despite the troubling facets of Baldwin's corpus as it pertains to women and femininity, reflective of his "existentialist" tendencies,[153] Baldwin argues that the human being is not fixed, but that it is the human's responsibility to trouble the essentialized "cage[s]" of identity "bequeathed us at our birth." In other words, human life "demands" a "new act of creation."[154]

The ability to create ourselves anew, in Baldwin's estimate, is a marker of the peculiar nature of the human being. He believes:

. . . it is not possible for the human being to be as simple as a stallion or a mare, because the human imagination is perpetually required to examine, control and redefine reality, of which we must assume ourselves to be the center and the key. Nature and revelation are perpetually challenging each other; this relentless tension is one of the keys to human history and to what is known as the human condition.[155]

Therefore, in the human being's ability to transcend the "descriptive statements" which ground our contemporary understandings of the human, out of which normative understandings of masculinity find their hegemonic power, Baldwin contains in his work the possibility for disrupting the very masculinity that seemed so impossible for him to escape. In other words, we can use Baldwin against Baldwin, pulling from his work the tools that we need to disrupt his sexism, misogynoir, and commitment to gender normativity.

Thus, rather than denying difference, or placing it in a secondary space to a type of generic human, it can and perhaps must be excavated, deconstructed, and created anew in ways that contribute to the flourishing of human life. Baldwin provides some building blocks for this task, particularly in his notion of "androgyny." However, he clearly cannot do this alone, but a robust engagement of Baldwin must always occur *with* black feminist, womanist, and queer thought. It is out of this space that the human being might begin to be reimagined and re-created, and perhaps reimagined and re-created yet again.

5

Jimmy's (A)Theology:
Toward a Black Agnostic Mysticism

According to El Kornegay, James Cone, the father of black theology, claimed that alongside Martin Luther King Jr. and Malcolm X, James Baldwin was one of the "trinity" of figures who most directly influenced his theological project.[1] In fact, Cone states that it was Baldwin who "taught me how to write,"[2] while also serving as a "theological mentor."[3] Yet, despite being named as foundational to the discourse of black theology, James Baldwin did not show up *in* black theology in any substantive fashion in the opening decades of the discourse. Ironically, the man who taught Cone how to write, is not written about. I am not the first to note this, for El Kornegay, in his work *A Queering of Black Theology: James Baldwin's Blues Project and Gospel Prose*, discusses at length Baldwin's "invisibility" within black theological discourse, and the consequences of that "erasure," despite his having been a major influence on the life and thinking of James Cone.[4] The last twenty years have shown an increased engagement with Baldwin's work within the discourse, with several monographs[5] being dedicated to theological explorations of Baldwin's understanding of religion. However, although many of these monographs were written from the disciplinary space of theology, one must recognize the inability of theology as such to *hold* Baldwin. His discourse, if properly examined, is the epitome of *not* theology, in that it pushes against what Ashon Crawley calls the "categorical distinction" to which theology as a discourse is beholden, an epistemology birthed in modernity that seeks to understand theological discourse as a "categorically pure [zone] of thought."[6]

This chapter examines Baldwin's relationship to the sacred, while refusing to place him within the thought world of Christian theological discourse. We will explore the primary thesis that Baldwin, in an apophatic fashion, offers a resounding "no" to god and god-talk, engaging in a type of "refusal"[7] in arguing that god is a construct of the human imagination. What Baldwin articulates is more properly described as a *mysticism*, one committed to the experience/ pursuit of a mysterious "something" (more will be said about Baldwin's use of this term below) which is always and already sensually present. In other words, Baldwin displaces the sacred from the realm of "belief" to that of *feeling* or affect[8]—feeling in the sense of a deeply embodied experience, one that pulls upon the whole of the senses. After examining Baldwin's rejection of the construct "god," we will then proceed to explore his religious sensibilities as a form of mysticism, or to borrow Crawley's language, a mysticism "otherwise"[9]—a deeply affective, aesthetic, and robustly agnostic reality.

What will be demonstrated is that black mysticism, as laid out in the work of Baldwin and Crawley, is about *sociality*.[10] Baldwin, disidentifying[11] with the category of salvation in his essay "To Crush a Serpent," argues that salvation is about "connection" and "union" as opposed to escape, and this is not simply a connection with other human beings but "with all that is or has been or will ever be."[12] In other words, the connection to what Baldwin calls "something out there"[13] is a call for radical human connectivity, a call for "sociality." Crawley articulates something similar, for black mysticism is rooted in a "renunciation of the singular," and is a "retreat *into* rather than away from the social."[14] Again, the black mysticism of Baldwin and Crawley is, in fact, about the social, those profoundly sensual moments in which black lives commune one with another.

Baldwin and the (De)Construction of God

Baldwin's close friend and biographer David Leeming recounts one of Baldwin's final conversations, which took place approximately a week before his death, concerning the role of the church and of god in his personal life. Leeming states:

> During the night he wanted to talk about religion. He realized that the church's role in his life had been significant, especially with respect to what he called his "inner vocabulary." As for the larger questions, he did not "believe" in God, but he felt—especially when he was alone— that there was "something out there."[15]

This statement will serve as an important starting point, for it will become clear that for Baldwin, *belief in* god is impossible and ultimately rejected, but the *feeling* of "something out there" speaks to a kind of agnostic possibility which allows us to glimpse a mysticism undergirding Baldwin's understanding of a "power" outside of human "control."[16]

For Baldwin to claim that he does not "'believe' in God," yet *feels* "something out there" highlights the paradoxical nature of his relationship to, and language concerning, the divine, a reality also noted by Josiah Ulysses Young III. Young's work, *James Baldwin's Understanding of God: Overwhelming Desire and Joy,* is important to discuss here because he takes seriously Baldwin's rejection of god-talk. In Young's text, he focuses on the ambiguity of belief and unbelief in Baldwin's literary corpus as it pertains to god. He states, "Throughout this book, I will place 'God' between quotation marks to indicate that I have found no evidence that Baldwin believed in 'God' in a traditional sense." He goes on to say: "[Baldwin] did not, that is, believe in YHWH, the Trinity, or Allah. He believed that 'God' revealed, for the most part, who *we* are rather than a Supreme Being somewhere above us. He did hold, however, that a mysterious force was at work in the cosmos."[17] What is most important for our purposes is that Young also makes special mention of Baldwin's language of "something" and "something out there,"[18] connecting that "something" to what he understands to be "Baldwin's credo," which is none other than Baldwin's "belief" in love.[19] Young states, "I have no reason to doubt, and this book has largely been about the fact that I do not doubt, that this *something out there* was for him a wise and creative love."[20] I will approach the topic in a similar fashion, although expanding beyond Young in theorizing the meaning of this "something."

Part of the paradoxical nature of Baldwin's language concerning god and the divine, lay in the fact that Baldwin consistently, from his early essay "Preservation of Innocence" to his final novel *Just Above My Head,* articulated what Young called a "Feuerbach-like"[21] understanding of god as a construct of the human mind. In other words, Baldwin views god as an outgrowth of human wants and needs. In his famous work *Essence of Christianity,* Ludwig Feuerbach claims that "consciousness of God is self-consciousness," thus god is an outgrowth of the human imagination, a type of projection of human consciousness made ultimate.[22] For instance, in the statement "God is love," what is important for Feuerbach is the "predicate" love which is attached to the "subject" god.[23] He states, "Thou believest in love as a divine attribute because thou thyself lovest; thou believest that God is a wise, benevolent being because thou knowest nothing better in thyself than benevolence and wisdom."[24] It is the predicate, love, which reveals the human value of love, and god simply serves as the *imaginary* means of giving that value ultimate meaning.[25] Returning to Feuerbach briefly, "What the subject is lies only in the predicate; the predicate is the *truth* of the subject—the subject only the personified, existing predicate, the predicate conceived as existing."[26] In other words, for both Feuerbach and

Baldwin, god is a human construct, not *real* in an ontological or metaphysical sense, but a symbol which takes on the characteristics and values of the various communities that create the deity.[27] This is why Young states: "For Baldwin, 'God' is predicate. 'God' is not love for him; love, rather, is 'God.'"[28] Therefore, it stands to reason that god constructs arising out of a western culture birthed in white supremacy would bear the marks of white supremacist racialization. That racialization of god, reflective of the US American logic of race, is one of the primary reasons for Baldwin's rejection of the symbol.

As early as 1949, Baldwin's theory of god being a "creation" of the human mind was readily apparent,[29] as seen in his essay "Preservation of Innocence."[30] This essay, which deals in part with the question of the "nature" of humanity, particularly as it relates to the "the problem of the homosexual,"[31] argues that god sprang to life out of human attempts at contending with the indifference of nature in relation to human existence. Baldwin points out that:

> Instantly the Deity springs to mind, in much the same manner, I sus-
> pect, that he sprang into being on the cold, black day when we discov-
> ered that nature cared nothing for us. His advent, which alone had the
> power to save us from nature and ourselves, also created a self-
> awareness and, therefore, tensions and terrors and responsibilities with
> which we had not coped before. It marked the death of innocence. . . .
>   We are forced to consider this tension between God and nature and
> are thus confronted with the nature of God because He is man's most
> intense creation and it is not in the sight of nature that the homosexual
> is condemned, but in the sight of God.[32]

Baldwin is making clear that god arose out of the need of human beings to contend with and create meaning in an uncaring natural world, and out of that "creation" human beings were now judged according to the standard of that deity. However, Baldwin goes beyond simply calling the deity a human "creation." Based on the fact that "an incalculable number of the world's hu-mans are thereby condemned to something less than life," (i.e., queer humans) based on the judgement of that construct, Baldwin claims that god is a "pro-found and dangerous failure of concept."[33]

This theme continues to arise over the years, echoed again by Baldwin during a 1963 public dialogue with Christian ethicist Reinhold Niebuhr, which took place in the aftermath of the infamous bombing of the 16th Street Baptist Church in Birmingham, Alabama. When asked if he saw any "meaning" or significance in the fact that the face of Christ was blown out of one of the church's large stained-glass windows during the bombing, Baldwin states:

It suggests to me several meanings. If I were going to be cynical this
morning, I would say that the absence of the face is something of an
achievement, since we've been victimized so long by an alabaster
Christ. And it suggests, much more seriously, something else, and to
me it sums up the crisis that we're living through. If Christ has no face,
then perhaps it is time that we, who in one way or another *invented*
and are *responsible for* our deities, give him a new face, give him a new
consciousness.[34]

We see again this language of "invention" and "responsibility," for Baldwin
continued to hold to the idea that human beings are the source of god, and if
human beings have the power to make gods, they also have the power to remake
or unmake them.[35] Clarence Hardy is indeed correct in naming that "for Baldwin, God largely becomes an outgrowth of humanity's own collective creative
powers."[36]

However, Baldwin's critique moves beyond a simple dismissal of god based
upon the idea that humans have made "Him," for in Baldwin's estimate humans can, and perhaps should, engage in this work "to expand and transform
God's nature,"[37] making god "larger, freer, and more loving."[38] Therefore,
the problem is not that humans have made god *per se*, but that the gods they
have made are far too small, reflective of the myopic machinations of white
supremacy and heterosexism. In his essay "In Search of a Majority," Baldwin
claims:

I suggest that the role of the Negro in American life has something to
do with our concept of what God is, and from my point of view, this
concept is not big enough. It has got to be made bigger than it is because God is, after all, not anybody's toy. To be with God is really to
be involved with some enormous, overwhelming desire, and joy, and
power which you cannot control, which controls you. I conceive of
my own life as a journey toward *something* I do not understand, which
in going toward, makes me better. I conceive of God, in fact, as a
means of liberation and not a means to control others.[39]

Baldwin seeks to name here that god constructs, perhaps even the task of theology itself, are at their root, often poor attempts at controlling a mystery which
cannot be named or approximated. In other words, capital "G" "God" fails
because the human imagination which has conjured that "God" lacks the
ability to capture the vastness of the "otherwise possibilities"[40] contained in
the symbol. Baldwin is on a journey toward *something*, that something being
representative of a power that god-talk fails to capture.

Baldwin and the Apophatic "Something"

Moving away from what Baldwin rejects toward that which he affirms, one place to begin our examination of Baldwin's "something" is his 1976 essay, *The Devil Finds Work*. In this text, Baldwin returns to the scene of his conversion, offering what is, arguably, a softer treatment than that found in *The Fire Next Time*. In this passage, Baldwin explores the "power" that he and other black Pentecostals encounter(ed) through the practice/experience of "pleading the blood."[41] "Pleading the blood" refers to the mystical moment in which "the soul of the sinner" is "locked in battle with Satan," as the saints, i.e., those who have already "passed through" this experience, "plead the blood" and bring the sinner "through" this turbulent trial.[42] On the floor of his Pentecostal church almost thirty years prior, Baldwin was "prayed through" by the saints. Reflecting on that moment, Baldwin states: "I had been prayed through, and I, then, prayed others through: had testified to having been born again, and, then, helped others to be born again."[43] However, what is important for us to note here is that in this 1976 retelling of his conversion narrative, Baldwin calls this experience a "reality," a much different tone than that found in *The Fire Next Time* in which he comes to the realization on the floor of the church that God . . . is white.[44] In offering this language of "the real," Baldwin is making clear that black Christians, and black Pentecostals in particular, are in fact experiencing "something," for blacks "did not so much use Christian symbols as recognize them—recognize them for what they were before the Christians came along—and, thus, reinvested these symbols with their original energy."[45]

Baldwin goes on to say that what he experienced in his conversion is not a matter of "belief," pointing again to his rejection of a type of *belief in* deity, for the language of "belief" "ineptly approaches the reality to which I am referring."[46] However, this experience, according to Baldwin, is a matter of "revelation." He states:

> The word "revelation" has very little meaning in the recognized languages: yet, it is the only word for the moment I am attempting to approach. This moment changes one forever. One is confronted with the agony and the nakedness and the beauty of a power which has no beginning and no end, which contains you, and which you contain, and which will be using you when your bones are dust. One thus confronts a self both limited and boundless, born to die and born to live. The creature is, also, the creation, and responsible, endlessly, for that perpetual act of creation which is both the self and more than the self. One is set free, then, to live among one's terrors, hour by hour and day

by day, alone, and yet never alone. *My soul is a witness!*—so one's ancestors proclaim, and in the deadliest of the midnight hours.[47]

*This is not a moment of belief, but a moment of confrontation with something
both in oneself and without.* This does not indicate that Baldwin reversed himself radically regarding his feelings about his conversion experience. However,
what is indicated is that Baldwin is allowing himself the room to see that what
he experienced in black Pentecostal worship, something the experience of
"pleading the blood" allowed, is a confrontation with "something," a power
both inside and outside oneself that cannot be contained or circumscribed, a
mystery that defies language.[48]

This language, which I argue gets to the root of Baldwin's relationship to
what he understands as sacred, reads as a type of apophatic evasion as he attempts to paradoxically allow that which is ultimate to remain "unnameable,"[49]
while proceeding to *name* the ultimate, that "power," by means of the intentionally vague language of "something." Michael A. Sells in his work *Mystical
Languages of Unsaying*, discusses the tradition of apophatic discourse, also
called "negative theology." In offering a general definition of apophatic discourse and the paradox underlying it, Sells ascertains:

> It is negative in the sense that it denies that the transcendent can be
> named or given attributes. The formal denial that the transcendent
> can be named must in some sense be valid, otherwise ineffability
> would not become an issue. Insofar as it is valid, however, the formal
> statement of ineffability turns back upon itself, and undoes itself. To
> say "X is beyond names," if true, entails that it cannot then be called
> by the name "X." In turn, the statement "it cannot be called X" be-
> comes suspect, since the "it," as a pronoun, substitutes for a name, but
> the transcendent is beyond all names. As I attempt to state the aporia
> of transcendence, I am caught in a linguistic regress. . . . The regress is
> harnessed and becomes the guiding semantic force, the *dynamis*, of a
> new kind of language.[50]

That new language is *"apophasis,"* a Greek term signifying both "negation"
and "un-saying or speaking-away."[51]

I am not the first to note Baldwin's relationship to apophatic discourse.
Vincent Lloyd, in his work *Religion of the Field Negro: On Black Secularism
and Black Theology*, also highlights Baldwin's tendency toward apophatic discourse / negative theology. He states:

> . . . James Baldwin transformed, rather than rejected, his father's
> Christianity. The components of that Christianity—ideas about

innocence, salvation, sin, truth, and much else—are reworked by
Baldwin and in their new form they are inextricably linked with Baldwin's political vision. . . . The theology that Baldwin offers in its place
is negative, part of the long tradition of Christian negative theology
for which the only true thing that can be said about God is what God
is not.[52]

However, as this quote makes clear, Lloyd seeks to place Baldwin in "the long
tradition of Christian negative theology," thus understanding Baldwin as par-
ticipating in the tradition rather than offering something profoundly novel.
Lloyd, like El Kornegay and others, seeks to place Baldwin within the normative
structures of Christian theology, therefore missing the truly agnostic potential
of Baldwin's mysticism.

With that in mind, it is important to note that I am not claiming that Baldwin is an apophatic theologian proper, for to do so would be to inappropriately
baptize Baldwin into the discourse of theology. However, despite the danger
of utilizing the language of apophasis in describing Baldwin, he is, in fact,
engaging in a type of apophatic *practice* in a truly remarkable sense, in that
he is refusing to speak of god in any substantive sense, thus eschewing god-talk
of any variety. Baldwin is engaging in a type of refusal in that he will not attempt to circumscribe or describe that which cannot be named. Baldwin's
refusal makes theology impossible, theology being the task of describing the
divine. However, in claiming a lack of belief in god, while also naming that
which is ultimate as something outside of our control, Baldwin *is* in fact positing an understanding of the sacred. However, that positive claim about the
sacred is still outside of the bounds of theological discourse, for Baldwin is not
attempting to make a claim about god/goddesses/divine beings as such, but
rather displaces the sacred from the realm of "belief" to that of *feeling*—"he
did not '*believe*' in God, but he *felt* . . . 'something out there'"[53]—feeling in the
sense of a deeply embodied experience, one that pulls upon the whole of the
senses. In other words, Baldwin's encounter with the unnameable is a sensual
experience.

A Black Mysticism of the Unnameable

As Baldwin states, "belief" is language that fails in relation to the unnameable,
yet "something" can be encountered by means of "feeling" and "revelation" (a
type of embodied confrontation). In deploying this language, I argue that
Baldwin is moving in the register of the mystical and, more specifically, a type
of black agnostic mysticism. William James, in his classic work *The Varieties*

of Religious Experience, argues that "mysticism" or "mystical states" bear four "qualities" or "marks."[54] First is *"ineffability,"* for the experience itself "defies expression" and "no adequate report of its contents can be given in words."[55] Much like the experience of love, in that "one must have been in love one's self to understand the lover's state of mind," the mystical must be "directly experienced" in order to have a sense of its meaning.[56] Connected to this is the fact that the experience is a matter of affect—"more like states of feeling," rather "than like states of intellect."[57] Second, mysticism bears a *"noetic quality,"* for the experience brings "illuminations" or "revelations" to the mystic, a "knowledge" or "insight" that is "unplumbed by the discursive intellect."[58] In James's estimate, the presence of these two qualities are enough for a phenomenon to qualify as "mystical."[59] The other two markers, *"transiency"*—reflecting the momentary nature of the experience, "they fade into the light of common day," and *"passivity"*—speaking to the sense of being "grasped and held by a superior power," are also present in many mystical experiences, but are not required.[60] For Baldwin, all four of these realities are present in the "confrontation" with "something," for Baldwin argues that this experience defies the cognition of belief, but must be *felt* or *confronted* (ineffability), bringing about a *revelation* (noetic quality) of a "power" "which contains you, and which you contain"[61] (passivity). However, the experience, for Baldwin, does "fade," and must "be reaffirmed every day and every hour"[62] (transience). Thus, what we see in Baldwin is a type of religious orientation not unlike that of mysticism.

However, it is important to highlight that William James's understanding of mysticism is inadequate in grounding Baldwin's distinct take on the mystical encounter. There are limits to what Joy Bostic, in her work *African American Female Mysticism: Nineteenth-Century Religious Activism*, calls an "'essentialist' position," of which William James would be an example. She defines this essentialism as such:

> In the study of mysticism, an essentialist view is one in which a scholar begins with the assumption that all mystical experience is essentially the same and that either the descriptions "reflect underlying similarities" or that even where language differs across cultural and/or religious traditions the fundamental experience is still the same.[63]

In other words, Bostic is pointing out that scholars such as William James presume that all mystical experience is "the same" at its core, while she demonstrates that mysticism is marked, in a profound sense, by the cultures and peoples out of which it springs.[64] She states, ". . . the language and constructs of how African Americans describe and interpret mysticism have both informed and have been informed by the various cultural strains that have converged in North America over the course of the last five centuries."[65] Therefore, following Bostic's lead, this chapter will speak to the peculiarity and specificity of the people and practices that came to mark Baldwin's distinct mystical mode of being. In order to do that, we must now turn to an examination of Ashon Crawley's understanding of "Blackpentecostalism" and black mysticism in order to gain an understanding of the contours of Baldwin's black agnostic mysticism.

It was through the language and thought world of Pentecostalism that Baldwin articulated his relationship to the unnamed something that we have been exploring thus far. Douglas Field is correct in noting that we must take Baldwin's Pentecostalism seriously, for he argues that "Baldwin's writing was shaped by key features of Pentecostalism."[66] Ashon Crawley helps us go further, for rather than simply linking Baldwin to Pentecostalism, Crawley makes clear the distinct lifeworld that is *black* Pentecostalism, or what he calls "Blackpentecostalism." Crawley's language of Blackpentecostal might lead to the misunderstanding that Crawley is only referring to the specific movement that begins with William Seymour in 1906, serving as one of the sparks of the modern Pentecostal movement.[67] However, Crawley is, in fact, utilizing the language of Blackpentecostalism in an expansive manner. He states:

> Blackpentecostalism does not belong to those Saints called Blackpentecostal, those Saints that attend traditionally considered Pentecostal church spaces. Rather, Blackpentecostalism belongs to all who would so live into the fact of the flesh, live into this fact as a critique of the violence of modernity, the violence of the Middle Passage and enslavement, the violence of enslavement and its ongoing afterlife, live into the flesh as a critique of the ongoing attempt to interdict the capacity to breathe.[68]

Crawley also claims:

> Blackpentecostalism is an intellectual practice grounded in the fact of the flesh, flesh unbounded and liberative, flesh as vibrational and always on the move. Such practice constitutes a way of life. The practices I analyze are a range of sensual, affective, material experiences: "shouting" as dance; "tarrying" as stilled intensity and waiting, as well as raucous praise noise; "whooping" (ecstatic, eclipsed breath) during prayer and preaching; as well as, finally, speaking in tongues. . . . I ultimately argue that these choreographic, sonic, and visual aesthetic practices and sensual experiences are not only important objects of study for those interested in alternative modes of social organization,

but they also yield a general hermeneutics, a methodology of reading culture.[69]

In other words, for Crawley, the specific aesthetic practices found in Black-pentecostal spaces are reflective of the broader contours of the resistant mode of being in the modern world called blackness.[70] These "performative prac-tices," which include sound and song, "constitute a disruptive force, generative for imagining otherwise modes of social organization and mobilization."[71]

However, for our purposes, what is most important is what marks Blackpen-tecostalism, and one could argue blackness itself, as mystical. Crawley, in both his 2017 work *Blackpentecostal Breath* and his 2020 text *The Lonely Letters*, calls our attention to the reality of a black mystical tradition, or what he calls "a sorta Black Radical *Mystical* Tradition,"[72] one which is linked to Blackpen-tecostal life and practice. To get at the mysticism of Crawley's thought, one must center the category of "feeling." According to Crawley, "Black religiosity" (again, one could argue blackness itself) is, at its core, "all about feeling."[73] Another way of framing this would be to utilize the language of the "sensual," for Crawley is not using the language of "feeling" to signify an emotional state, but there is a deep materiality to Crawley's understanding of feeling, for it is a "sense [experience]" involving "taste, touch, smell, sight, hearing."[74] What makes this mystical is the way in which black religion broadly, and Blackpen-tecostalism in particular, is a matter of "feeling *something*," something un-nameable. Crawley states, "Blackpentecostal believers often talk about 'feeling something,' where 'something' cannot necessarily be described with precision," but it is "registered on and in the flesh."[75] This is an experience of *something* in the flesh, and that *something* is *felt* through the medium of black aesthetic practices, practices which "[constitute] a way of life."[76] These practices, reflec-tive of that unnamed *something*, "[exceed] capture" in the logics of theological discourse and nomenclature.[77] In addition, we will see that this is far from a type of individual experience, for it leads to "social organization and mobilization."[78]

Bridging the broad understanding of mysticism offered by William James (mysticism as an experience of *ineffability*—i.e., "more like states of feeling") and the black mysticism illuminated by Ashon Crawley (the experience of "feeling something"), we can begin to see a framework through which to read Baldwin's own mysticism. Baldwin's understanding of the mystical encounter is also centered on "the sensual," for that *something* which is felt is experienced in the flesh.[79] This raises the question, what is this "something," this "power," and how do people connect to this "unnameable" reality? We must proceed with caution, for any attempt at offering a robust definition of this "something" would violate Baldwin's apophatic inclinations. However, Baldwin does offer a glimpse as to what this "something" might be, found in his reimagining of the category "salvation" in his essay "To Crush a Serpent." Baldwin states:

> Salvation is not flight from the wrath of God; it is accepting and recip-rocating the love of God. Salvation is not separation. It is the beginning of *union with all that is or has been or will ever be.*
>
> . . . Salvation is as real, as mighty, and as impersonal as the rain, and it is as private as the rain in one's face. It is never accomplished; it is to be reaffirmed every day and every hour. There is absolutely no salvation without love: this is the wheel in the middle of the wheel. Salvation does not divide. *Salvation connects, so that one sees oneself in others and others in oneself.* It is not the exclusive property of any dogma, creed, or church. It keeps the channel open between oneself and however one wishes to name That which is greater than oneself.[80]

This passage, one of the few places that Baldwin engages the symbol "God" in a positive sense,[81] offers a glimpse into what is encountered, and the out-growth of that encounter. For here we see Baldwin disidentifying with salvation in arguing that the goal of salvation is not escape, but salvation is about con-nection and "union," not just with other human beings but "with all that is or has been or will ever be."[82] This bears profound resonance with Crawley's black mysticism, for Crawley is clear that black mysticism differs from other traditions of western mysticism in that, rather than centering the "pattern of withdrawal-purgation-transformation,"[83] black mysticism is rooted in a "renunciation of the singular," and is a "retreat *into* rather than away from the social."[84] What I am attempting to signify here is that Baldwin's mysticism, in his calls for *unification* and *connection,* is signifying what Crawley's calls "sociality."[85]

Crawley, in his essay "Susceptibility," states:

> Black life is about relation, about sociality, in orbit. Because of the circum-sacred, what is marked is the deep and complex relationship between that which is considered to be black religiosity and that which is considered to be, on the other side and categorically distinct, black sociality. This division, I argue, is illusory and unnecessary, impossible to order, impossible to enclose, impossible to maintain.[86]

Elsewhere, Crawley, building on the work of Hortense Spillers, refers to this as "the intramural," "the internal relation, the interior relation, the way Black folks are with one another."[87] In other words, this is a mysticism that is rooted in the unification/connection of (black) humanity together, it points to the ways in which black persons exist with one another. To solidify the point made by Crawley, this sociality should not, and cannot, be distinguished from black religiosity, for to attempt to separate black sociality and black religiosity would be an attempt to make black religion something "categorically distinct"[88] from black life writ large. Black religiosity is, simply, another name for the materiality of black life. This is why Charles Long, in his work *Significations: Signs, Symbols, and Images in the Interpretation of Religion*, argues that to understand black religiosity, one must understand the "experience, expression, motivations, intentions, behaviors, styles, and rhythms" of the black community.[89] Black religiosity is black life, and black mysticism signifies the ways in which blackness is always and already about the pursuit of life together.

Returning to Baldwin, his "power" or "something" is rooted in the idea of *unification*, and this unification is nothing other than the knitting together of life together, black social life, black religious life. If one thinks back to the previous chapters, it should become clear that, with the exception of Baldwin's failed attempt to escape "Man" in Chapter 4, every chapter is about the importance of, and the necessity to create, the social—signified as the erotic touch between lovers (Chapter 1), the building of black sociality through the arts (Chapter 2), and the hope for a black eschatological future (Chapter 3).[90] The remainder of this chapter will be dedicated to exploring how Baldwin's religious thought reveals a mysticism rooted in the *affective*, the *aesthetic*, and the *agnostic*, all of which bear within them the goal of unification—i.e., black sociality.

Beginning with the *affective*, as has already been clearly shown, Baldwin centers his religious sensibilities in "feeling," or what Crawley calls "fleshed feeling."[91] The encounter with the sacred is not a matter of belief, but it is always and already about that which is felt in the body, reflective of Baldwin's Blackpentecostal past. Baldwin himself speaks to this in *The Fire Next Time*, when he notes that "there is still, for me, no pathos quite like the pathos of those multicolored, worn, somehow triumphant and transfigured faces."[92] He continues on:

> I have never seen anything to equal the fire and excitement that sometimes, without warning, fill a church, causing the church, as Leadbelly and so many others have testified, to "rock." Nothing that has happened to me since equals the power and the glory that I sometimes felt when, in the middle of a sermon, I knew that I was somehow, by some miracle, really carrying, as they said, "the Word"—when the church and I were one. Their pain and their joy were mine, and mine were theirs—they surrendered their pain and joy to me, and I surrendered mine to them.[93]

What one sees in this passage, through the deeply affective language of "pathos," "pain," and "joy," is Baldwin indicating that even in the black church, a space that he found to be a deeply compromised space, there was the possibility for a profound knitting together of community. Somehow, mysteriously, mystically, black pain and joy were shared in that space. Somehow, black community, black sociality, was manifest in the gathering of "the Saints" together.

However, this was not limited to the church, for Baldwin refuses to draw a hard and fast distinction between black life inside and outside of the black church. He states:

> Perhaps we were, all of us—pimps, whores, racketeers, church members, and children—bound together by the nature of our oppression, the specific and peculiar complex of risks we had to run; if so, within these limits we sometimes achieved with each other a freedom that was close to love. I remember, anyway, church suppers and outings, and, later, after I left the church, rent and waistline parties where rage and sorrow sat in the darkness and did not stir, and we ate and drank and talked and laughed and danced and forgot all about "the man." We had the liquor, the chicken, the music, and each other, and had no need to pretend to be what we were not. This is the freedom that one hears in some gospel songs, for example, and in jazz.[94]

With a very subtle sleight of hand, Baldwin bridges the space of the black church and the outside. Whether in the Blackpentecostal church, a space of preaching and praise, or the rent party, a space of abundant drink and secular music, *there was a sharing of space, a sharing of experience*—"we had . . . each other." *Baldwin calls this "love" and "freedom."* This is the affective quality of black mysticism, for in the sharing of pain, joy, excitement, laughter, and sorrow, black sociality is pursued and created. That togetherness, that sociality, superseded the myopic machinations of a theology that would divide those in the church from those outside, in fact it rendered theology unnecessary.

Yet, as previously mentioned, affect and feeling are a matter of the body, or, again, what Crawley calls "fleshed feeling." This passage from Crawley resonates with the affective quality of Baldwin's mysticism. Crawley states:

> Perhaps we have been trained away from, we have been taught to give up, the possibility for mystical experience. Which is to say perhaps we have been trained, have been taught, to give up the possibility for touch, for touching feeling, for touching friendship, for touching relationship,

unless under very strict control, by the state for example, mediated by a
god or a state or an institution that says its ok.[95]

Touch—whether that offered in friendship, romance, or sexuality *is* sociality,
it is the expansion outside of, or through, oneself to feel, experience, recognize,
and know the other. Returning to the subject of this book's Chapter 1, erotic
touch is mystical in that the mutual recognition of the humanity of the other
that can take place in the sex act lays the groundwork for a unity much greater
than the two individuals involved, it provides an opportunity to "[see] oneself
in others and others in oneself."[96] As Douglas Field states, "Baldwin's emphasis
on 'touch' is both physical and spiritual, suggesting being moved (to be touched)
but also the physical act of reaching out to another."[97] Remember, the courage
to touch—to caress and embrace—another person, provides an opportunity for
revelation, or as Baldwin states: "you see everyone else very differently than
you saw them before—perhaps I only mean to say that you begin to *see*."[98] What
Baldwin is attempting to name here is that touch, "touching feeling," erotic
touch, allows for the mystical possibility of connection and unification. The
touch of Arthur and Crunch, Crunch and Julia, and Fonny and Tish (to name
only a few examples) created worlds in which the characters found salvation,
which was none other than the deep and enduring knowledge of oneself and
the other, and oneself *in relation to* the other.

However, Baldwin's mysticism is also *aesthetic*. Just as William James
argues that "the simplest rudiment of mystical experience" can be discovered
in "lyric poetry and music,"[99] Baldwin, too, understood black aesthetic expression, and music in particular, to be a vehicle for mystical unification.
Saadi A. Simawe in his article, "What Is in a Sound? The Metaphysics and
Politics of Music in *The Amen Corner*," posits that for Baldwin, "music is
associated with liberation, security, *mystical power*, self-reconciliation, a more
democratic divine power, unrestricted humanism, and sexuality that is inseparable from spirituality."[100] The mysticism of aesthetic expression for
Baldwin stems from its mysterious ability to connect/unify human beings
one to another.[101] As stated in Chapter 2, blackness, for Baldwin, is an aesthetic reality carried in the sound, beat, rhythms, and *tone* of black music in
the United States.[102] That sound can be recognized in the musical genres of
gospel, jazz, blues, soul, and others. Baldwin, like Crawley, does not draw a
distinction between so-called sacred vs. secular forms of music production—
all of them have the potential to build connection between one human and
another.[103] Crawley states:

> Because of the illusory division between black religiosity and black soci-
> ality, what black popular culture, in general, reaches and strives for is

the affective mood and movement (but not, it must be said and maintained, the doctrinal and theological thought) of Blackpentecostal energy, fervor, and verve. Blackpentecostalism is *an* example—not the
only one, of course—of what black life performs, practices, produces in
terms of joy, love, relation. The spirit, the movement, and verve desired
in religious Blackpentecostal performance is reached for and desired for
all black performance.[104]

What Crawley is signifying here is that Blackpentecostalism has always bore
within it a particular "energy, fervor, and verve" that other forms of black artistic
production also seek to express. Baldwin, captivated as a child by the sound
and energy of black art as found in the church, came to recognize that same
energy, a sacred energy, outside of it—in literature, the blues, jazz, soul. It was
sacred for Baldwin because what Blackpentecostalism performs/offers, what
Crawley calls "circum-sacred performance," "is about marking relation, existence, or being *with*, a presence that is about sociality as the ground of irreducibly plural existence."[105] This is why Baldwin grounds blackness in sound,
rhythm, and tone, for black art broadly, and black sound in particular, has always
provided the means through which the black community was, and continues
to be, expressed.[106] For Crawley, "this circum-sacred is that which black life is
gathered around but is, like vibration detected as sound and song of music
some might call nothing, there but barely raised to the level of detection though
it is sensed, felt, known."[107] Thus, we see, yet again, the inextricable link between the aesthetic and the affective, that which is felt/sensed, and sociality.
This is why Clarence Hardy argues that "For Baldwin, it seems, the power
associated with true religion does not come with God but with the music
sweating, suffering bodies produce—just as true love does."[108] Music provides
the possibility of partaking in this unity by moving the listener into a space
that shows their connection "with all that is or has been or will ever be."[109]

    Lastly, Baldwin's mysticism is *agnostic.* Inherent in Baldwin's reluctance to
name the divine is his belief that no person, and no single tradition, can control
that "unnameable" "something." Returning again to the essay, "To Crush a
Serpent," Baldwin argues that "salvation . . . is not the exclusive property of
any dogma, creed, or church. It keeps the channel open between oneself and
however one wishes to name That which is greater than oneself."[110] Crawley
makes a similar point, stating: "The sacred does not belong to particular religious traditions or to the zone and category and enclosure called the religious
itself."[111] As this chapter has made clear, Baldwin believes that the Christian
god, like all gods, is created by communities of people. Baldwin does not privilege any god construct over another, which is why he emphatically stated on

the eve of his death that he does not, in fact, "'believe' in god." Therefore, any attempt to place Baldwin within a monotheistic or Christian framework when speaking of his mysticism is a misrepresentation of his thought and writing.

This brings us, yet again, back to Crawley's work on black mysticism. In *The Lonely Letters*, Crawley laments that "Mystical traditions, at least the western ones, run up against their own limit," that limit being reflective of the need on the part of these traditions to bolster and produce a "normative Christianity."[112] He states:

> I'm not looking for a New Age individuation, not looking to enlarge my territory or to have health, wealth, and blessings unending, theologies of conspicuous consumption and acquisition that discard the histories and practices from which certain mysticisms emerge. But I guess I have the same problem with mysticisms that I have with what I guess we could call, imprecisely of course, nonmystical traditions. (Does such a thing even exist?) Mystical traditions, at least the western ones, seem to run up against their own limit, seem to be about the production of normative function and form.
>
> The limit, I guess, in Eckhart would be a kind of normative Christianity. And his aloneness, his negativity, his nothingness all emerge from *that* limit even if he is trying to approach something otherwise. Because for his experience to be *about* Christianity, such experience is against the very interconnectedness of all things mysticism presumes to seek.[113]

What makes Crawley's musings regarding mysticism so helpful here is that he seeks to decouple black mysticism from any particular *Christian* tradition. To locate this black mysticism within Christianity is to place it within a tradition marked by a "normative function and form," a "limit." Christianity, particularly those dominant traditions found within the western world, operate, according to Sylvester Johnson, under a "principle of scarcity." In his work, *African American Religions*, he argues that according to "the dominant sensibilities of Christianity":

> The worship of any gods other than the Christian deity was arguably the most incriminating action in the Christian imagination. Its theological importance easily outweighed that of such horrendous acts as murder, pillaging, sexual violence, or genocide. In Christian grammar, it was an exceptional category—idolatry—and it constituted the most direct form of rebellion against the Christian deity.[114]

What this indicates is that the Christian god often, though not always, stands alone. "He" stands as the measure by which all other conceptions and understandings of the divine are evaluated. Baldwin's "refusal,"[115] reflected also in Crawley's "refusal," is rooted in the pursuit of unity and "interconnectedness." Thus, in Baldwin's black mysticism, one does not need to commune with a singular divine figure as the ground of the mystical experience, for "interconnectedness," one with another, is that which grounds the experience of "something out there." Baldwin's mysticism does not require that one embrace a life of solitude in order to gain access to a singular god. Access to a power outside of one's "control" only comes about through the experience of life together, through "the possibility for touch, for touching feeling, for touching friendship, for touching relationship."[116]

Coda[1]

This book sought to answer the question, *what is James Baldwin doing with and through his literary deployment of religious language and symbols?* In the previous chapters, I set out to explore the ways in which Baldwin, throughout the whole of his public career, continually disidentifies[2] with and queers the religious symbols of his youth in calling the US American empire to "the self-confrontation of prayer, the cleansing breaking of the heart which precedes atonement."[3] In essence, I show that Baldwin seeks *transformation*—a transformation of individuals and the larger culture through a strategic disidentification with symbols rich in theological and religious meaning, including but not limited to, conversion, love, "the people of God,"[4] the sacred, the human being, and "the New Jerusalem."[5] Despite Baldwin's recurring critiques and public claims of disaffiliation with Christianity and its god, he continues to find the symbols of the faith, "his inner vocabulary,"[6] efficacious in articulating a novel religious vision, one in which queer sexuality signifies the depth of love's transforming possibilities; the arts serve as the (religious) medium of knitting human community together; an "unnameable"[7] "power" disrupts the "smallness" of the gods of the United States;[8] "androgyny" troubles the gender binary;[9] and a black child bears within it the hope for a world made new.[10] Baldwin's vision is *religious*, for it seeks to create a world in which human beings, all human beings, have the freedom to live into their "complex subjectivities."[11]

It is important to stress that Baldwin does not consider himself a Christian, nor does he utilize these symbols in an attempt to bolster the Christian faith. But, in disidentifying with these symbols Baldwin seeks to imagine both religion and the world "otherwise." As stated in the Introduction, "otherwise" or "otherwise possibilities," a concept articulated by Ashon Crawley, signifies that "infinite alternatives exist," for "what *is*, what exists, is but one of many."[12] Therefore, Baldwin's vision of religion, interpreted through the lens of Crawley's concept of "otherwise possibilities," can be understood as an alternative to "what is," an alternative to religion as a site of oppression, an alternative to a society fueled by the machinations of white supremacy. For Baldwin, enlivened by the language and symbols of the religious faith of his youth, is always "working toward the New Jerusalem," a world of human flourishing.[13]

In addition, Baldwin's disidentificatory practice also offers a methodology for theorizing theology "otherwise," for it moves within the register of "the impure,"[14] transgressing the boundaries of "pure thought" and "pure difference."[15] In other words, it disrupts attempts at categorizing and demarcating what theology *is* in an essentialized and fixed manner. Baldwin's praxis provides a method through which to see religion and the theological in the mundane, in the pleasure of orgasm, in the sounds of raucous laughter, in the sting of whiskey in one's throat—diverse and deeply material sites from which, and through which, to think theologically.[16] This is Baldwin's disidentificatory practice, his vision of religion "otherwise," his, and now our, means of engaging religious phenomena *queerly*.

Disidentification does not destroy religious or theological symbols, but "exposes the encoded message's universalizing and exclusionary machinations and recircuits its workings to account for, include, and empower minority identities and identifications."[17] In other words, "disidentification scrambles and reconstructs"[18] the symbol, allowing it to take on "new life."[19] This makes Baldwin's methodology relevant, not only for marginalized people of religious communities and traditions, but also for theologians committed to working both in the academy and religious communities. It is also useful for those who choose to remain *in* traditional religious spaces. In Baldwin's corpus, one finds a means of recognizing and troubling the "exclusionary machinations" of theological notions and concepts typically used to bolster the oppression of those on the margins, particularly people of color and queer and trans persons, without *destroying* those symbols which have deep and enduring meaning for persons of faith.

However, theologians and "believers" (i.e., those who remain in traditional religious spaces), can only engage in this practice of Baldwinian disidentification by troubling their own relationships with the discourse of theology, and the faith traditions in which they are a part. Although Baldwin's method of disidentification does not destroy the theological symbol, it is *not* interested in maintaining the symbol in any of its traditional meanings. Therefore, one cannot engage in this work from the *secure* (read: safe and steady) position of

"Christian theologian" or "Christian believer," for these categories lose their solidity within the disruptive method articulated by Baldwin. For Baldwin, the "Christian" is most profoundly glimpsed in the "unchristian" (Luke in *The Amen Corner*), the "believer" most clearly observed in the "unbeliever" (Tish's family in *Beale Street*), the "holy" most readily apparent in the "sacrilegious" (Arthur and Crunch's queer lovemaking in *Just Above My Head*). Therefore, the theologian must be prepared to move in the register of the "*a*theological,"[20] and the believer in the space of unbelief, engaging in courageous acts of theological imagination that trouble the orthodox, corrupt the pure, and desanctify the holy.

Acknowledgments

No book is the author's alone, but like many scholars I was "reared" in varying communities, academic and otherwise, that shepherded this work from beginning to end. It was during the early years of my PhD education that I began to ask questions about James Baldwin, which later blossomed into the primary focus of my research agenda. I must first thank my PhD advisor, and now dear friend, Nancy Bedford. Nancy was willing to take on a quite strange and headstrong PhD student, and I am eternally grateful for the immeasurable number of hours that she committed to studying with me, teaching me, arguing with me, and closely reading and critiquing my early Baldwin work. Her brilliance, grace, and support shaped me into the scholar that I am today. In addition, a special thanks to Sylvester Johnson, Stephen Ray, Linda Thomas, and Clarence Hardy for their care and critique of this project in its earliest stages. There are a number of others I must thank for engaging my early musings about Baldwin including, but not limited to, Larry Murphy, El Kornegay, Alexander Weheliye, and the late Theodore Jennings. In addition, I thank Ed Pavlić, Roger Sneed, Leonard Curry, Eric Thomas, and Kirsten Collins for engaging and offering feedback on my Baldwin work over the years.

I am grateful to FTE (The Forum for Theological Exploration) for funding not one but two fellowships which provided me with both community and financial support throughout my PhD program. I also want to offer a special thank you to Matthew Wesley Williams, former vice president of strategic initiatives for FTE, for believing in my work and offering guidance and support. Furthermore, I must thank the Iliff School of Theology for awarding me the Elizabeth Iliff-Warren Fellowship for two consecutive years. In addition, I want to thank my Colorado College Religion Department colleagues, Pamela Reaves,

Yogesh Chandrani, Peter Wright, Tracy Coleman, and David Gardiner for their ongoing support and friendship. I also must thank Dean Emily Chan who awarded me the Mrachek Fellowship and the Humanities Executive Committee of Colorado College who granted me funding, both of which allowed for research trips and writing retreats. A big thank you to my student research assistant, River Clarke, whose careful eye and research skills contributed greatly to this project. I also owe much to the students in the varying iterations of my "James Baldwin and Religion" course taught at Colorado College. Their excitement and brilliant insights on Baldwin's literature was a constant reminder of why I love doing this work. There are many other scholars who contributed, both directly and indirectly, to this project, including Theodore Vial, Anne Joh, Miguel De La Torre, Xavier Pickett, Amy Barbour, Bill Mullen, Elyse Ambrose, and John Kutsko. I also want to offer a special thank you to Richard Morrison of Fordham University Press for believing in this project, and to Ingrid Yuzly Mathurin, the brilliant artist whose painting serves as the cover for the book.

Finally, I must thank my family, which includes my biological family, dear friends, and queer kin. I thank my partner Shannon Hunt, for this book is as much hers as mine. Shannon spent years dialoguing with me about Baldwin, reading countless drafts of papers, and even volunteered to be my unpaid "research assistant" in working through the Baldwin papers at the Schomburg Center for Research in Black Culture. Not only that, but for years her labor allowed me the luxury of engaging in academic research. I could not ask for a better life partner, I love you. To Miles, my brilliant child, whose love, hilarious jokes, and welcome interruptions gave me the energy to keep this project going—being your dad is the greatest thing to ever happen to me. I love you, Bug. I must thank my parents, Chris and Cynthia Hunt, for being the first to instill in me a love of learning, and for always being willing to entertain the never-ending questions of their child. I am forever grateful for your love and support. I am also thankful for my big brother Justin Hunt, who has always believed in my work and shown me unconditional love. To Cameron Mais, I am so very grateful for your love, and for the way that you have never stopped believing in the importance of my work. A big thanks to my dear friend Stephen Readus, who I met by chance while perusing the religion section in the Seminary Co-op Bookstore in Chicago, for always being willing to share his encyclopedic knowledge of Baldwin's work, while also being a true friend. I must also thank Mesha Arant and Kate Hanch, not only for how they stretch me intellectually, but for their deep and enduring friendships. A very special thank you to Ashon Crawley who has read numerous iterations of my Baldwin work over the years, offering guidance and critique which only served to shape this project for the better. I am truly grateful for your friendship, Ashon. Lastly, a number of other friends and family members contributed to this project—Steve Stull, Janet Stull, Stephen Stull, Laura Stull, Leah Lopez, Christy Collier, Troy Collier, the late K. Eugene Spicer, and the late Marvin Baker. To all of you, I say thank you.

Notes

Preface

1. *James Baldwin: The Price of the Ticket*, directed by Karen Thorsen (American Masters, 1990), 1:23:31 to 1:24:13, https://www.kanopy.com/en/coloradocollege/watch/video/116250.

2. David Leeming, in *James Baldwin: A Biography* (New York: Henry Holt & Company, 1994), also refers to Baldwin's "gospel" (201).

3. A number of brilliant reviews and reflections on the documentary were written soon after its release that dealt with the topic of the documentary's erasure of Baldwin's queerness. One example would be this excellent piece by Preston Mitchem, "'I Am Not Your Negro' Erased the Sexuality of James Baldwin. What if it Wins an Oscar?," *ThinkProgress*, February 26, 2017, https://archive.thinkprogress.org/i-am-not-your-negro-erased-sexuality-baldwin-3b68fb881421/.

4. Douglas Field, *All Those Strangers: The Art and Lives of James Baldwin* (New York: Oxford University Press, 2015), 2.

5. James Baldwin and Richard Goldstein, "'Go the Way Your Blood Beats:' An Interview with James Baldwin," in *James Baldwin: The Last Interview and Other Conversations* (New York: Melville House Publishing, 2014), 73.

Introduction

1. In referencing "possibilities" in the title, I am borrowing Ashon Crawley's understanding of "otherwise possibilities." See Ashon T. Crawley's *Blackpentecostal Breath: The Aesthetics of Possibility* (New York: Fordham University Press, 2017), 2.

2. Douglas Field, *All Those Strangers: The Art and Lives of James Baldwin* (New York: Oxford University Press, 2015), 82–83.

3. Throughout the book I do not capitalize "god" unless directly quoting an author who does. This goes against standard conventions in which the monotheistic deity of the Judaic and Christian faiths is typically written with a capital "G." This is intentional on my part and is reflective of the agnostic positioning of this text (which is inspired by Baldwin's own agnostic inclinations, which will be engaged in Chapter 5).

4. Clarence E. Hardy III, *James Baldwin's God: Sex, Hope, and Crisis in Black Holiness Culture* (Knoxville: The University of Tennessee Press, 2003), xi. This book was invaluable when I first set out to explore the religious themes in Baldwin's work.

5. José Esteban Muñoz, *Disidentifications: Queers of Color and the Performance of Politics* (Minneapolis: University of Minnesota Press, 1999), 11–12.

6. Muñoz, *Disidentifications*, 12.

7. Muñoz, *Disidentifications*, 4–5, 31, 39.

8. Queer of color critique is particularly helpful theoretically. According to Roderick A. Ferguson in his work, *Aberrations in Black: Toward a Queer of Color Critique* (Minneapolis: University of Minnesota Press, 2004), "queer of color analysis has to debunk the idea that race, class, gender, and sexuality are discrete formations, apparently insulated from one another" (4). In engaging Muñoz's queer of color critique, this text also seeks to read Baldwin through the intersecting realities of race, gender, sexuality, and I would add, religion.

9. Muñoz, *Disidentifications*, 11; and Michel Pêcheux, *Language, Semantics, and Ideology* (New York: St. Martin's Press, 1982).

10. Muñoz, *Disidentifications*, 21–22; and Cherríe Moraga and Gloria Anzaldúa, eds., *This Bridge Called My Back*, 4th ed. (Albany: SUNY Press, 2015).

11. Muñoz, *Disidentifications*, 12, 25.

12. Muñoz, *Disidentifications*, 31.

13. Muñoz, *Disidentifications*, 25.

14. Muñoz, *Disidentifications*, ix.

15. Muñoz, *Disidentifications*.

16. Muñoz, *Disidentifications*.

17. Muñoz, *Disidentifications*, 18.

18. James Baldwin, *The Devil Finds Work*, in *James Baldwin: Collected Essays*, ed. Toni Morrison (New York: The Library of America, 1998), 481.

19. Baldwin, *The Devil Finds Work*, 482; and Muñoz, *Disidentifications*, 15.

20. Muñoz, *Disidentifications*, 18.

21. Baldwin, *The Devil Finds Work*, 482.

22. Muñoz, *Disidentifications*, 18.

23. Muñoz, *Disidentifications*.

24. Cheryl J. Sanders, *Saints in Exile: The Holiness-Pentecostal Experience in African American Religion and Culture* (New York: Oxford University Press, 1996). Sanders defines the "Sanctified church" as including "Holiness, Pentecostal, and Apostolic" church groups. Sanders states, "Although some of these churches [speaking of the Holiness, Pentecostal, and Apostolic churches] practice speaking in

tongues and some baptize only in Jesus' name, all adhere to some form of doctrine and practice of sanctification; thus, the term 'Sanctified church' is inclusive of them all" (5).

25. It is important to note that "queering" and disidentification are not the same, although disidentification is sometimes a means of "queering" a phenomenon. By "queering," I am referring to the usage of "queer" as a verb. In defining queer as a verb, Donald E. Hall, in his work *Queer Theories* (New York: Palgrave Macmillan, 2003), argues: ". . . 'queering' does pose a particular threat to systems of classification that assert their timelessness and fixity. It may not destroy such systems but it certainly presses upon them, torturing their lines of demarcation, pressuring their easy designations" (14). In other words, "queering" is a means of disruption, particularly for Hall in regard to "sexuality and desire," and I would add gender (14). This book will make clear that Baldwin is utilizing a method of disidentification, which in turn sometimes "queers" Christian symbols, troubling and sexually disrupting them. However, disidentification cannot be reduced to queering, but can be utilized to engage and reimagine many different socio-cultural and political phenomena.

26. Christopher Z. Hobson also notes Baldwin's tendency to "revise" Christian ideas and concepts, although he links this to what he understands to be the "long African American practice of taking authority over the dominant culture's beliefs." He argues:

> Baldwin's appropriation and revision of biblical language situate him within a long African American practice of taking authority over the dominant culture's beliefs and turning them to African Americans' own purposes. Absalom Jones and Richard Allen, for example, were taking authority in this way when, in 1794, they spoke of "how hateful slavery is in the sight of that God, who hath destroyed kings and princes, for their oppression of the poor slaves," as was James H. Cone, in 1970, in appropriating Matthew 11:28 for his own foundational statement that "it is impossible to speak of the God of Israelite history, who is the God revealed in Jesus Christ, without recognizing that God is the God *of* and *for* those who labor and are overladen." These thinkers were selecting and emphasizing Bible teachings so as to reshape Christianity. Baldwin similarly reinterprets and reapplies biblical ideas so as to take authority over, largely humanize, and extend and radicalize them (9).

Elsewhere, Hobson states that ". . .Baldwin applies the method of 'taking authority,' recasting an oppressive word as one of freedom; doing so in relation to sexuality and homosexuality means he is revising much African American church teaching as well as Paul's" (13). This, clearly, has some resonance with disidentification. Christopher Z. Hobson, *James Baldwin and the Heavenly City: Prophecy, Apocalypse, and Doubt* (East Lansing: Michigan State University Press, 2018), 9, 13.

27. Muñoz, *Disidentifications*, 19.

28. James Baldwin and David C. Estes, "An Interview with James Baldwin," in *Conversations with James Baldwin*, ed. Fred L. Standley and Louis H. Pratt (Jackson: University Press of Mississippi, 1989), 278.

29. Muñoz, *Disidentifications*, 19.

30. Muñoz, *Disidentifications*.

31. David Leeming, *James Baldwin: A Biography* (New York: Henry Holt & Company, 1994), 333–34; and Muñoz, *Disidentifications*, 19.

32 Muñoz, *Disidentifications*, 19–20.

33. Muñoz, *Disidentifications*, 20.

34. Leeming, *James Baldwin: A Biography*, 374.

35. James Baldwin and Jewell Handy Gresham, "James Baldwin Comes Home," in *Conversations with James Baldwin*, 163, emphasis mine.

36. Baldwin and Gresham, "James Baldwin Comes Home," 163.

37. Anthony B. Pinn, *Terror and Triumph: The Nature of Black Religion* (Minneapolis: Fortress Press, 2003), 157, 173.

38. Pinn, *Terror and Triumph*, 158.

39. Pinn, *Terror and Triumph*, 22.

40. Pinn, *Terror and Triumph*, 175.

41. Pinn, *Terror and Triumph*, 173.

42. Pinn, *Terror and Triumph*.

43. Pinn, *Terror and Triumph*.

44. Pinn, *Terror and Triumph*, 174.

45. Pinn, *Terror and Triumph*, 173.

46. Crawley, *Blackpentecostal Breath*, 4.

47. Ashon T. Crawley, *The Lonely Letters* (Durham, NC: Duke University Press, 2020), 25.

48. Crawley, *Blackpentecostal Breath*, 109–24.

49. Crawley, *Blackpentecostal Breath*, 121, emphasis mine.

50. Crawley, *Blackpentecostal Breath*, 24–25.

51. James Baldwin, "Everybody's Protest Novel," in *James Baldwin: Collected Essays*, 13.

52. Baldwin, "Everybody's Protest Novel," 13. David Leeming, in *James Baldwin: A Biography*, makes a similar point, arguing: "In criticizing Stowe and Wright, Baldwin is laying the foundation for his own position as a novelist and spokesperson. . . . As Baldwin sees it, the artist's job is to absorb and re-create not only the deeds of humanity but the motivations for those deeds, which spring from human ambiguity, human complexity" (65).

53. Anthony B. Pinn, *Varieties of African American Religious Experience: Toward a Comparative Black Theology*, 20th anniv. ed. (Minneapolis: Fortress Press, 2017), xxv.

54. See also Anthony B. Pinn, *The End of God-Talk: An African American Humanist Theology* (New York: Oxford University Press, 2012). Pinn offers a similar definition of theology in this text, positing: "Theology is a method for critically engaging, articulating, and discussing the deep existential and ontological issues

endemic to human life. So defined, African American nontheistic humanist theology is a way for African American humanists to speak and critique their collective life stories as these stories are guided by the structures and practices of nontheistic humanism as a quest for complex subjectivity" (6).

55. Pinn, *Varieties of African American Religious Experience*, xxv.

56. Crawley, *Blackpentecostal Breath*, 17.

57. Crawley, *Blackpentecostal Breath*, 11–12, 30.

58. Crawley, *Blackpentecostal Breath*, 11.

59. Crawley, *Blackpentecostal Breath*, 11–12.

60. Crawley, *Blackpentecostal Breath*, 11.

61. Crawley, *Blackpentecostal Breath*, 30.

62. Crawley, *Blackpentecostal Breath*, 11.

63. Crawley, *Blackpentecostal Breath*, 11, 86–87.

64. Crawley, *Blackpentecostal Breath*, 5.

65. Crawley, *Blackpentecostal Breath*, 11–12.

66. Crawley, *Blackpentecostal Breath*, 12.

67. Crawley, *Blackpentecostal Breath*.

68. I use terms such as "the West" and "western" not to connote a geographic region, but to signify what Ashon Crawley, in *Blackpentecostal Breath*, calls "the epistemology of western civilization" (12). In other words, I am signifying certain hegemonic ways of "knowing" and "being" which were birthed in the moment(s) of European colonial and imperial expansion.

69. Crawley, *Blackpentecostal Breath*, 13–17.

70. Crawley, *Blackpentecostal Breath*, 12.

71. Crawley, *Blackpentecostal Breath*, 13.

72. Crawley, *Blackpentecostal Breath*.

73. Crawley, *Blackpentecostal Breath*.

74. Crawley, *Blackpentecostal Breath*, 14.

75. Crawley, *Blackpentecostal Breath*, 15.

76. Crawley, *Blackpentecostal Breath*, 18.

77. Crawley, *Blackpentecostal Breath*, 12.

78. Crawley, *Blackpentecostal Breath*, 17.

79. Crawley, *Blackpentecostal Breath*, 2.

80. Crawley, *Blackpentecostal Breath*, 14–15.

81. Crawley, *Blackpentecostal Breath*, 20.

82. Crawley, *Blackpentecostal Breath*, 3.

83. Crawley, *Blackpentecostal Breath*, 4, 17–18.

84. Crawley, *Blackpentecostal Breath*, 11.

85. Baldwin, *The Devil Finds Work*, 566.

86. I was first inspired to think about the "religion that is blackness" by Dr. Stephen Ray. However, that phrase also brings to mind J. Kameron Carter's recent text, *The Anarchy of Black Religion: A Mystic Song* (Durham, NC: Duke University Press, 2023). My project on Baldwin resonates deeply with Carter's "black study of

religion," which "subject[s] religion to black study, revealing the modern (re)invention
of religion to be an idea of enclosure" (15).

87. I borrow this language of "transfigure" and "recycle" from Muñoz, *Disidentifications*, 39.

88. See Sylvester A. Johnson's, *The Myth of Ham in Nineteenth-Century
American Christianity: Race, Heathens, and the People of God* (New York: Palgrave
Macmillan, 2004), for an excellent examination of how notions of peoplehood, and
specifically being "the people of God," becomes inextricably linked to racial logics.
See also Sylvester A. Johnson, *African American Religions, 1500–2000: Colonialism,
Democracy, and Freedom* (New York: Cambridge University Press, 2015).

89. James Baldwin, "White Racism or World Community?," in *James Baldwin:
Collected Essays*, 753.

90. James Baldwin, "Many Thousands Gone," in *James Baldwin: Collected
Essays*, 33.

91. I borrow the language of "alterity," hence "alterity creating/creation," from
Johnson's *The Myth of Ham*.

91. I borrow the language of "alterity," hence "alterity creating/creation," from
Johnson's *The Myth of Ham*.

92. I borrow the convention of capitalizing the O in "Other" or "the Other" from
Regina M. Schwartz, *The Curse of Cain: The Violent Legacy of Monotheism*
(Chicago: The University of Chicago Press, 1997). Schwartz seemingly does this to
signify the mode of being through which a people are "violently" made Other. She
states: "This book is about violence. It locates the origins of violence in identity
formation, arguing that imagining identity as an act of distinguishing and
separating from others, of boundary making and line drawing, is the most frequent
and fundamental act of violence we commit. Violence is not only what we do to the
Other. It is prior to that. Violence is the very construction of the Other" (5). This
understanding directly informs my use of the language of "alterity creation" and
"the Other," hence the capital O signifies a mode of being constituted through
violent modes of "othering." In addition, I was also inspired by Michelle M. Wright's
use of "Other" in her essay, "'Alas, Poor Richard!' Transatlantic Baldwin, the Politics
of Forgetting, and the Project of Modernity," in *James Baldwin Now*, ed. Dwight A.
Mcbride (New York: NYU Press, 1999). She states: "By 'Other,' I mean the
representation of the black as wholly the result of white racism. Theoretically
speaking, the black as Other is structured as the antithesis of the white Self, as all
that the white Self rejects, hates, fears and secretly (and consciously) desires" (209).

93. The language and concept of "divine peoplehood" is borrowed from
Johnson, *The Myth of Ham*.

94. Ed Pavlić, *Who Can Afford to Improvise? James Baldwin and Black Music, the
Lyric, and the Listeners* (New York: Fordham University Press, 2016), 70.

95. Crawley, *Blackpentecostal Breath*, 18.

96. James Baldwin and Richard Goldstein, "'Go the Way Your Blood Beats': An
Interview with James Baldwin," in *James Baldwin: The Last Interview and Other
Conversations* (New York: Melville House Publishing, 2014), 73.

97. James Baldwin, "The Uses of the Blues," in *The Cross of Redemption: Uncollected Writings*, ed. Randall Kenan (New York: Vintage International, 2011), 73.

98. Baldwin, "The Uses of the Blues," 70.

99. Jürgen Moltmann, *A Theology of Hope: On the Grounds and Implications of Christian Eschatology*, trans. James W. Leitch (Minneapolis: Fortress Press, 1993).

100. James Baldwin and Nikki Giovanni, *A Dialogue* (Philadelphia: J.B. Lippincott, 1973), 45. https://search.alexanderstreet.com/view/work/bibliographic_entity%7C bibliographic_details%7C4390030.

101. James Baldwin, "No Name in the Street," in *James Baldwin: Collected Essays*, 475.

102. Josiah Ulysses Young III, *James Baldwin's Understanding of God: Overwhelming Desire and Joy* (New York: Palgrave Macmillan, 2014), 161.

103. See chapter eleven, entitled "The Black Issue of the Holy Ghost," in Young, *James Baldwin's Understanding of God*; See also James Baldwin, "*The Black Scholar* Interviews James Baldwin," in *Conversations with James Baldwin*.

104. Sylvia Wynter, "Unsettling the Coloniality of Being/Power/Truth/Freedom: Towards the Human, After Man, Its Overrepresentation—An Argument," *CR: The New Centennial Review* 3, no. 3 (2003). http://www.jstor.org/stable/41949874.

105. Matt Brim, *James Baldwin and the Queer Imagination* (Ann Arbor: University of Michigan Press, 2014), 74.

106. Brim, *James Baldwin and the Queer Imagination*, 73–75.

107. Brim, *James Baldwin and the Queer Imagination*, 74.

108. Wynter, "Unsettling the Coloniality of Being," 260–63, 315–17, 323. "Descriptive statements" is a concept Wynter borrows from the work of Gregory Bateson, as seen in "Unsettling the Coloniality of Being," 262, 267–68. See also Wynter's essay "On How We Mistook the Map for the Territory, and Reimprisoned Ourselves in Our Unbearable Wrongness of Being, of Desêtre: Black Studies Toward the Human Project," in *I Am Because We Are: Readings in Africana Philosophy*, revised edition, ed. Fred Lee Hord (Mzee Lasana Okpara) and Jonathan Lee Scott (Amherst and Boston: University of Massachusetts Press, 2016), 277.

109. Wynter, "Unsettling the Coloniality of Being," 260–63, 315–17, 323.

110. Baldwin, *No Name in the Street*, 390–93.

111. James Baldwin, "Freaks and the American Ideal of Manhood," in *James Baldwin: Collected Essays*, 814.

112. Several examples of this will be examined, one of the earliest instances being found in James Baldwin, "Preservation of Innocence," in *James Baldwin: Collected Essays*.

113. I borrow the language of "unnamed" and "unnameable" from Michael A. Sells, *Mystical Languages of Unsaying* (Chicago: The University of Chicago Press, 1994).

114. Please see Leeming, *James Baldwin: A Biography*, 384, for an example of Baldwin's usage of the term "something."

115. I am indebted to Ashon T. Crawley's work *The Lonely Letters* in helping me see the importance of "feeling" in Baldwin's mysticism.

116. See *The Lonely Letters* for Crawley's most robust treatment of mysticism. By "otherwise," I am building on Crawley's concept offered in *Blackpentecostal Breath*, 2.

117. Ashon Crawley, "Susceptibility," *GLQ: A Journal of Lesbian and Gay Studies* 27, no. 1 (2021): 11, muse.jhu.edu/article/777706.

Chapter 1. Jimmy's Queer "Threshing-Floor": Transformation and the Role of Disidentification in Baldwin's Fiction

1. "The Threshing-Floor" is taken from Part III of James Baldwin's *Go Tell It on the Mountain*, in *James Baldwin: Early Novels and Stories*, ed. Toni Morrison (New York: The Library of America, 1998), 183, 185. A version of Chapter 1 of this book was originally published as "'Somebody Touched Me:' Disidentification, Conversion, and the Promise of Queer Transformation in James Baldwin's Fiction," *Black Theology: An International Journal* 21, no. 3 (2023): 205–23, https://doi:10.1080/14769 948.2023.2255774.

2 James Baldwin, *The Fire Next Time*, in *James Baldwin: Collected Essays*, ed. Toni Morrison (New York: The Library of America, 1998), 304.

3. Clarence E. Hardy III, *James Baldwin's God: Sex, Hope, and Crisis in Black Holiness Culture* (Knoxville: The University of Tennessee Press, 2003), 18.

4. Douglas Field, *All Those Strangers: The Art and Lives of James Baldwin* (New York: Oxford University Press, 2015), 90.

5. Michael F. Lynch, "A Glimpse of the Hidden God: Dialectical Vision in Baldwin's *Go Tell It on the Mountain*," in *New Essays on Go Tell It on the Mountain*, ed. Trudier Harris (Cambridge: Cambridge University Press, 1996), 52.

6. Hardy, *James Baldwin's God*, 18.

7. In *James Baldwin's God*, Hardy also speaks of "the empty promise of conversion" (42). More will be said about this later.

8. James Baldwin and Richard Goldstein, "'Go the Way Your Blood Beats': An Interview with James Baldwin," in *James Baldwin: The Last Interview and Other Conversations* (New York: Melville House Publishing, 2014), 73.

9. El Kornegay, Jr.'s work, *A Queering of Black Theology: James Baldwin's Blues Project and Gospel Prose* (New York: Palgrave Macmillan, 2013) was the first text to explore Baldwin's literature as a means of queering black Christianity and theological discourse. Kornegay also discusses Baldwin's "queering conversion" in chapter five of his text. In essence, Kornegay argues that blackness, in and of itself, is a queer mode of being, and that "everything that comes into contact with blackness is itself queered: this includes black theology and conversion" (99). Not only that, but Kornegay also claims that "the importance of queering to my project is not centered on Baldwin as a queer subject" (99). I believe that Baldwin as a queer person, and the queer modes of being of his characters, are essential for understanding Baldwin's queer project. Baldwin queers Christian theological symbols in particular moments in his novels with the express purpose of calling attention to the sacred nature of queerness, particularly queer sexual expression.

10. José Esteban Muñoz, *Disidentifications: Queers of Color and the Performance of Politics* (Minneapolis: University of Minnesota Press, 1999), 11, 31, 39.

11. Muñoz, *Disidentifications*, 31.

12. Kornegay, in *A Queering of Black Theology*, makes a similar claim, positing: "For Baldwin, the body is itself a site of the sacred. Queering conversion liberates black bodies from depravity" (111).

13. Hardy, *James Baldwin's God*, 17–18.

14. Albert J. Raboteau, *Slave Religion: The "Invisible Institution" in the Antebellum South*, updated ed. (New York: Oxford University Press, 2004), 97–98.

15. Raboteau, *Slave Religion*, 98, 103, 128–32; and Anthony B. Pinn, *Terror and Triumph: The Nature of Black Religion* (Minneapolis: Fortress Press, 2003), 83–84.

16. Raboteau, *Slave Religion*, 120, 132–33.

17. Raboteau, *Slave Religion*, 132–33.

18. Raboteau, *Slave Religion*, 120, 130–33.

19. Hardy, *James Baldwin's God*, 18. Again, I want to note that, according to Hardy, many black Christians do not experience conversion in the exact fashion that Baldwin describes. He argues, ". . . many practitioners of Afro-Protestantism then as now did not experience the singular, traumatic event of conversion that Baldwin describes in his essays and fiction" (17). What is most important is that, despite how one experiences conversion, the rite of conversion itself is deeply important to black Protestants.

20. David Leeming, *James Baldwin: A Biography* (New York: Henry Holt & Company, 1994), 24–25; and Hardy, *James Baldwin's God*, 4–5.

21. Hardy, *James Baldwin's God*, 4.

22. Although Baldwin converted under Horn's ministry, he served as a minister at the Fireside Pentecostal Assembly. See Bill V. Mullen, *James Baldwin: Living in Fire* (London: Pluto Press, 2019), 4; David Leeming, *James Baldwin: A Biography*, 24–25; and Josiah Ulysses Young III, *James Baldwin's Understanding of God: Overwhelming Desire and Joy* (New York: Palgrave Macmillan, 2014), 47–49.

23. Cheryl J. Sanders, *Saints in Exile: The Holiness-Pentecostal Experience in African American Religion and Culture* (New York: Oxford University Press, 1996), 5.

24. Sanders, *Saints in Exile*, 58.

25. Sanders, *Saints in Exile*, 58.

26. Baldwin, *Go Tell It on the Mountain*, 9.

27. Baldwin, *The Fire Next Time*, 296.

28. Baldwin, *Go Tell It on the Mountain*, 31–32.

29. This is clearly seen in the character John's anxiety and excitement as he attends a movie in part 1 of *Go Tell It on the Mountain*. For a discussion of Baldwin's introduction to, and love for, the arts, see chapter 1 of James Baldwin's, *The Devil Finds Work*, in *James Baldwin: Collected Essays*.

30. Baldwin, *The Fire Next Time*, 297.

31. Baldwin, *Go Tell It on the Mountain*, 183.

32. Baldwin, *Go Tell It on the Mountain*, 187.

33. Baldwin, *Go Tell It on the Mountain*, 187–200.

34. Hardy, *James Baldwin's God*, 19. The communal aspect of Baldwin's conversion cannot be overstated. As Keri Day notes in her work *Azuza Reimagined: A Radical Vision of Religious and Democratic Belonging* (Stanford, CA: Stanford University Press, 2022), the type of service in which John converted was a tarry service. In describing a tarry service, a practice that Day notes "black women stood at the center of," she states: "Tarrying was a key marker of religious experience at Azusa. . . . Tarrying lasted from one to two hours in the middle or after a service. This practice included praying, songs, supplications, special invocations and specific rules and expectations." For our purposes, what is most relevant to note is Day's claim that "what is most important about tarrying is that the person could only have a conversion or encounter with God *through the community*. Communal leaders midwifed personal experiences of the Spirit" (92). This is consistent with Baldwin's description of John's conversion, for the whole of the gathered community (with the exception of his father) sought to usher John through the experience.

35. Baldwin, *Go Tell It on the Mountain*, 214–15.

36. Michael F. Lynch, "Staying Out of the Temple: Baldwin, the African American Church, and *The Amen Corner*," in *Re-Viewing James Baldwin: Things Not Seen*, ed. D. Quentin Miller (Philadelphia: Temple University Press, 2000), 37.

37. Baldwin, *The Fire Next Time*, 304–5, 309–10.

38. Hardy, *James Baldwin's God*, 35.

39. For an example of this, see James Baldwin, "Everybody's Protest Novel," in *James Baldwin: Collected Essays*, 17–18; See also Kelly Brown Douglas's examination of Baldwin's *Go Tell It on the Mountain* in *What's Faith Got to Do with It? Black Bodies/Christian Souls* (Maryknoll, NY: Orbis Books, 2005), 168–85. Hardy, in *James Baldwin's God*, also engages this subject, and his project is, in fact, an extended examination of Baldwin's critique of black holiness culture and the ways in which that evangelical space contributes to black "disfigurement." He states:

> But even as Baldwin relied on Christian rhetoric in his quest for social justice, his work, considered as a whole, suggests that while black evangelicalism embodies a posture of resistance against a hostile white world, its redemptive value ultimately fails to overcome the extent to which Christianity has contributed to African disfigurement. This complex relationship with Christianity is the core concern that animates my inquiry (xi).

See also Hardy, *James Baldwin's God*, 25–36.

40. In *James Baldwin's God*, Hardy calls this "the empty promise of conversion" (42). For Hardy, the failure of conversion lay in the fact "that despite this earth-shattering conversion experience black suffering remains intractable" (43). I, however, believe that the primary failure of conversion for Baldwin lay in the fact that it failed to make Christians more loving. In other words, it failed to actually change them for the better. See Baldwin, *The Fire Next Time*, 308–10.

41. In *A Queering of Black Theology*, El Kornegay makes a similar claim in regard to "conversion" and "transformation." He states, "In the works of James Baldwin,

conversion can be likened to transformation, in that the primary outcome of any cultural-religious endeavor should transform the person and their god(s) into becoming larger, freer, and more loving" (102).

42. In *James Baldwin's God*, Hardy notes David Leeming's recollection of how Baldwin would often treat his white friends and "acquaintances" as "congregations" that he would confront with the truth of his message. Hardy states, "Baldwin challenged, confronted, and ushered members of both sets of 'congregations'— black first and then white—toward the emotional release typically promised by the salvation offered in evangelical churches" (85–86). This serves as another confirmation that Baldwin sought a kind of conversion/transformation in the United States.

43. James Baldwin, "The Price of the Ticket," in *James Baldwin: Collected Essays*, 839.

44. Baldwin, "The Price of the Ticket," 839–40; Hardy, in *James Baldwin's God*, speaks to this as well, stating: ". . . Baldwin suggests that while intense conversions may air out repressed emotions and fear and self-loathing, they do not fundamentally change lives for the better. In describing the often 'transitory' character of conversion he shows how 'the reformed' drunk and others addicted to self-destructive behaviors often return 'to their former ways.' In fact, in Baldwin's view, the effects of intense conversions can be worse than a meaningless form of emotional release; it may, in fact, foster a dangerous self-righteousness" (23).

45. Muñoz, *Disidentifications*, 12.

46. Lynch, "Staying Out of the Temple," 47. Lynch's article offers an excellent examination of *The Amen Corner*. In his "dialectical" reading of Baldwin, Lynch takes seriously Baldwin's critique of the church while also arguing that Baldwin wrote the play to "[explore] the possibility of an individual's retaining essentially Christian ideals [while] pursuing one's vocation outside the church" (37). He is correct in arguing that Baldwin is attempting to show that the play's main characters must find life and meaning outside the confines of the church. However, Lynch believes the play reflects Baldwin's "hope for Christian faith," a claim which my analysis emphatically rejects (67).

47. Lynch, "Staying Out of the Temple," 47.

48. David Leeming, *James Baldwin: A Biography*, 24–25; and Hardy, *James Baldwin's God*, 4–5.

49. Sanders, *Saints in Exile*, 5.

50. Rosa A. Horn, "What is Holiness? A Complete Life in Christ," in *Daughters of Thunder: Black Women Preachers and Their Sermons, 1850–1979*, by Bettye Collier-Thomas (San Francisco: Jossey-Bass Publishers, 1998), 191.

51. James Baldwin, *The Amen Corner* (New York: Vintage Books, 1998), 24–26.

52. Baldwin, *The Amen Corner*, 9.

53. Baldwin, *The Fire Next Time*, 296.

54. Saadi A. Simawe, "What Is in a Sound? The Metaphysics and Politics of Music in *The Amen Corner*," in *Re-Viewing James Baldwin: Things Not Seen*. Simawe refers to Luke as "an apostle of human love" (23).

55. Simawe, in "What Is in a Sound?," also refers to this as a conversion. He states, ". . . the worldly musician [Luke] is able not only to effectively preach human love and sexuality, but also to ultimately seduce and convert the pastor [Margaret] to the world" (23). Later, Simawe claims that "Luke the jazz musician is more honest, more life-affirming, and more spiritual than Margaret the Pastor" (24).

56. I borrow the phrase "religion of love" from Trudier Harris, "The Eye as Weapon in *If Beale Street Could Talk*," in *Critical Essays on James Baldwin*, ed. Fred L. Standley and Nancy V. Burt (Boston: G. K. Hall & Co., 1988), 212.

57. Baldwin, *The Amen Corner*, 62.

58. Baldwin, *The Amen Corner*, 59–60.

59. Baldwin, *The Amen Corner*, 59.

60. Baldwin, *The Amen Corner*, 59–60.

61. Baldwin, *The Amen Corner*, 13.

62. Baldwin, *The Amen Corner*, 14.

63. Baldwin, *The Fire Next Time*, 304–5.

64. Young, in *James Baldwin's Understanding of God*, makes a similar point. He states, "I take Baldwin to mean that Sister Margaret had attempted to escape her love for Luke and the stillborn infant produced by that love by transferring this painful love to the 'Lord'" (72).

65. This passage from Young's *James Baldwin's Understanding of God* captures the "irony" of the moment. He states:

> In the dialogue between Luke and Sister Margaret, Baldwin presents a choice. Who is saved, Luke or Margaret? Baldwin couches this choice in more irony. Luke's salvation is tubercular and confined in a tiny dark room. Sister Margaret's salvation is self-righteous and self-anointed. Regardless of what the audience decides, I think Luke—despite his condition—is better off (72).

However, I think Baldwin's messaging is much clearer than Young alludes to here, for Baldwin *wants* his audience to frame Luke as saved and Margaret as unsaved. In essence, Baldwin does not just present the audience with a choice framed as a question, but he answers the question.

66. Baldwin, *The Amen Corner*, 57–58.

67. Sanders, *Saints in Exile*, 58.

68. James Baldwin, "Notes for the Amen Corner," in *The Amen Corner*, xvi.

69. Baldwin, *The Amen Corner*, 57.

70. Baldwin, *The Amen Corner*, 81.

71. Baldwin, *The Amen Corner*, 82.

72. Lynch, in "Staying out of the Temple," also refers to this as a "conversion." However, he understands it to be a "conversion to the true spirit of Christianity" (63–64).

73. Baldwin, *The Amen Corner*, 86.

74. Baldwin, "Notes from the Amen Corner," in *The Amen Corner*, xvi.

75. Leeming, in *James Baldwin: A Biography*, states: "In the character David, Baldwin clearly is considering his own condition as a teenager vis-à-vis the church and home" (108).

76. Baldwin, *The Amen Corner*, 42.

77. Baldwin, *The Amen Corner*, 42–43.

78. Hardy, in *James Baldwin's God*, uses the language of "calling" when referring to Baldwin's pull to the arts. He states, "His interest in the written word and literary imagination became his new calling and pushed him not so gently out of the world revealed in the biblical stories and rhythmic words of worship and song toward an outside world filled with sinful pleasures" (7).

79. Baldwin, *The Amen Corner*, 44.

80. Baldwin, *The Fire Next Time*, 306–7.

81. Baldwin, *The Devil Finds Work*, 502–3.

82. Baldwin, *The Devil Finds Work*, 503. Also, David Leeming, in *James Baldwin: A Biography*, notes Baldwin's sense of being "called" to the life of being a "witness" (xii–xiii). He states, "Like it or not, he was called, and to the extent that he attempted to refuse the call in his life he found himself psychologically trapped in the belly of the whale" (xiii).

83. In "What Is in a Sound?," Saadi A. Simawe makes a similar claim, stating: "Baldwin embraced the world of art with the same religious passion with which he had earlier embraced the church . . ." (18).

84. Field, *All Those Strangers*, 95. Elsewhere, Field notes, "Baldwin's distrust and disillusionment with the institution of the church is illustrated through characters such as Arthur in *Just Above My Head* and Luke in *The Amen Corner*, both of whom represent a spiritual authenticity that stems from outside the church. Yet, neither Luke nor Arthur can accurately be described as secular, since both protagonists are musicians, suggesting a more authentic spirituality that can be found through jazz and gospel. By illustrating the power of music, a medium that fosters an open community that contrasts sharply with the stifling division of institutional piety, Baldwin suggests the close relationship between blues, jazz, gospel, and spirituality" (93).

85. Hardy, *James Baldwin's God*, 58.

86. Simawe, "What Is in a Sound?," 13.

87. Baldwin, *The Amen Corner*, 79–80.

88. Baldwin, *Go Tell It on the Mountain*, 195.

89. Leeming, in *James Baldwin: A Biography*, makes a similar claim: "And then David says something that seems to tie his new life as a musician with a larger mission. He articulates the connection between his author's need to write and the prophetic quest reflected in such scenes as the flashbacks of *Go Tell It on the Mountain* and the incidents recorded in 'Notes of a Native Son': 'Every time I play,' he says, 'every time I listen, I see Daddy's face and yours, and so many faces—who's going to speak for all that, Mama? Who's going to speak for all of us'" (109).

90. Simawe, "What Is in a Sound?," 29.

91. Baldwin, *The Amen Corner*, 88.

92. Lynch makes a similar claim in "Staying out of the Temple." He states:

> Although Baldwin uses David's development as a completion of *Go Tell It*
> and as a rationale for Baldwin's personal evolution, he positions Margaret
> as the protagonist to suggest the possibility of even a spiritually corrupt
> minister's reformation and discovery of the heart of the gospel. However, as
> Baldwin himself learned, and as David and Margaret do also, the sanctity
> and peace promised by the church are attainable only outside it, either
> through a commitment to the sacred nature of art (David) or through a
> revised but identifiably Christian dedication to serve others (Margaret) (58).

Field, in *All Those Strangers*, also points out that for Baldwin, "authentic
spirituality and redemption can be—and indeed must be—found outside of the
church" (110).

93. Simawe, in "What Is in a Sound?," also refers to Baldwin's work in *The Amen
Corner* as being reflective of a kind of "reversal." He states, "Because *The Amen
Corner* is a tragedy in the Aristotelian sense with powerful irony, reversal, and
recognition, it begins by underscoring the pride and dignity of the dominant
dramatic characters, who are unaware of their fatal tragic flaws" (25).

94. Young, *James Baldwin's Understanding of God*, 71.

95. James Baldwin and Margaret Mead, *A Rap on Race* (New York: Dell
Publishing, 1971), 89.

96. Ed Pavlić, in *Who Can Afford to Improvise?: James Baldwin and Black Music,
the Lyric and the Listeners* (New York: Fordham University Press, 2016), calls *Just
Above My Head* "[Baldwin's] most fully and explicitly musical novel and his most
deeply realized and profound exploration of human erotic, moral, and political
experience" (168).

97. This scene is also explored in Kornegay's *A Queering of Black Theology*. His
interpretation of this scene served as an inspiration for my own reading, particularly
in his understanding of the sacred as being revealed in Arthur and Crunch's "flesh"
as they make love (111–14). However, key differences will be shown between my
reading and Kornegay's. Field, in *All Those Strangers*, also notes that Baldwin uses
"language . . . strongly evocative both of religious conversion . . . and sexual
intimacy" in *Just Above My Head* (111). Christopher Z. Hobson, in *James Baldwin
and the Heavenly City*, also explores this scene and the sex scene between Tish and
Fonny in *If Beale Street Could Talk*, which I also discuss in this section, as reflective
of Baldwin's tendency to "treat sexuality both mimetically and through extended
applications of religious language to suggest varied states factually or symbolically
comparable to elements of Christian deliverance." Christopher Z. Hobson, *James
Baldwin and the Heavenly City: Prophecy, Apocalypse, and Doubt* (East Lansing:
Michigan State University Press, 2018), 88–90.

98. Field, *All Those Strangers*, 99. Field does an excellent job in pointing out
how Baldwin, throughout the whole of his corpus, "increasingly suggested that

redemption could, and perhaps indeed must, be achieved through mutual love and companionship. By emphasizing the sanctity of sexual love (as opposed to sex), Baldwin developed what he had hinted at through the stunted attempts of John and Elisha in *Go Tell It* and Johnnie and David in 'The Outing'" (106). However, Field understands Baldwin as trying to gesture back to some type of pure Christianity (107), while I believe that Baldwin is radically reimagining the symbols. Despite this difference, Field's excellent chapter on Baldwin and religion resonates with my own work.

99. Kornegay, in *A Queering of Black Theology*, states: "Nakedness here is not intended to be simply bare-skinned, but uncovered in the sense that labels, the shadows of race, sexuality, and gender, are set aside allowing for uninhibited interaction between humans. This interaction was most sacred to Baldwin and central to his sense of identity as a human being" (111). In addition, Field in *All Those Strangers* is correct in noting that "In Baldwin's later fiction, nakedness is not only holy, but the fear of judgement is replaced by the act of complete surrender to another lover. Thus, authentic sexual love becomes itself an act both of revelation and redemption" (108).

100. James Baldwin, in *Just Above My Head*, in *James Baldwin: Later Novels*, ed. Darryl Pinckney (New York: The Library of America, 2015) states, through the narrator Hall Montana: "He [Arthur] hated to be naked in front of anyone, even me—perhaps, especially me; I had sometimes given him his bath: but that had been under another condition, for which he had not been responsible, and which he was not compelled to remember. Nakedness had not, then, been a confession, or a vow" (699). See also Kornegay's discussion of this moment of "confession" in *A Queering of Black Theology*, 112–13. Hardy, in *James Baldwin's God*, also notes that "The very language Baldwin uses to describe sexual intimacy—as an 'act of confession'—suggests a deep connection between his understanding of sex and religion" (64).

101. Leeming, in *James Baldwin: A Biography*, notes the importance of confession throughout Baldwin's corpus, and the need for people to "face truths about" themselves (375). He claims, "It was the lack of confession—the failure to risk the necessary lowering of barriers—that had destroyed David in *Giovanni's Room* and which Baldwin had complained of in Tony Maynard. It was confession that he demanded of his lovers and was so often refused. It was confession that Ida had demanded of Vivaldo and confession that saved Tish and Fonny. The refusal to risk the danger of confession was at the base of the great social failure revealed by American racism" (375).

102. Baldwin, *Just Above My Head*, 700, 703.

103. Kornegay, *A Queering of Black Theology*, 112.

104. Baldwin, *Just Above My Head*, 702–3. It was the brilliant scholar Leonard Curry who pointed out in conversation the similarities between this scene and the Eucharist.

105. Baldwin uses the language of "fear" and "terror," and variations of these terms, throughout the whole of this scene in *Just Above My Head* (698–704).

106. Baldwin, *Just Above My Head*, 703. Kornegay, in *A Queering of Black Theology*, highlights the role of terror as well, positing: "The terror is not caused by the body itself, but the inheritance of the racial, sexual, and religious prohibitions against black bodies, which makes us see our own nakedness as an exposure of our depravity" (112–13).

107. Baldwin, *Just Above My Head*, 703.

108. I am in agreement with Douglas Field who notes in *All Those Strangers*: "In both *Beale Street* and *Just Above*, Baldwin invokes gospel music to signal and define a sexual love that retains a spiritual purity" (111). Field also states, "In *Just Above*, Baldwin again uses gospel song as an expression of sexual love. In his last novel, however, gospel music becomes a way of sanctifying love between men: a medium that facilitates otherwise prohibited relationships" (111).

109. Baldwin, *Just Above My Head*, 703.

110. Baldwin, *Just Above My Head*, 703–4.

111. Kornegay makes a similar claim in *A Queering of Black Theology*, stating: "Baldwin makes this interaction a sacred act and the body a vessel for the revelation of the sacred" (113).

112. It is important to note that Hardy, in *James Baldwin's God*, understands "sexually revelatory" experiences to be marked by a "fundamental ambiguity." He states:

> Surprisingly, Baldwin often characterizes the sexually revelatory as a moment filled with anguish even for those in pursuit of authentic and unrepressed sexual expression. While he accepts the sacred dimensions of love, Baldwin, the very apostle of bodily love, seems captive to a perspective that considers the coupling of human bodies to be a principal source for profound alienation as well (66).

However, in my view, this does not take away from the power of the sexual moment, but only shows that Baldwin remains skeptical that any revelation, salvation, or transformation is a once and for all and complete reality. That is why, in "To Crush a Serpent" in *The Cross of Redemption: Uncollected Writings*, ed. Randall Kenan (New York: Vintage International, 2011), Baldwin makes clear that "it [salvation] is never accomplished; it is to be reaffirmed every day and every hour" (203). Also, Douglas Field, in *All Those Strangers*, highlights the intersection of religious transformation and sex in Baldwin's literature, positing: "The references to queer desire are important, particularly in the way that Baldwin connects religious transformation with sexual desire" (103).

113. Kornegay, in *A Queering of Black Theology*, also mentions the indispensable role of sexuality in revealing the sacred (113–14).

114. Baldwin, *Just Above My Head*, 702.

115. Baldwin, *Just Above My Head*, 703–4.

116. Baldwin, *Just Above My Head*, 707–8.

117. Field, in *All Those Strangers*, is correct in noting that "in Baldwin's later fiction, nakedness is not only holy, but the fear of judgement is replaced by the act of

complete surrender to another lover. Thus, authentic sexual love becomes itself an act both of revelation and redemption" (108).

118. Field, *All Those Strangers*, 96.

119. Field, *All Those Strangers*.

120. Field, *All Those Strangers*. In addition, Hardy, in *James Baldwin's God*, also notes the way in which conversion is linked to sex in Baldwin's novel *Another Country*. He argues, "Sexual expression, it seems from *Another Country*, can disturb and shape one's identity in ways that suggest the conversions of old" (64).

121. Kornegay, *A Queering of Black Theology*, 2. Kornegay understands his work to be "a generational (black) theological project that is the next (logical) evolution beyond a black theology of liberation and black womanist theology" (2).

122. Kornegay, *A Queering of Black Theology*, 18–31, 33.

123. Kornegay, *A Queering of Black Theology*, 3–4.

124. Kornegay, *A Queering of Black Theology*, 7.

125. Kornegay, *A Queering of Black Theology*, 40. For a full description of Baldwin's "allegorical defense," see 31–38.

126. Kornegay, *A Queering of Black Theology*, 32.

127. Kornegay, *A Queering of Black Theology*, 31.

128. Kornegay, *A Queering of Black Theology*, 26.

129. Kornegay, *A Queering of Black Theology*, 21–31. Kornegay uses the language of "metaphorical blackness" throughout the text, one example being page 45.

130. Kornegay, *A Queering of Black Theology*, 35.

131. Kornegay, *A Queering of Black Theology*, 32.

132. Kornegay, *A Queering of Black Theology*, 40–41.

133. Kornegay, *A Queering of Black Theology*, 41.

134. Kornegay, *A Queering of Black Theology*, 41.

135. Kornegay, *A Queering of Black Theology*, 42.

136. Kornegay, *A Queering of Black Theology*, 43. Kornegay borrows this language of "reinvest" from Baldwin's essay *The Devil Finds Work*.

137. Kornegay, *A Queering of Black Theology*, 99, 101.

138. Kornegay, *A Queering of Black Theology*, 110.

139. Kornegay, *A Queering of Black Theology*, 110.

140. Kornegay, *A Queering of Black Theology*, 99.

141. Kornegay, *A Queering of Black Theology*, 102. He goes on to say: "Baptism is the actual imbibing of the psychological trap of puritanism and metaphorical blackness. Christianity actually converts black bodies into immoral bodies devoid of moral courage and imbibes the black psyche and spirit with the rejection of the moral courage . . . to challenge Christianity" (102).

142. Hardy, *James Baldwin's God*, 25–36.

143. Hardy, *James Baldwin's God*, 35.

144. Hardy, *James Baldwin's God*, 33.

145. Kornegay, *A Queering of Black Theology*, 105.

146. Kornegay, *A Queering of Black Theology*, 102.

147. Kornegay, *A Queering of Black Theology*, 111.

148. Kornegay, A *Queering of Black Theology*, 110.

149. Kornegay, A *Queering of Black Theology*, 108–9. On page 102 of A *Queering of Black Theology*, Kornegay states: "Though conversion is a stratagem used for safety, it resists pragmatic resolution to the messiness of black life. Therefore Baldwin's understanding of conversion widens the road of faith and changes human messiness into a liberating force yet unseen in black religion and theology." It is also important to note that Kornegay links conversion to "safety," which Kornegay understands, building on Baldwin's comments in *The Fire Next Time*, to be the purpose of religion (103–4). He posits, "To be saved, to acquire safety, is the revelatory moment of the presence of the divine with blues bodies. Baldwin reveals that blues bodies are not saved by casting a blind eye on their messiness: they are saved by accepting it" (109). However, safety is not "an attainable ideal. But the *hope* for safety fuels growth and the acceptance of our humanity" (109).

150. Kornegay, A *Queering of Black Theology*, 31–38.

151. Kornegay, A *Queering of Black Theology*, 40.

152. Kornegay, A *Queering of Black Theology*, 33.

153. Muñoz, *Disidentifications*, ix, 18.

154. Kornegay, A *Queering of Black Theology*, 111–14; It is important to note that "confession" and "vow" is the language Baldwin uses in describing the scene in *Just Above My Head*, 699.

155. Kornegay, A *Queering of Black Theology*, 112–13.

156. Kornegay, A *Queering of Black Theology*, 113. Although Kornegay claims that god is "reimagined/recreated in the sexual intimacy between bodies" (113), god remains central and normative in Kornegay's theology. In Baldwin's literature, god is not necessary.

157. Kornegay, A *Queering of Black Theology*, 113.

158. Kornegay, A *Queering of Black Theology*. I make this claim despite Kornegay's takes on the "unstable and ungiven . . . God in exile" (66) in chapter three, and his attempts at "queering monotheism" (138) in chapter six. In the end, Kornegay still stands on normative Christian concepts, reflected in this claim made in the conclusion of the book: "God manifest in Jesus is created, revealed, and sustained in the midst of sensuousness and not marginalized because of it" (146).

159. Kornegay, A *Queering of Black Theology*. In addition, Kornegay is also correct in claiming that in Baldwin's literature, "conversion can . . . be seen as a sexual act" (106). However, how he fleshes out that claim misses Baldwin's point. Kornegay highlights the conversion experience in *Go Tell It on the Mountain*, arguing that the experience of conversion, for John, at the altar of the sanctified church of his youth, is a sexual encounter. Kornegay states:

> The altar like the Avenue, is therefore a dirty space, impossible to make or keep clean. The altar, like the threshing floor, is covered with the dust of sex acts. It is a place overrun with sexual encounters. In the space of the altar the divine actively communes with sexualized selves. In *Go Tell It on the Mountain*, John Grimes sees the gods as a part of the dirt: God created

the dirt and humanity from the dirt. The altar is the bed of the divine
where the convert becomes God's consort. It is where the convert lets the
divine have *His* way with the convert. As the convert remembers all that
he/she is sexually, the divine revels in those memories, washing over the
convert *fucking him/her* with it (106–7).

What this reading misses is that Baldwin, throughout *Go Tell It on the Mountain*
and the rest of his literary corpus, never frames the church as a space of unironic
sexual release, lasting conversion, or freedom. Conversion, as brought about by the
sex act, always takes place *outside* of the institutional church in Baldwin's literature.

160. Baldwin, *Just Above My Head*, 733–34.

161. Baldwin, *Just Above My Head*, 734.

162. Field, *All Those Strangers*, 108.

163. James Baldwin, *If Beale Street Could Talk*, in *James Baldwin: Later Novels*, 423.

164. Baldwin, *If Beale Street Could Talk*, 423.

165. Baldwin, *If Beale Street Could Talk*, 425.

166. Harris, "The Eye as Weapon," 211. Harris also notes the way in which
Baldwin utilizes gospel songs in relation to lovemaking in *Beale Street*. She states:

Time and again [Tish's] sentences are redolent with phrases from gospel
songs. She describes the atmosphere around them being changed after
their discovery of love (—as in the song of religious conversion—"I looked
at my hands, my hands looked new. I looked at my feet, they did too"), the
"sacramental air" and "vows" of their love and the transforming power of
sex—"Fonny caressed me and called my name and he fell asleep. I was very
proud. I had crossed my river. Now, we were one" (213).

Harris returns again and again to the theme of conversion throughout the article.

167. Trudier Harris, *Black Women in the Fiction of James Baldwin* (Knoxville:
The University of Tennessee Press, 1985), 160. It is important to note that this is not
without its problems in the way that Baldwin frames it. As will be made apparent in
Chapter 4 of this book, Baldwin's portrayal of Tish is riddled with sexism and
misogynoir, and Fonny does not simply initiate her into a "love religion," but,
according to Harris, functions as her "Lord and Master" (160).

168. Harris, "The Eye as Weapon," 213.

169. Baldwin, *If Beale Street Could Talk*, 425.

170. Field, *All Those Strangers*, 100.

171. Field, *All Those Strangers*, 109.

172. Baldwin, *Just Above My Head*, 588. Field also notes this passage in making a
similar claim in *All Those Strangers*, 109.

173. Kornegay, in *A Queering of Black Theology*, notes: "Love seen in this way
helps with understanding the difference between sentimental love and love
according to Baldwin which is a state of toughness and daring required for living
with the masks (race, sex, sexuality, and gender) removed we *fear we cannot live
without and know we cannot live within*" (124).

174. Roger A. Sneed, *Representations of Homosexuality: Black Liberation Theology and Cultural Criticism* (New York: Palgrave Macmillan, 2010), 94–95.

175. Baldwin, *The Devil Finds Work*, 571. Hardy, in *James Baldwin's God*, in relation to this same quote, adds: "Perhaps what distinguishes love from other revelatory experiences, Baldwin suggests, is that love is contingent on a basic self-awareness and transparency that the religious variety does not demand. Baldwin knows his lover's soul trembles precisely because he accepts that his own soul trembles as well" (66).

176. James Baldwin, *No Name in the Street*, in *James Baldwin: Collected Essays*, 366.

177. Baldwin, *No Name in the Street*.

178. Baldwin, *No Name in the Street*.

179. Ashon T. Crawley, *The Lonely Letters* (Durham, NC: Duke University Press, 2020), 117.

180. Field, *All Those Strangers*, 100.

181. Roderick Ferguson, "The Nightmares of the Heteronormative," *Cultural Values* 4, no. 4 (October 2000), https://doi:10.1080/14797580009367210. It is also worth noting that Ferguson speaks of Baldwin's "reinterpretation of Christian salvation" in the article, linking salvation to Baldwin's revaluation of "nonheteronormative intimate relations" in *Go Tell it on the Mountain* (439).

182. Ferguson, "The Nightmares of the Heteronormative," 423.

183. Ferguson, "The Nightmares of the Heteronormative."

184. Ferguson, "The Nightmares of the Heteronormative," 420.

Chapter 2. Jimmy's Communion: Race, Peoplehood, and the Tone of (Black) Community

1. James Baldwin, "Anti-Semitism and Black Power," in *The Cross of Redemption: Uncollected Writings*, ed. Randall Kenan (New York: Vintage Books, 2011), 251. According to David Leeming, in *James Baldwin: A Biography* (New York: Henry Holt & Company, 1994), this piece was based on the open letter that Baldwin sent to the *Liberator*, condemning the publications growing antisemitism (273–74). For further discussion of this quote/letter, see Eddie S. Glaude Jr., *Begin Again: James Baldwin's America and Its Urgent Lessons for Our Own* (New York: Crown Publishing, 2020), 90; Ed Pavlić, *Who Can Afford to Improvise? James Baldwin and Black Music, the Lyric, and the Listeners* (New York: Fordham University Press, 2016), 68–69; Michael Oliver, "James Baldwin and the 'Lie of Whiteness': Toward an Ethic of Culpability, Complicity, and Confession," *Religions* 12, no. 6 (2021): 447, https://doi.org/10.3390/rel12060447.

2. I borrow this idea from Regina M. Schwartz's, *The Curse of Cain: The Violent Legacy of Monotheism* (Chicago: The University of Chicago Press, 1997). She states, "Violence is not only what we do to the Other. It is prior to that. Violence is the very construction of the Other" (5).

3. I use the term "theo-racial" to signify that racial identities were birthed out of particular Christian theological ideas. This is informed by, although not limited to, the scholarship of Willie James Jennings, *The Christian Imagination: Theology and the Origins of Race* (New Haven, CT: Yale University Press, 2010); J. Kameron Carter, *Race: A Theological Account* (New York: Oxford University Press, 2008); Sylvester A. Johnson, *The Myth of Ham in Nineteenth-Century American Christianity: Race, Heathens, and the People of God* (New York: Palgrave Macmillan, 2004), and *African American Religions, 1500–2000: Colonialism, Democracy, and Freedom* (New York: Cambridge University Press, 2015); and Geraldine Heng, "The Invention of Race in the European Middle Ages I: Race Studies, Modernity, and the Middle Ages," *Literature Compass* 8, no. 5 (2011): 315–31, https://doi.org/10.1111/j.1741-4113.2011.00790.x, and "The Invention of Race in the European Middle Ages II: Locations of Medieval Race," *Literature Compass* 8, no. 5 (2011): 332–50, https://doi.org/10.1111/j.1741-4113.2011.00795.x.

4. The language of "nexus" I borrow from Sylvester Johnson's *African American Religions*. For an excellent discussion of the role of commerce in the early period of European colonialism in West Africa, see chapter one, entitled "Black Atlantic Religion and Afro-European Commerce," in Johnson's *African American Religions*.

5. See Johnson, *The Myth of Ham* for an excellent examination of how notions of peoplehood, and specifically being "the people of God," becomes inextricably linked to racial logics. See also Johnson's *African American Religions*.

6. I am not the first to use the language of "theo-political" or "theopolitical." One notable use of this term is found in Erin Runions's *The Babylon Complex: Theopolitical Fantasies of War, Sex, and Sovereignty* (New York: Fordham University Press, 2014).

7. James Baldwin, "White Racism or World Community?," in *James Baldwin: Collected Essays*, ed. Toni Morrison (New York: The Library of America, 1998), 753; El Kornegay, Jr., in *A Queering of Black Theology: James Baldwin's Blues Project and Gospel Prose* (New York: Palgrave Macmillan, 2013), makes a similar claim in stating: "Baldwin recognizes the liabilities of a history that was (re)invented for black people. Baldwin locates the source of the historical (re)invention of the Negro in Protestant Puritanism" (36).

8. James Baldwin, "Many Thousands Gone," in *James Baldwin: Collected Essays*, 33.

9. Kathryn Gin Lum, *Heathen: Religion and Race in American History* (Cambridge, MA: Harvard University Press, 2022); Johnson, *The Myth of Ham*; Johnson, *African American Religions*. It is also worth noting El Kornegay's treatment of a similar topic in *A Queering of Black Theology*. In chapter one of his text, Kornegay claims that "puritan religious ideology" (23) utilizes "metaphor" or "metaphors of oppression" (24) in conflating black identity with "damnation" (30) and "depravity" (102) among other negative symbols. Kornegay states:

The metaphorical equation presupposes that blackness cannot be compared equally to whiteness and must therefore be likened to something that is less than and unequal to it. As such, the metaphorical equation makes blackness the dumping ground for all that puritanism deems unrighteous. In other words blackness becomes the shadow side of whiteness (22).

For a discussion of Kornegay's "metaphors of oppression," see chapter one of *A Queering of Black Theology*, entitled: "The Prolonged Religious Crisis."

10. Cheryl J. Sanders, *Saints in Exile: The Holiness-Pentecostal Experience in African American Religion and Culture* (New York: Oxford University Press, 1996). Sanders defines the "Sanctified church" as including "Holiness, Pentecostal, and Apostolic" church groups (5).

11. The language and concept of "divine peoplehood" is borrowed from Johnson, *The Myth of Ham*.

12. Pavlić, *Who Can Afford to Improvise?*, 70.

13. Ashon T. Crawley, *Blackpentecostal Breath: The Aesthetics of Possibility* (New York: Fordham University Press, 2017), 18.

14. Eddie Glaude, in his work *Begin Again*, utilizes the language of "the lie" in referring to US American collective identity. He states:

Baldwin's understanding of the American condition cohered around a set of practices that, taken together, constitute something I will refer to throughout the book as *the lie*. The idea of facing the lie was always at the heart of Jimmy's witness, because he thought that it, as opposed to our claim to the shining city on a hill, was what made America truly exceptional. The lie is more properly several sets of lies with a single purpose. If what I have called the "value gap" is the idea that in America white lives have always mattered more than the lives of others, then the lie is a broad and powerful architecture of false assumptions by which the value gap is maintained. These are the narrative assumptions that support the everyday order of American life, which means we breathe them like air. We count them as truths. We absorb them into our character (7).

I too will utilize this language of "the lie" in discussing the deception and falsehoods that ground white identity in the US.

15. Crawley, *Blackpentecostal Breath*, 2.

16. My use of the terms "Christian imagination" and/or "imaginary" are inspired by the Willie Jenning's work, *The Christian Imagination*.

17. James Baldwin, "Everybody's Protest Novel," in *James Baldwin: Collected Essays*, 16.

18. Michelle M. Wright, "'Alas Poor Richard!' Transatlantic Baldwin, the Politics of Forgetting, and the Project of Modernity," in *James Baldwin Now*, ed. Dwight A. McBride (New York: NYU Press, 1999), 210.

19. Wright, "'Alas Poor Richard!,'" 209–10.

20. James Baldwin, *No Name in the Street*, in *James Baldwin: Collected Essays*, 470–72.

21. Judith Weisenfeld, *New World A-Coming: Black Religion and Racial Identity During the Great Migration* (New York: NYU Press, 2016).

22. Robert Birt, "Existence, Identity, and Liberation," in *Existence in Black: An Anthology of Black Existential Philosophy*, ed. Lewis R. Gordon (New York: Routledge, 1997), 205.

23. James Baldwin, *Nobody Knows My Name*, in *James Baldwin: Collected Essays*, 136.

24. Clarence E. Hardy III., *James Baldwin's God: Sex, Hope, and Crisis in Black Holiness Culture* (Knoxville: The University of Tennessee Press, 2003), 47, 73; Cornel West, "Philosophy and the Afro-American Experience," in *Blackwell Companions to Philosophy: A Companion to African-American Philosophy*, ed. Tommy L. Lott and John P. Pittman (Oxford: Blackwell, 2006), https://doi.org/10.1002/9780470751640.ch1, includes Baldwin as part of "the Afro-American existentialist tradition" (20–24).

25. Baldwin, "White Racism or World Community?," 749.

26. Anthony B. Pinn, *Terror and Triumph: The Nature of Black Religion* (Minneapolis: Fortress Press, 2003), 82.

27. Baldwin, "White Racism or World Community?," 749.

28. Baldwin, "White Racism or World Community?," 752.

29. Baldwin, "White Racism or World Community?," 752–53.

30. Baldwin, "White Racism or World Community?," 753.

31. Baldwin, "White Racism or World Community?"

32. James Baldwin and Kenneth B. Clark, "A Conversation with James Baldwin," in *Conversations with James Baldwin*, eds. Fred L. Standley and Louis H. Pratt (Jackson: University Press of Mississippi, 1989), 45.

33. Hardy notes this "technique" in *James Baldwin's God*. He states, "Here [in reference to the introduction of *Blues for Mister Charlie*] Baldwin uses a technique that he used extensively in *Notes of a Native Son* more than a decade before. He obscures his own position in America's racial hierarchy as a black man and adopts a literary perspective that assumes the position of the white majority. From this vantage point Baldwin proceeds from within a white identity to dismantle the psychological underpinnings of white supremacy" (90).

34. James Baldwin, "Many Thousands Gone," 23.

35. That is why scholars such as Clarence Hardy, in *James Baldwin's God*, argue:

> Baldwin sees Christian conversion not simply as an initiation rite into a new faith, but as an emblem of displacement for those Africans snatched from their homeland and forced into a "New World." For these displaced Africans and perhaps for many of their progeny, the principal backdrop of Christian conversion is shame, not hope (33).

Hardy goes on to say that in the essay "Many Thousands Gone," reflecting on the same quote that I shared from the essay, "Baldwin demonstrates just how closely aligned he believes the psychology of black self-hatred to be with the very act of Christian conversion itself" (34). For more on this topic, see Hardy, *James Baldwin's God*, 33–36.

36. Johnson, *The Myth of Ham*, 135 (fn. 1).

37. Kathryn Gin Lum, *Heathen: Religion and Race in American History* (Cambridge, MA: Harvard University Press, 2022), 14.

38. Lum, *Heathen*, 1.

39. Johnson, *African American Religions*, 13, 27.

40. Johnson, *African American Religions*, chapter one.

41. Johnson, *African American Religions*, 37, 39–40.

42. Johnson, *African American Religions*, 19.

43. Johnson, *African American Religions*, 51.

44. Johnson, *African American Religions*, 58.

45. Johnson, *African American Religions*, 91.

46. Johnson, *African American Religions*, 89–90.

47. Johnson, *African American Religions*, 89.

48. Johnson, in *African American Religions*, states: "This colonial relation of power is the form of political order through which a polity (viz., a state, be it monarchical or democratic) rules a population by treating its members as political aliens. This means the dominated population is governed as a political unit whose relationship to the political community of the ruling state is denied a pristine status. Racialization is achieved through this colonial form of political order when this dominated population is marked as perpetually, ineluctably alien. They are treated as incapable of truly belonging to the state" (394).

49. Johnson, *African American Religions*, 90. Johnson is not alone in linking racialization to political processes, nor is he alone pointing to the role of religion in marking particular people groups as radically Other. See Geraldine Heng's 2011 two-part essay entitled: "The Invention of Race in the European Middle Ages I: Race Studies, Modernity, and the Middle Ages" and "The Invention of Race in the European Middle Ages II: Locations of Medieval Race."

50. James Baldwin, "A Talk to Teachers," in *James Baldwin: Collected Essays*, 682, emphasis mine.

51. Johnson, *The Myth of Ham*, xiii.

52. Johnson, *The Myth of Ham*, 4.

53. Johnson, *The Myth of Ham*, 20.

54. Johnson, *The Myth of Ham*.

55. Johnson, *The Myth of Ham*, 21.

56. Johnson, *The Myth of Ham*, 5.

57. Johnson, *The Myth of Ham*, 21.

58. Johnson, *The Myth of Ham*.

59. Johnson, *The Myth of Ham*, 11.

60. Johnson, *The Myth of Ham*, 12.

61. James Baldwin, *The Fire Next Time*, in *James Baldwin: Collected Essays*, 307; David Leeming, in *James Baldwin: A Biography*, also notes Baldwin's "fascination" with the Hamitic narrative (85).

61 James Baldwin, *Go Tell It on the Mountain*, in *James Baldwin: Early Novels and Stories*, ed. Toni Morrison (New York: The Library of America, 1998), 191.

63. Hardy, *James Baldwin's God*, 33.

64. Johnson, *The Myth of Ham*, 28–29.

65. Johnson, *The Myth of Ham*, 31.

66. Again, for discussions of "divine peoplehood" in relation to white and black communities in the United States, see Johnson's *The Myth of Ham*.

67. Lum, *Heathen*, 16.

68. Hardy echoes this point in *James Baldwin's God*, arguing: "In reframing America's long-standing 'race' problem into a question of white identity, Baldwin's political and moral rhetoric, always infused with a sense of the apocalypse, now found its central emphasis. Baldwin saw the United States and the West teetering on the edge of ruin because of white people's willful ignorance" (84); Leeming, in *James Baldwin: A Biography*, states: "Baldwin took a certain pleasure in 'setting these liberals straight' about the 'Negro Problem,' which he reminded them was a 'white problem'" (185); In addition, Glaude, in *Begin Again*, argues: "By the publication of *The Fire Next Time*, Baldwin had turned this question on its head. The problem wasn't black people or simply reconciling our practices with our creed. The problem was white people. For Baldwin, there was no such thing as 'the Negro problem'" (104–5).

69. Baldwin and Clark, "A Conversation with James Baldwin," 45; Baldwin makes a similar statement in the essay, "A Talk to Teachers." He argues: "In order for me to live, I decided very early that some mistake had been made somewhere. I was not a 'nigger' even though you called me one. But if I was a 'nigger' in your eyes, there was something about *you*—there was something *you* needed. I had to realize when I was very young that I was none of those things I was told I was. . . . *I had been invented by white people*, and I knew enough about life by this time to understand that whatever you invent, whatever you project, is you!" (682, emphasis mine).

70. In *The Fire Next Time*, Baldwin states: "But it is not permissible that the authors of devastation should also be innocent. It is the innocence which constitutes the crime" (292).

71. James Baldwin, *No Name in the Street*, 386.

72. James Baldwin, *No Name in the Street*.

73. Baldwin, *The Fire Next Time*, 341.

74. Baldwin, *No Name in the Street*, 386.

75. Baldwin, "Many Thousands Gone," 20.

76. Hardy offers an excellent analysis of the "self-deluded innocence" (95) of whiteness through an examination of David in *Giovanni's Room*. See *James Baldwin's God*, 91–95.

77. Baldwin, *No Name in the Street*, 432.

78. Baldwin, "A Talk to Teachers," 683–84.

79. Lewis R Gordon's, *Bad Faith and Antiblack Racism* (New York: Humanity Books, 1995), 8.

80. Hardy rightfully notes that white ignorance is "self-imposed." In *James Baldwin's God*, Hardy states: "[Baldwin] first acknowledges the ignorance of the benefactors of white supremacy even as he simultaneously suggests that this

ignorance is self-imposed in an insidious effort to avoid any real sense of culpability" (90); This also brings to mind a quote from "Anti-Semitism and Black Power," in which Baldwin states: ". . . the American Republic has told us nothing but lies. But the Republic has told *itself* nothing but lies" (252).

81. Baldwin, *The Fire Next Time*, 292.

82. Baldwin, *The Fire Next Time*, 346–47.

83. Baldwin, *The Fire Next Time*, 294.

84. Baldwin, *The Fire Next Time*, 299–300.

85. Baldwin, *The Fire Next Time*, 341.

86. Lum, *Heathen*, 1.

87. Lum, *Heathen*, 16.

88. See Johnson, *African American Religions*, chapter 4.

89. Leeming, *James Baldwin: A Biography*, 24–25; and Hardy, *James Baldwin's God*, 4–5.

90. Sanders, *Saints in Exile*, 5.

91. Baldwin, *The Fire Next Time*, 296–97. Baldwin does not explicitly mention same-gender attraction here, but it is evident in his fictional retelling of this period in *Go Tell It on the Mountain*, in *James Baldwin: Early Novels and Stories*, 16.

92. Baldwin, *The Fire Next Time*, 296.

93. Baldwin, *The Fire Next Time*, 297.

94. Baldwin, *The Fire Next Time*, 299.

95. Kelly Brown Douglas, *What's Faith Got to Do with It?: Black Bodies/Christian Souls* (Maryknoll, NY: Orbis Books, 2005), 178.

96. Douglas, *What's Faith Got to Do with It?*, 180–81.

97. Baldwin, in *The Fire Next Time*, states: ". . . I also supposed that God and safety were synonymous. The word 'safety' brings us to the real meaning of the word 'religious' as we use it" (296).

98. Baldwin, *The Fire Next Time*, 301.

99. Baldwin, *The Fire Next Time*, 296–306.

100. Baldwin, *The Fire Next Time*, 304–5; 309–10; Douglas Field also notes Baldwin's rejection of the black church on the basis of it lacking "love" in *All Those Strangers: The Art and Lives of James Baldwin* (New York: Oxford University Press, 2015), 92.

101. Baldwin, *The Fire Next Time*, 304–5.

102. Baldwin, *The Fire Next Time*, 309–10. Also Hardy, in *James Baldwin's God*, rightly states: "In their refusal to accept everyone, black churches like their white counterparts expose the narrow parochialism at the heart of traditional Christianity. Baldwin would in fact ask in *Fire* whether heaven was 'merely another ghetto.' With this question, Baldwin challenges black churches' insularity and their uneasy relationship with the demands and broad universal reach of love. Because of this insularity, Baldwin asserts that in fact there is 'no love in the church'" (69).

103. Baldwin, *The Fire Next Time*, 308.

104. Sanders, *Saints in Exile*, 58.

105. Baldwin, *The Fire Next Time*, 310.

106. Baldwin, *The Fire Next Time*, emphasis mine.

107. Josiah Ulysses Young III, in *James Baldwin's Understanding of God* (New York: Palgrave Macmillan, 2014), is correct in pointing out: "When Baldwin puts Ham and Cain together . . . he is, therefore, evaluating the theologies that reject certain people and elect others" (112–13).

108. James Baldwin, *If Beale Street Could Talk*, in *James Baldwin: Later Novels*, ed. Darryl Pinckney (New York: The Library of America, 2015), 385.

109. Baldwin, *If Beale Street Could Talk*, 383, emphasis mine.

110. Baldwin, *If Beale Street Could Talk*, 412.

111. Trudier Harris, in *Black Women in the Fiction of James Baldwin* (Knoxville: University of Tennessee Press, 1985), notes: "The woman [Mrs. Hunt] is physically and philosophically ugly to us. As Baldwin's representative of everything that is wrong with the church and with the hypocritical professors of Christianity, she serves well. . . . Mrs. Hunt is able to reject her son precisely in the name of Christianity and the idea of being dutiful ('If thy right eye offend thee, pluck it out.' 'One should reject father, mother, husband, and children for the sake of God.')" (140); See also Sylvester Johnson's *The Myth of Ham*, particularly chapter 4 entitled: "Becoming the People of God," for a discussion of how black people came to view Christian identity as part of God's plan to "uplift the race" (75).

112. James Baldwin, *The Evidence of Things Not Seen* (New York: Henry Holt & Company, 1995), 121.

113. Baldwin, *The Evidence of Things Not Seen*, 121–22.

114. Baldwin, *The Evidence of Things Not Seen*, 122.

115. Douglas Field, in *All Those Strangers*, also discusses Buddy (who Field incorrectly calls "Billy") (92–93). He states, "Billy serves to illuminate the reasons for the author's exile from the institution of the church. Not only did Baldwin rail against white Christianity, stating that 'I became a Christian by not imitating white people,' but he also viewed all institutionalized religion as hypocritical and ineffectual" (93).

116. Baldwin, *The Evidence of Things Not Seen*, 122.

117. Baldwin, *The Evidence of Things Not Seen*, emphasis mine.

118. Baldwin, *The Evidence of Things Not Seen*.

119. Pavlić, *Who Can Afford to Improvise?*, 70.

120. Crawley, *Blackpentecostal Breath*, 18.

121. I borrow this language of "constitutive" in relation to black communal identity from Crawley's, *Blackpentecostal Breath* (4–5).

122. Michael F. Lynch, "A Glimpse of the Hidden God: Dialectical Vision in Baldwin's *Go Tell It on the Mountain*," in *New Essays on Go Tell It on the Mountain*, ed. Trudier Harris (Cambridge: Cambridge University Press, 1996), mentions the ability of the "artist" to "save others" (53); Hardy, *James Baldwin's God*, 54–58.

123. Pavlić, *Who Can Afford to Improvise?*, 9. Pavlić offers, "To listen is very often to encounter links between (as well as within) human interiors. Part of the

action of what we mean when we say 'lyrical' lives in those links. In *Go Tell It on the Mountain*, Florence hears the saints in the Temple of the Fire Baptized sing '*Standing in the need of prayer*' and 'gained again from the song the meaning it had held for her mother, and gained a new meaning for herself.' Such lyrical links turn upon repetition. . . . Close and repeated listening links personal interiors to each other and opens renewed engagements with the worlds within and around them" (9).

124. Hardy, *James Baldwin's God*, 54.

125. James Baldwin and Nikki Giovanni, *A Dialogue* (Philadelphia: J.B. Lippincott, 1973), 68–69, https://search.alexanderstreet.com/view/work/bibliographic_entity%7C bibliographic_details%7C4390030.

126. Pavlić, *Who Can Afford to Improvise?*, 9.

127. Baldwin and Giovanni, *A Dialogue*, 74.

128. Baldwin, "Many Thousands Gone," 19; Saadi A. Simawe also cites and discusses this passage in "What Is in a Sound? The Metaphysics and Politics of Music in *The Amen Corner*," in *Re-Viewing James Baldwin: Things Not Seen* (Philadelphia: Temple University Press, 2000), 15.

129. Simawe, "What Is in a Sound?," 15.

130. James Baldwin, "The Uses of the Blues," in *The Cross of Redemption: Uncollected Writings*, 70. Baldwin states, "Now, I am claiming a great deal for the blues; I'm using them as a metaphor—I might have titled this, for example, 'The Uses of Anguish' or 'The Uses of Pain.' But I want to talk about the blues not only because they speak of this particular experience of life and this state of being, but because they contain the toughness that manages to make this experience articulate" (70).

131. Baldwin, "The Uses of the Blues," 70–71.

132. James Baldwin, *Just Above my Head*, in *James Baldwin: Later Novels*, 611.

133. Simawe, in "What Is in a Sound?," states: "Another essential component of the ideal condition of the blues, as Baldwin defines it, is its ability to make people learn, mature, and ultimately gain wisdom from suffering, which may be seen as the blues connection to the Biblical concept of suffering as a way to wisdom" (16); Young, in *James Baldwin's Understanding of God* states: "The music is really about the human experience. That may not be a popular apprehension, but Baldwin suggests that his insight—*our suffering is a bridge to one another*—is as *basic* as breathing and is more primal than religion" (172).

134. Baldwin, "The Uses of the Blues," 70–71.

135. Pavlić, *Who Can Afford to Improvise?*, 69.

136. Pavlić, *Who Can Afford to Improvise?*

137. Pavlić, *Who Can Afford to Improvise?*, 70.

138. Baldwin, "Anti-Semitism and Black Power," 252.

139. Pavlić, *Who Can Afford to Improvise?*, 69.

140. Crawley, *Blackpentecostal Breath*, 19.

141. Crawley, *Blackpentecostal Breath*, 17–18.

142. James Baldwin and Studs Terkel, "An Interview with James Baldwin," in *Conversations with James Baldwin*, 4.

143. Baldwin and Terkel, "An Interview with James Baldwin," 4–5; Crawley, *Blackpentecostal Breath*, 17–18.

144. Crawley, *Blackpentecostal Breath*, 18–19.

145. It is worth noting at this point a claim made by Kornegay in A *Queering of Black Theology*, which resonates with this ongoing discussion. He states:

> Baldwin's work represents a hermeneutical break with puritan religious mythology and the black religious response to it. The hermeneutical rupture is the path to the "recreation" or reconstitution of the black self via the "tone and cadence" of language. Baldwin says it is "a cadence . . . a question of the *beat*" of what it meant to be an American Negro. Baldwin seeks to privilege a blues hermeneutic position that dispelled the suspicion and lies which buried him beneath a whole fantastic image of himself that was not his, "but white people's image" of him. Baldwin constructs a hermeneutical circle that privileges the cadence—the blues as gospel—the beat of what it means to be an American Negro. Such hermeneutical independence reveals a quest for safety. However, you cannot overlook the fact that for Baldwin a true religion depends on whether or not it can offer safety—moral authority—to black bodies from puritanism (24).

Elsewhere, Kornegay makes a similar claim: "For Baldwin, the hermeneutical model—black religious vernacular—is the blues. The language of the blues becomes a starting point for building a language that accounts for black bodies in a way that liberates them from the psychological trap of metaphorical blackness and connects to a protective and liberating God" (45). As is apparent from these quotes, Kornegay also views a particular "beat," "tone," and "the blues," all of which he seemingly connects to "language," as something which can liberate black people from the destructive images created by white people.

146. Crawley, *Blackpentecostal Breath*, 4, 41–42.

147. Crawley, *Blackpentecostal Breath*, 4.

148. Crawley, *Blackpentecostal Breath*, 5, emphasis mine.

149. Crawley, *Blackpentecostal Breath*, 45.

150. Baldwin, *No Name in the Street*, 470.

151. Baldwin and Giovanni, *A Dialogue*, 75.

152. Baldwin, *The Fire Next Time*, 306.

153. Baldwin, *The Fire Next Time*, 305.

154. Hardy, *James Baldwin's God*, 58.

155. Baldwin and Giovanni, *A Dialogue*, 74–75.

156. Hardy, in *James Baldwin's God*, notes, "For Baldwin, it seems, the power associated with true religion does not come with God but with the music sweating, suffering bodies produce—just as true love does" (58).

157. Baldwin, "The Uses of the Blues," 70.

158. Pavlić, *Who Can Afford to Improvise?*, 38.

159. Baldwin, *No Name in the Street*, 471.

160. Baldwin, *No Name in the Street*, 470–71.

161. Baldwin, *No Name in the Street*, 471.

162. Baldwin and Terkel, "An Interview with James Baldwin," 21.

163. Baldwin, "Anti-Semitism and Black Power," 252–53.

164. Baldwin, "White Racism or World Community?," 754.

165. Baldwin, *Just Above My Head*, 781.

166. Ed Pavlić, in *Who Can Afford to Improvise?*, discusses the inability of the white character Vivaldo to truly *hear* what his black lover, Ida, is communicating through song (149–61). Pavlić states:

> It's pretty clear . . . that Ida *is* complexly attacking [Vivaldo] partly for his passive role in her brother's death, partly to protect herself from the grief-stricken song in *her* ear. But, she is also attacking him for not knowing anything about the sky and ocean of a lover, a best friend, a million strangers who live, technically, in the same city that he does (151).

In other words, Ida is attacking her white lover for being unable, and perhaps unwilling, to hear the song of blackness. In a similar fashion, Matthew Brim, in his work *James Baldwin and the Queer Imagination* (Ann Arbor: The University of Michigan Press, 2014), also draws attention to Vivaldo's inability to truly hear the blackness undergirding the blues. Brim states:

> In Ida's experience, people, both black and white, make the cheap trade. They pay with their money or with their bodies rather than entering into the more difficult and perhaps impossible exchange by which blacks and whites might actually attempt to know each other. She tells Vivaldo, who insists that he wants to spend the rest of his life finding out about her, that he is not truly willing to do so. "And, listen," Ida concedes, "I don't blame you for not being willing. I'm not willing, nobody's willing. Nobody's willing to pay their dues." The price, she knows, would be too high. Throughout the novel, Vivaldo listens to the blues, but in his liberal innocence, he does not truly hear; Ida, however, sings the blues as the song of experience. She therefore sees Vivaldo's attempt to recover Rufus (and redeem himself) as a white liberal fantasy that blacks, who know the score, cannot afford to share (103).

167. James Baldwin, "Mass Culture and the Creative Artist: Some Personal Notes," in *The Cross of Redemption: Uncollected Writings*, 6–7.

168. Leeming, in *James Baldwin: A Biography*, points to the liberating work of the black artist through an examination of "Sonny's Blues." He states, "Sonny's brother has a revelation; he sees that the artist, especially the black artist, is a prophet of freedom, not only of freedom for his own race but of freedom for all those suffocating under the repressive blanket of emotional safety and innocence" (136); Pavlić, in *Who Can Afford to Improvise?*, makes a similar point when discussing Baldwin's 1973 performance with Ray Charles entitled "The Hallelujah

Chorus." He states, "'The Hallelujah Chorus' would present black music as a kind of phenomenological Virgil guiding people back to a living sense of themselves and each other" (174). See also the whole of Pavlić's chapter 6, for his examination of "The Hallelujah Chorus" shows the ways in which Baldwin and Charles's performance "unearthed connections between music and experience, connections that were political and personal" (178).

169. Baldwin, *The Fire Next Time*, 305.
170. Baldwin, *The Fire Next Time*, 296, 339.
171. Baldwin, "The Uses of the Blues," 70–71.
172. Baldwin, *The Fire Next Time*, 339.
173. Baldwin and Terkel, "An Interview with James Baldwin," 5–6.

Chapter 3. Jimmy's Eschaton: Hope in "the New Jerusalem"

1. James Baldwin, "Civil Rights—James Baldwin—Interview—Mavis on Four," *Mavis on Four*, February 12, 1987, Thames Television, video, 17:21–17:40, https://www.youtube.com/watch?v=YUMrEDNiy3I. The date of this interview and other identifying information was confirmed utilizing the "James Baldwin Digital Resource Guide," Smithsonian, National Museum of African American History & Culture, https://nmaahc.si.edu/explore/exhibitions/chez-baldwin/digital-resource-guide.

2. James Baldwin, "The Uses of the Blues," in *The Cross of Redemption: Uncollected Writings*, ed. Randall Kenan (New York: Vintage International, 2011), 73. I must acknowledge the problematic nature of the ableist and stigmatizing language of "madness." Although I would not use this term, what Baldwin is attempting to signify is the psychological toll anti-blackness exacts from the black person. Baldwin understood his own father's mental illness to be a result, in part, of white supremacy.

3. Baldwin, "The Uses of the Blues," 70–71.
4. Baldwin, "The Uses of the Blues," 70.
5. One important text in examining the role of "the New Jerusalem" in Baldwin's literature is Christopher Z. Hobson's work, *James Baldwin and the Heavenly City*. In that text, he rightly notes: "The governing idea in James Baldwin's six novels is the pursuit of the heavenly city, New Jerusalem, 'that city which the people from heaven had made their home' . . . . The city, then, is a renovated earth, and the revelations of its possible future existence come not from angels but from a double descent into the lower world: that of the body and its sexuality and that of the nation and its night places that reveal truths hidden by day." Christopher Z. Hobson, *James Baldwin and the Heavenly City: Prophecy, Apocalypse, and Doubt* (East Lansing: Michigan State University Press, 2018), 1–2; James Baldwin and Richard Goldstein, "'Go the Way Your Blood Beats': An Interview with James Baldwin," in *James Baldwin: The Last Interview and Other Conversations* (New York: Melville House, 2014), 73.

6. José Esteban Muñoz, *Disidentifications: Queers of Color and the Performance of Politics* (Minneapolis: University of Minnesota Press, 1999).

7. Jürgen Moltmann, A *Theology of Hope: On the Grounds and Implications of Christian Eschatology*, trans. James W. Leitch (Minneapolis: Fortress Press, 1993).

8. James Baldwin and Nikki Giovanni, A *Dialogue* (Philadelphia: J.B. Lippincott, 1973), 45, https://search.alexanderstreet.com/view/work/bibliographic_entity%7C document%7C4390032.

9. Josiah Ulysses Young III, in *James Baldwin's Understanding of God: Over-whelming Desire and Joy* (New York: Palgrave Macmillan, 2014), 161.

10. See chapter eleven, entitled "The Black Issue of the Holy Ghost," in Young, *James Baldwin's Understanding of God*; See also James Baldwin, *"The Black Scholar* Interviews James Baldwin" in *Conversations with James Baldwin*, eds. Fred L. Standley and Louis H. Pratt (Jackson: University Press of Mississippi, 1989).

11. Young, *James Baldwin's Understanding of God*, 161.

12. Baldwin, "The Uses of the Blues," 70–71.

13. Baldwin, "The Uses of the Blues," 70.

14. Baldwin, "The Uses of the Blues," 73–74.

15. I use the language of "black parent" in opposition to Baldwin's sexist inclination to often frame the necessity of providing for the black family as a distinct problem and anxiety for men. See Chapter 4 of this book for an extended discussion of Baldwin's sexism.

16. Baldwin, "The Uses of the Blues," 73–74.

17. Baldwin, "The Uses of the Blues."

18. Baldwin, "The Uses of the Blues."

19. Leeming, in *James Baldwin: A Biography*, notes: "Suicide formed a strange leitmotif in Baldwin's life . . . . The suicidal tendency usually emerged during long periods of depression, and the incidents were in almost every instance preceded by a major fight with a lover." David Leeming, *James Baldwin: A Biography* (New York: Henry Holt & Company, 1994), 120. Throughout the biography, Leeming recounts numerous suicide attempts.

20. James Baldwin, "Equal in Paris," in *James Baldwin: Collected Essays*, ed. Toni Morrison (New York: Library of America, 1998), 101–3.

21. Leeming, *James Baldwin: A Biography*, 72–73.

22. Leeming, *James Baldwin: A Biography*, 72–73.

23. Baldwin, "Equal in Paris," 116. Leeming, in *James Baldwin: A Biography*, notes that this incident led Baldwin to a broader understanding of "blackness." He states, "Taken to Fresnes prison outside of Paris, deprived of shoelaces and a belt and, therefore, of dignity, Baldwin was placed in a cell with a number of 'common criminals' condemned to shuffle about holding up their trousers, and forced, in effect, to undergo several days of a kind of purgatory in which he was faced by a more universal definition of blackness than he had been aware of before" (71–72).

24. It is important to mention that I am not at all claiming that suicide is always a result of despair, or that the act of suicide is always the outgrowth of "injustice." The ongoing ethical debates concerning the morality of suicide are outside of the scope of this project. However, I want to be clear that Baldwin is

discussing suicide that is a direct result of the despair caused by white supremacy. He, nor I, are discussing suicide in an all-encompassing fashion, nor are we attempting to make a moral argument concerning suicide in and of itself.

25. James Baldwin, "Notes of a Native Son," in *James Baldwin: Collected Essays.* Pages 65–67 describe David Baldwin's mental illness.

26. Young, in *James Baldwin's Understanding of God*, states that David Baldwin was diagnosed with paranoid schizophrenia toward the end of his life (40).

27. Leeming, *James Baldwin: A Biography*, 7.

28. Baldwin, "Notes of a Native Son," 65; Clarence E. Hardy III, in *James Baldwin's God: Sex, Hope, and Crisis in Black Holiness Culture* (Knoxville: The University of Tennessee Press, 2003), supports this claim, positing: "With his father's untimely death, Baldwin could see the impact of white supremacy in the wreckage of his father's life. As Baldwin writes, 'When he died I had been away from home for a little over a year. In that year I had had time to become aware of the meaning of all my father's bitter warnings, had discovered the secret of his proudly pursed lips and rigid carriage: I had discovered the weight of white people in the world'" (91).

29. Baldwin, "Notes of a Native Son," 65.

30. James Baldwin, "White Racism or World Community?," in *James Baldwin: Collected Essays*, 753.

31. Baldwin and Giovanni, *A Dialogue*, 36–37.

32. Baldwin and Giovanni, *A Dialogue*, 37.

33. Baldwin, "The Uses of the Blues," 73.

34. James H. Cone, *Black Theology and Black Power* (Maryknoll, NY: Orbis Books, 1997), 8–9; Albert Camus, *The Myth of Sisyphus and Other Essays* (New York: Vintage International, 1991).

35. Cone, *Black Theology and Black Power*, 8–9.

36. Cone, *Black Theology*, 11.

37. Baldwin, "The Uses of the Blues," 70–71; Hardy, in *James Baldwin's God*, discusses Baldwin's view of "cosmic indifference," which bears some resonance with notions of "the absurd." He states, "In addition, Baldwin believes that black people have been forced to grapple with cosmic indifference in ways whites have not. That there are those of European descent who refuse to grapple with this indifference only reveals the breathtaking extent of white arrogance and denial. . . . Baldwin suggest that if black people 'delude' into thinking that the world owes them something—that is, act white—they will self-destruct and meet the same fate as Baldwin's father did; like David Baldwin, they will become steadily more and more detached from reality and lose their sanity before a white god who has refused in the end to return their love" (96–97).

38. Baldwin, "The Uses of the Blues," 73.

39. Cornel West, *Race Matters* (Boston: Beacon Press, 1993), 15. In this same passage, West states: "The first African encounter with the New World was an encounter with a distinctive form of the Absurd" (15).

40. Lewis R. Gordon, *Existentia Africana: Understanding Africana Existential Thought* (New York: Routledge, 2000), 13.

41. An example of this can be found in Frank B. Wilderson III's work *Afropessimism* (New York: Liveright, 2020). In one section, Wilderson recounts an exchange with his grandmother as she celebrates the actions of a black "rioter" on the television (37–43). Wilderson asks his grandmother, "Why are we mad?" (39). After a brief exchange, he and his grandmother proclaim together: "We're mad at the world!" (40). He goes on to say:

> It would, though, be a stretch to say that my grandmother was an Afropessimist. But Afropessimism isn't a church to pray at, or a party to be voted in and out of office. Afropessimism is Black people at their best. "Mad at the world" is Black folks at their best. Afropessimism gives us the freedom to say out loud what we would otherwise whisper or deny: that no Blacks are in the world, but, by the same token, there is no world without Blacks. The violence perpetrated against us is not a form of discrimination; it is necessary violence; a health tonic for everyone who is not Black (40).

Later, Wilderson offers: ". . . we weren't mad for the reasons people who suffered class oppression, gender discrimination, or colonial domination were mad. Their anger had grounding wires internal to the world. We were the world's grounding wire. . . . Human life is dependent on Black death for its existence and for its coherence" (41–42). In other words, for Wilderson, it is anti-blackness which constitutes "the world."

42. Fred Moten, "Blackness and Nothingness (Mysticism in the Flesh)," *The South Atlantic Quarterly* 112, no. 4 (2013): 752, https://doi.org/10.1215/00382876-2345261.

43. James Baldwin and James Mossman, "Race, Hate, Sex, and Colour: A Conversation with James Baldwin and Colin MacInnes," in *Conversations with James Baldwin*, 51.

44. Hardy, *James Baldwin's God*, 109.

45. *James Baldwin: The Price of the Ticket*, directed by Karen Thorsen (American Masters, 1990), 1:24:22 to 1:24:55, https://www.kanopy.com/en/coloradocollege/watch/video/116250.

46. Baldwin and Goldstein, "Go the Way Your Blood Beats," 72–73.

47. Hobson, *James Baldwin and the Heavenly City*, 9.

48. Wes Howard-Brook and Anthony Gwyther, *Unveiling Empire: Reading Revelation Then and Now* (Maryknoll, NY: Orbis Books, 1999), xxiv.

49. Howard-Brook and Gwyther, *Unveiling Empire*, 157.

50. Howard-Brook and Gwyther, *Unveiling Empire*.

51. Howard-Brook and Gwyther, *Unveiling Empire*, 169–70.

52. Howard-Brook and Gwyther, *Unveiling Empire*, 176–77.

53. Howard-Brook and Gwyther, *Unveiling Empire*, 171–76.

54. Howard-Brook and Gwyther, *Unveiling Empire*, xxiii.

55. Brian K. Blount, *Can I Get a Witness? Reading Revelation Through African American Culture* (Louisville, KY: Westminster John Knox Press, 2005), ix.

56. Blount, *Can I Get a Witness?*, x.

57. Howard-Brook and Gwyther, *Unveiling Empire*, 184.

58. Howard-Brook and Gwyther, *Unveiling Empire*.

59. All quotations of the Bible are taken from *The Hebrew-Greek Key Study Bible*, New American Standard Bible, Red Letter Edition, ed. Spiros Zodhiates, (Chattanooga, AMG Publishers, 1984), unless specified otherwise.

60. Howard-Brook and Gwyther, *Unveiling Empire*, 191.

61. Howard-Brook and Gwyther, *Unveiling Empire*, 191.

62. Young, *James Baldwin's Understanding of God*, 24.

63. Young, *James Baldwin's Understanding of God*, 24; James Baldwin, "Notes on the House of Bondage," in *James Baldwin: Collected Essays*, 807.

64. Baldwin, "Notes on the House of Bondage," 806.

65. Baldwin, "Notes on the House of Bondage," 804–5.

66. Revelation 21:5 states, "And He who sits on the throne said, 'Behold, I am making all things new.' And He said, 'Write, for these words are faithful and true'" (NASB).

67. José Esteban Muñoz, *Cruising Utopia: The Then and There of Queer Futurity*, 10th anniv. ed. (New York: NYU Press, 2019), 10.

68. Muñoz, *Cruising Utopia*, 2–4.

69. Muñoz, *Cruising Utopia*, 11.

70. Muñoz, *Cruising Utopia*, 10, 20–21.

71. Muñoz, *Cruising Utopia*, 3.

72. Muñoz, *Cruising Utopia*, 1.

73. Muñoz, *Cruising Utopia*.

74. Muñoz, *Cruising Utopia*, 3, 21.

75. Leeming, *James Baldwin: A Biography*, 384.

76. Muñoz, *Cruising Utopia*, 6.

77. Baldwin, "Notes on the House of Bondage," 806.

78. Moltmann, *Theology of Hope*, 15.

79. Moltmann, *Theology of Hope*, 16.

80. Moltmann, *Theology of Hope*, 99.

81. Moltmann, *Theology of Hope*, 100.

82. Hobson, *James Baldwin and the Heavenly City*, 115.

83. Hobson, *James Baldwin and the Heavenly City*.

84. Moltmann, *Theology of Hope*, 18.

85. Moltmann, *Theology of Hope*.

86. Moltmann, *Theology of Hope*.

87. Heb. 11:1 (KJV)

88. Baldwin and Goldstein, "Go the Way Your Blood Beats," 73.

89. Hardy, *James Baldwin's God*, 97; Hobson, in *James Baldwin and the Heavenly City*, makes a similar claim: "The 'city' he envisions will come into being—if it does—not in response to divine judgement but out of human actions" (12). Elsewhere, Hobson claims, "At the same time, since Daniel and Revelation do not see human agents as initiating apocalyptic events—the initiative comes from

the world above—Baldwin naturalizes the sources for the change, finding them in conscious acceptance of what is deepest in the psyche and in acts of love and rebellion in the social world" (16).

90. Muñoz, *Disidentifications*, 11.

91. Moltmann, *Theology of Hope*, 104.

92. Baldwin, *The Fire Next Time*, in *James Baldwin: Collected Essays*, 346–47.

93. Baldwin and Mossman, "Race, Hate, Sex, and Colour," 48.

94. Baldwin and Giovanni, *A Dialogue*, 45.

95. Moltmann, *Theology of Hope*, 16.

96. Baldwin, "Civil Rights—James Baldwin—Interview—Mavis on Four;" Baldwin, "*The Black Scholar* Interviews James Baldwin," 157.

97. Baldwin, "Civil Rights—James Baldwin—Interview—Mavis on Four."

98. Baldwin, *The Fire Next Time*, 339.

99. Baldwin and Giovanni, *A Dialogue*, 21.

100. Baldwin and Giovanni, *A Dialogue*, 22.

101. For further exploration of these "Christological underpinnings," see the section in this chapter entitled: "Despair and Hope in *If Beale Street Could Talk*."

102. James Baldwin, *The Devil Finds Work*, in *James Baldwin: Collected Essays*, 490. It is important to note that this quote is located in a longer passage in which Baldwin discusses the hypocrisy of "the civilized" who prohibit abortion for the so-called "civilized," touting the "'sanctity' of human life," yet they create the conditions (what he calls "population-control programs") in which "the wretched" are left with no other choice (489). Now, this passage might read as an apologetic against abortion, but I do not think that is what Baldwin is arguing. I believe that Baldwin is simply pointing out the hypocrisy of "the civilized," and the defiance of the black community in the face of that hypocrisy.

103. Young, *James Baldwin's Understanding of God*, 161.

104. Baldwin, "*The Black Scholar* Interviews James Baldwin," 156.

105. Baldwin, "*The Black Scholar* Interviews James Baldwin," 157; Young also quotes a portion of this section in *James Baldwin's Understanding of God*, 161.

106. Baldwin, "*The Black Scholar* Interviews James Baldwin," 157; Young, *James Baldwin's Understanding of God*, 161.

107. Baldwin, "*The Black Scholar* Interviews James Baldwin," 157.

108. Baldwin, "*The Black Scholar* Interviews James Baldwin," 158.

109. Young, *James Baldwin's Understanding of God*, chapter 11.

110. James Baldwin, *Tell Me How Long the Train's Been Gone*, in *James Baldwin: Later Novels*, ed. Darryl Pinckney (New York: The Library of America, 2015), 84.

111. Baldwin, *Tell Me How Long*, 85.

112. Baldwin, *Tell Me How Long*, 85–86.

113. Baldwin, *Tell Me How Long*, 86.

114. Baldwin, *Tell Me How Long*.

115. Baldwin, *Tell Me How Long*, 87.

116. Baldwin, *Tell Me How Long*.

117. Muñoz, *Cruising Utopia*, 1.

118. Muñoz, *Cruising Utopia*, 7.

119. James Baldwin, *Just Above My Head*, in *James Baldwin: Later Novels*, 671.

120. Baldwin, *Just Above My Head*, 704–7.

121. Baldwin, *Just Above My Head*, 704.

122. Muñoz, *Cruising Utopia*, 6.

123. Moten, "Blackness and Nothingness," 752.

124. Muñoz, *Cruising Utopia*, 6.

125. Baldwin, *Just Above My Head*, 706–7.

126. Baldwin, *Just Above My Head*, 707.

127. Baldwin, *Just Above My Head*, 692–94; Hobson, in *James Baldwin and the Heavenly City*, offers a broad overview of the "apocalyptic-eschatological ideas" (79) in Baldwin's literature, while also speaking of the "utopian possibility" found in *Just Above My Head* (154). However, he argues that "sexual love's anticipatory experiences of a new existence," as seen in the sexual relationship of Arthur and Crunch, "remain transient" in the novel (158). In addition, he argues that the novel displays "the need to choose between hope and skepticism, even while recognizing the intellectual validity of both" (146). Another relevant quote comes from the Introduction to his book, for he argues, "the novels do not, in the end, take us to the city. They only point somewhere 'up the road,' expressing doubt about what lies there and blinding sorrow for the fallen. There is no sure guide to this road, nor can there be, since Baldwin's tenuous conviction is only of possibility" (3). Therefore, what is important is "possibility," not certainty, in Baldwin's eschatological and utopian vision.

128. James Baldwin and Kenneth B. Clark, "A Conversation with James Baldwin," in *Conversations with James Baldwin*, 45.

129. James Baldwin, *No Name in the Street*, in *James Baldwin: Collected Essays*, 475.

130. Young, *James Baldwin's Understanding of God*, 158–62.

131. Young, *James Baldwin's Understanding of God*, 159.

132. Young, *James Baldwin's Understanding of God*, 161.

133. Young, *James Baldwin's Understanding of God*, 159. Young also explicitly names Fonny and Tish's unborn child as "the new world 'kicking in the belly of its mother'" (159–60).

134. James Baldwin, *If Beale Street Could Talk*, in *James Baldwin: Later Novels*, 445.

135. Baldwin, *If Beale Street Could Talk*, 506.

136. Baldwin, *If Beale Street Could Talk*, 439–40.

137. Baldwin, *If Beale Street Could Talk*, 440.

138. Baldwin, *If Beale Street Could Talk*, 492.

139. Baldwin, *If Beale Street Could Talk*, 442.

140. Baldwin, *No Name in the Street*, 413–14; David Leeming, *James Baldwin: A Biography*, 289–90.

141. Baldwin, *No Name in the Street*, 415–16.

142. Baldwin, *No Name in the Street*.

143. Baldwin, *No Name in the Street*, 423.

144. Baldwin, *No Name in the Street*, 424

145. Leeming, *James Baldwin: A Biography*, 328.

146. Baldwin, *If Beale Street Could Talk*, 442.

147. Trudier Harris, in *Black Women in the Fiction of James Baldwin* (Knoxville: The University of Tennessee Press, 1985), supports this claim, stating: "[Tish] views the conception of the baby as the giving of a portion of Fonny's life to her, a sacred trust comparable to that of God and the Virgin Mary" (161). See also page 210; Vincent W. Lloyd, in *Religion of the Field Negro: On Black Secularism and Black Theology* (New York: Fordham University Press, 2018), refers to Tish as "Mary-like" (44).

148. Baldwin, *No Name in the Street*, 475.

149. Young, *James Baldwin's Understanding of God*, 161.

150. Baldwin, *If Beale Street Could Talk*, 390.

151. Baldwin, *If Beale Street Could Talk*, 398.

152. Baldwin, *If Beale Street Could Talk*, 400.

153. Young, *James Baldwin's Understanding of God*, 160.

154. Baldwin, *If Beale Street Could Talk*, 454; Young, in *James Baldwin's Understanding of God*, quotes part of this passage on page 160.

155. Baldwin, *If Beale Street Could Talk*, 500–504.

156. Baldwin, *If Beale Street Could Talk*, 509.

157. Baldwin, *If Beale Street Could Talk*, 509. Young, reflecting on this passage in *James Baldwin's Understanding of God*, states: "Was Fonny dreaming again in prison? Is he out of the Tombs? Whatever the case, the baby is no dream. He or she is the reason for Baldwin's hope that we can make the world better than it is" (161).

158. It is important to note that Hobson brings to our attention another connection between *Beale Street* and Baldwin's notion of "the New Jerusalem." He states:

> The implications of "Zion," Baldwin's title for the novel's brief second section, are richer. In evangelical tradition, Zion refers broadly to God's righteous kingdom, as in the Gospel source above. In this sense, Lynn Orilla Scott sees Zion in *Beale Street* as implying "the messianic promise of a future ideal community". . . . In its most far-reaching uses, in messianic chapters of Isaiah, Zion signifies a broadly apocalyptic national resurrection and the birth of a new world: "Awake and sing, ye that dwell in dust", the nation is told, "for thy dew is as the dew of herbs, and the earth shall cast out the dead"; and, "as soon as Zion travailed, she brought forth her children" (Isa. 26:19, 66:8). These images of resurrection and birth become part of Revelation, which takes up the theme of the woman in labor. Baldwin's use of "Zion" as part-title and controlling metaphor thus signifies future recompense for those who "dwell in dust" and the "righteous" who have aided them.
>
> This sense of "Zion" becomes the frame for Baldwin's second major apocalyptic symbol, Tish's labor and the birth of her child. The nine

months of the child's gestation, referred to throughout the narrative and in its final paragraph, coupled with the significance of birth as a "transformation" and references to apocalyptic change in the closing pages, present the birth as an apocalyptic event, symbolically the start of a culminating transformation in world history (130–31).

159. Ashon T. Crawley, *Blackpentecostal Breath: The Aesthetics of Possibility* (New York: Fordham University Press, 2017), 3.

160. Crawley, *Blackpentecostal Breath*, 1–2.

161. Crawley, *Blackpentecostal Breath*, 4.

162. Crawley, *Blackpentecostal Breath*, 5–7.

163. Crawley, *Blackpentecostal Breath*, 2, 6–7.

164. Crawley, *Blackpentecostal Breath*, 6–7.

165. Crawley, *Blackpentecostal Breath*, 34.

166. Gordon, *Existentia Africana*, 13.

167. Gordon, *Existentia Africana*, 14.

168. Baldwin and Clark, "A Conversation with James Baldwin," 45.

169. Lee Edelman, *No Future: Queer Theory and the Death Drive* (Durham, NC: Duke University Press, 2004), 2.

170. Edelman, *No Future*, 3.

171. Edelman, *No Future*.

172. Edelman in *No Future*, acknowledges that "the Child" may wear different "faces," including racial ones. He states, ". . . whatever the face a particular politics gives the baby to wear—Aryan or multicultural, that of the thirty-thousand-year Reich or of an ever expanding horizon of democratic inclusivity," they all seek "to secure, in the form of the future, the order of the same" (151). Baldwin is making clear that "the face" the child wears does, in fact, matter, for the Western world is established on the continued destruction of black children.

173. Eric A. Thomas, "The Futures Outside: Apocalyptic Epilogue Unveiled as Africana Queer Prologue," in *Sexual Disorientations: Queer Temporalities, Affects, Theologies*, ed. Kent L. Brintnall, Joseph A. Marchal, and Stephen D. Moore (New York: Fordham University Press, 2018), 90.

174. Thomas, "The Futures Outside," 96.

175. Thomas, "The Futures Outside."

176. Thomas, "The Futures Outside," 91.

177. Thomas, "The Futures Outside," 90.

178. Thomas, "The Futures Outside," 91.

179. Thomas, "The Futures Outside," 95.

180. Heb. 11:1 (KJV).

Chapter 4. Jimmy's "Man": The Problem of Sexism in Baldwin's Literature

1. James Baldwin, *No Name in the Street*, in *James Baldwin: Collected Essays*, ed. Toni Morrison (New York: Library of America, 1998), 136.

2. James Baldwin and James Mossman, "Race, Hate, Sex, and Colour: A Conversation with James Baldwin and Colin MacInnes" in *Conversations with James Baldwin*, ed. Fred L. Standley and Louis H. Pratt (Jackson: University Press of Mississippi, 1989), 48.

3. Sylvia Wynter, "Unsettling the Coloniality of Being/Power/Truth/Freedom: Towards the Human, After Man, Its Overrepresentation—An Argument," *CR: The New Centennial Review* 3, no. 3 (2003), http://www.jstor.org/stable/41949874.

4. I use the term "nonfeminine" alongside "masculine" to signify that although Baldwin troubles masculinity to a degree, he continues to understand femininity and "the feminine" as a problem for cisgender "men."

5. Matt Brim, *James Baldwin and the Queer Imagination* (Ann Arbor: The University of Michigan Press, 2014), 74.

6. Brim, *James Baldwin and the Queer Imagination*, 73–75.

7. Brim, *James Baldwin and the Queer Imagination*.

8. Wynter, "Unsettling the Coloniality of Being," 315–16, 323.

9. James Baldwin, "Freaks and the American Ideal of Manhood," in *James Baldwin: Collected Essays*.

10. "James Baldwin BBC Bookshelf Program Interview (1963)," *Bookstand* on BBC, 1963, 12:24 to 13:22. https://worldhistoryarchive.wordpress.com/2018/02/07/james-baldwin-bbc-bookshelf-program-interview-1963/. Emphasis mine.

11. I borrow this language of "center" from Baldwin's work, "Freaks and the American Ideal of Manhood." In that piece, Baldwin states:

> In other words, it is not possible for the human being to be as simple as a stallion or a mare, because the human imagination is perpetually required to examine, control and redefine reality, of which we must assume ourselves to be the center and the key. Nature and revelation are perpetually challenging each other; this relentless tension is one of the keys to human history and to what is known as the human condition (814–15).

As this quote makes clear, Baldwin views the human as "the center and the key" of "reality."

12. "James Baldwin BBC Bookshelf Program Interview," 13:24 to 13:25.

13. Brim, in *James Baldwin and the Queer Imagination*, also points to this piece as being one of the first places Baldwin shows "the tension between identity categories and 'the human being'" (58).

14. James Baldwin, "Everybody's Protest Novel," in *James Baldwin: Collected Essays*, 13.

15. Baldwin, "Everybody's Protest Novel," 12.

16. Baldwin, "Everybody's Protest Novel."

17. Baldwin, "Everybody's Protest Novel," 12–13.

18. Baldwin, "Everybody's Protest Novel," 16.

19. Baldwin, "Everybody's Protest Novel."

20. James Baldwin, *The Devil Finds Work*, in *James Baldwin: Collected Essays*, 537.

21. James Baldwin, "Stranger in the Village," in *James Baldwin: Collected Essays*, 122.

22. James Baldwin and Audre Lorde, "Revolutionary Hope: A Conversation Between James Baldwin and Audre Lorde," *The Culture*, http://theculture.forharriet .com/2014/03/revolutionary-hope-conversation-between.html.

23. Brim, *James Baldwin and the Queer Imagination*, 68.

24. Brim, *James Baldwin and the Queer Imagination*, 70.

25. James Baldwin, "Preservation of Innocence," in *James Baldwin: Collected Essays*, 600; Brim, *James Baldwin and the Queer Imagination*, 70.

26. Brim, *James Baldwin and the Queer Imagination*, 70.

27. Brim alludes to similar questions on pages 73–75 of *James Baldwin and the Queer Imagination*; For more on Baldwin as a humanist, see Anthony B. Pinn's edited volume, *By These Hands: A Documentary History of African American Humanism* (New York: NYU Press, 2001). Pinn is accurate in stating that "Baldwin's words seem to point to basic principles of humanism" broadly (228), and to Pinn's own understanding of African American humanism specifically (9–10). The distinctives of African American humanism can be found in the introduction to the text. Pinn posits:

> African American humanists in these pages are atheistic, agnostic, skeptical, and so on in perspective, yet, they share elements of a basic ethics defined by the following elements: (1) understanding of humanity as fully (and solely) accountable and responsible for the human condition and the correction of its plight; (2) suspicion toward or rejection of supernatural explanation and claims, combined with an understanding of humanity as an evolving part of the natural environment as opposed to its having been created; (3) tied to this is an appreciation for African American cultural production and a perception of traditional forms of Black religiosity as having cultural importance as opposed to any type of "cosmic" authority; (4) a commitment to individual and societal transformation; and (5) a controlled optimism that recognizes both human potential and human destructive activities (10).

Also, Clarence E. Hardy III, in *James Baldwin's God: Sex, Hope, and Crisis in Black Holiness Culture* (Knoxville: The University of Tennessee Press, 2003), frames Baldwin as pursuing "an intensely realized humanism" (80); Eddie Glaude, in *Begin Again*, speaks to Baldwin's "new kind of humanism shorn of constraining categories like race and sexuality." Eddie S. Glaude Jr., *Begin Again: James Baldwin's America and its Urgent Lessons for Our Own* (New York: Crown, 2020), 98.

28. Brim, *James Baldwin and the Queer Imagination*, 55.

29. Brim, *James Baldwin and the Queer Imagination*, 74.

30. Brim, *James Baldwin and the Queer Imagination*, 97.

31. Brim, *James Baldwin and the Queer Imagination*, 74.

32. Brim, *James Baldwin and the Queer Imagination*, 74–75.

33. James Baldwin and Richard Goldstein, "'Go the Way Your Blood Beats:' An Interview with James Baldwin," in *James Baldwin: The Last Interview and Other Conversations* (New York: Melville House Publishing, 2014), 61; and Brim, *James Baldwin and the Queer Imagination*, 57.

34. Brim, *James Baldwin and the Queer Imagination*, 71.

35. Brim, *James Baldwin and the Queer Imagination*, 74.

36. Brim, *James Baldwin and the Queer Imagination*.

37. Brim, *James Baldwin and the Queer Imagination*, 74–75

38. Brim, *James Baldwin and the Queer Imagination*, 74.

39. Brim, *James Baldwin and the Queer Imagination*, 75.

40. Brim, *James Baldwin and the Queer Imagination*.

41. Brim, *James Baldwin and the Queer Imagination*.

42. Brim is aware of this problem as well. On page 75 of *James Baldwin and the Queer Imagination*, he states: "Losing our sexual identities would mean losing an important opportunity either to connect at a detailed level of human experience or to face the fact of our sustained disconnection. It would also mean, as Sarah Schulman's unpublished play *The Lady Hamlet* dramatizes, leaving in place the unstated connection between a "universalizable" point of view and heterosexual male privilege."

43. Wynter, "Unsettling the Coloniality of Being," 263–64.

44. Wynter, "Unsettling the Coloniality of Being," 265–66.

45. Wynter, "Unsettling the Coloniality of Being," 263–64.

46. "Descriptive statements" is a concept Wynter borrows from the work of Gregory Bateson, as seen in "Unsettling the Coloniality of Being," 262, 267–68. See also Wynter's essay "On How We Mistook the Map for the Territory, and Reimprisoned Ourselves in Our Unbearable Wrongness of Being, of Desêtre: Black Studies Toward the Human Project," in *I Am Because We Are: Readings in Africana Philosophy*, revised edition, ed. Fred Lee Hord (Mzee Lasana Okpara) and Jonathan Lee Scott (Amherst and Boston: University of Massachusetts Press, 2016), 277.

47. Wynter, "Unsettling the Coloniality of Being," 267–68.

48. Wynter, "Unsettling the Coloniality of Being," 277.

49. Wynter, "Unsettling the Coloniality of Being," 269.

50. Wynter, "Unsettling the Coloniality of Being," 271.

51. Wynter, "Unsettling the Coloniality of Being."

52. Wynter, "Unsettling the Coloniality of Being," 305–6.

53. Wynter, "Unsettling the Coloniality of Being," 307–8.

54. In saying that the human is always and already "determined" is not to claim that understandings of the human go uncontested or do not shift over time. Wynter clearly shows the metamorphosis/evolution of varying understandings of the human, which are "both discontinuous and continuous" with those that came before. Wynter, "Unsettling the Coloniality of Being," 318.

55. Wynter, "Unsettling the Coloniality of Being," 286–87.

56. Wynter, "Unsettling the Coloniality of Being," 309–10, 315–16.

57. Wynter, "Unsettling the Coloniality of Being," 315.

58. Wynter, "Unsettling the Coloniality of Being," 315–16.

59. This is why Wynter argues that even in regard to "feminist studies" and its struggles against "patriarchy," the "issue is that of the genre of the human, the issue whose target of abolition is the ongoing collective production of our present ethnoclass mode of being human, Man." Wynter, "Unsettling the Coloniality of Being," 312–13.

60. Wynter, "Unsettling the Coloniality of Being," 316, emphasis mine.

61. Wynter, "Unsettling the Coloniality of Being," 323.

62. Lewis R. Gordon, *Bad Faith and Antiblack Racism* (New York: Humanity Books, 1995), 4.

63. Clarence Hardy also engages Baldwin's sexism in *James Baldwin's God*, 68–72, discussing his problematic reduction of the problem of race to the problem of black masculinity. He also spends some time discussing *No Name in the Street*, which I will also examine.

64. For more on the intersection of masculinity and white supremacy, see Baldwin's "Freaks and the American Ideal of Manhood."

65. James Baldwin, *The Fire Next Time*, in *James Baldwin: Collected Essays*, 330.

66. James Baldwin, *No Name in the Street*, in *James Baldwin: Collected Essays*, 390–93.

67. Baldwin, *No Name in the Street*, 390–91.

68. Baldwin, *No Name in the Street*, 391.

69. Baldwin, *No Name in the Street*.

70. Hardy, *James Baldwin's God*, 72.

71. Baldwin, *The Fire Next Time*, 330.

72. James Baldwin and Studs Terkel, "An Interview with James Baldwin," in *Conversations with James Baldwin*, 9.

73. Baldwin and Terkel, "An Interview with James Baldwin," 9.

74. Baldwin and Terkel, "An Interview with James Baldwin," 10.

75. Hardy, *James Baldwin's God*, 72.

76. Baldwin, *No Name in the Street*, 392. In *James Baldwin's God*, Hardy also points to this passage in his examination of Baldwin's sexism (70–71). Hardy argues that Baldwin is "blind to the crucial question of sexism in his analysis of white supremacy" (71). He continues on: "This blindness is highlighted in Baldwin's answer to a question a white woman posed at the end of his lecture at DePaul University in 1986, near the end of his life. When asked whether his analysis of racial oppression could be expanded to include women, 'Baldwin flatly responded that white women were not oppressed. And black women to the degree that they were oppressed, suffered the oppression of race.' Although Baldwin occasionally discussed the brutal use of black women's bodies by white slaveholders and their descendants, he generally did not confront the brutality many women faced from their black male companions" (71).

77. Baldwin, *No Name in the Street*, 392.

78. Hardy, *James Baldwin's God*, 71.

79. Hardy, in *James Baldwin's God*, argues that Baldwin's focus on the problem of black masculinity only intensifies in the aftermath of "attacks" on his sexuality by black nationalists (71–72). Hardy claims, "After these attacks, Baldwin makes clear that for him the prime effect of white supremacy was the loss of black manhood. Perhaps it was defensive of Baldwin, who in *No Name in the Street* declares white supremacy as most directly a problem of the black phallus" (72).

80. Brim, in his "trans-gay analysis" of *Giovanni's Room* (76), points out that the "threat" of femininity in relation to the gay man can be clearly glimpsed in the novel. He states, "Baldwin, perhaps inseparable from David in this respect, can only envision the person who transitions gender as threatening beast, not beauty" (83). See Brim, *James Baldwin and the Queer Imagination*, 76–91; Douglas Field, in *All Those Strangers: The Art and Lives of James Baldwin* (New York: Oxford University Press, 2015), also notes Baldwin's extreme, and I would argue deeply problematic, discomfort with gender nonconformity in his novel *Giovanni's Room*, stating:

> In Baldwin's description of the transvestite, the figure is terrifying because s/he cannot be located. Here, as elsewhere, Baldwin's writing troubles the critical romance of "fluid" identity: liminality or undecidability for the writer is rarely celebrated. The transvestite is a paradox: neither wholly female nor male, a figure who for David, the novel's protagonist, is both mesmerizing and repulsive. As Baldwin's writing reminds us, association with one identity category or other, such as black or homosexual, does not preclude a spectrum of reactions, attitudes, and seemingly contradictory responses (9).

81. Trudier Harris, *Black Women in the Fiction of James Baldwin* (Knoxville: University of Tennessee Press, 1985), 5.

82. Harris, *Black Women in the Fiction of James Baldwin*, 5.

83. Harris, *Black Women in the Fiction of James Baldwin*, 5. It is also important to note that Harris points out that the women in *If Beale Street Could Talk* are different in that they "are not tied down by their own notions of guilt about their actions" (130). She continues on, "Questions of morality are no longer simplistically two-sided; for these women, more complexity develops, and there is ample room for extenuating circumstances. By rejecting the morality of the fundamentalist black church, they represent characters who no longer believe themselves guilty beyond redemption" (130).

84. Harris, *Black Women in the Fiction of James Baldwin*, 5.

85. Harris, *Black Women in the Fiction of James Baldwin*, 8.

86. Harris, *Black Women in the Fiction of James Baldwin*, 9.

87. Harris, *Black Women in the Fiction of James Baldwin*.

88. James Baldwin, *The Amen Corner* (New York: Vintage International, 1968), xvi. It is also important to note that in using the language of "matriarch" to describe Margaret, language explicitly used in the broader US American context to pathologize

black women in particular, and the black community as a whole, Baldwin is parroting the logic infamously articulated in Daniel Moynihan's 1965 "report" entitled: "The Negro Family: The Case for National Action." In the report, Moynihan claims, "In essence, the Negro community has been forced into a matriarchal structure which, because it is to out of line with the rest of the American society, seriously retards the progress of the group as a whole, and imposes a crushing burden on the Negro male and, in consequence, on a great many Negro women as well." The Moynihan Report: "The Negro Family, the Case for National Action," *The Black Past*, https://www.blackpast.org/african-american-history/moynihan-report-1965/. (accessed January 20, 2024).

Now, critiques of this document span decades, so it is unnecessary for this project to engage in a thorough dismantling of Moynihan's faulty report. However, what *is* important to note is that Baldwin, in deploying a language and logic similar to that found in the report, is in fact engaging in what Hortense J. Spillers, in "Mama's Baby, Papa's Maybe: An American Grammar Book," in *Black, White, and in Color: Essays on American Literature and Culture* (Chicago: The University of Chicago Press, 2003), calls a "misnaming" (204) or "dehumanized naming" (210) of the black woman.

89. Baldwin, *The Amen Corner*, 58.

90. Baldwin, *The Amen Corner*.

91. Baldwin, *The Amen Corner*, 74, emphasis mine.

92. Baldwin, *The Amen Corner*, 81.

93. Baldwin, *The Amen Corner*, 83.

94. Baldwin, *The Amen Corner*, 84.

95. Magdalena J. Zaborowska, *Me and My House: James Baldwin's Last Decade in France* (Durham: NC: Duke University Press, 2018), 187.

96. Baldwin, *The Amen Corner*, xvi.

97. Baldwin, *The Amen Corner*, 82.

98. Baldwin, *The Amen Corner*, 86.

99. Baldwin, *The Amen Corner*, xvi.

100. Harris, *Black Women in the Fiction of James Baldwin*, 153. Interestingly, Harris posits that the more positive, although it will be shown still lacking, qualities of the black women in *Beale Street* could be the byproduct of Baldwin's "dialogue" with black feminist Nikki Giovanni (220, fn. 18).

101. See Harris, *Black Women in the Fiction of James Baldwin*, 157, 161. See the whole of chapter 4, entitled: "Bearing the Burden of the Blues: *If Beale Street Could Talk*," for Harris's examination of the women of *Beale Street*.

102. Harris, *Black Women in the Fiction of James Baldwin*, 158.

103. Harris, *Black Women in the Fiction of James Baldwin*, 158–59.

104. Harris, *Black Women in the Fiction of James Baldwin*, 159–60.

105. James Baldwin, *If Beale Street Could Talk*, in *James Baldwin: Later Novels*, ed. Darryl Pinckney (New York: The Library of America, 2015), 392.

106. Harris, in *Black Women in the Fiction of James Baldwin*, states, ". . . Tish accepts the order of things, the place and worth that Fonny has assigned her; that

role is the source of her fulfillment and underscores Tish's urgency in getting Fonny out of jail" (160).

107. Baldwin, *If Beale Street Could Talk*, 392.

108. This is why Harris, in *Black Women in the Fiction of James Baldwin*, makes special note of the way in which Fonny functions as Tish's "Lord" in the novel. She claims:

> The religion of love that Fonny and Tish create depends upon Fonny being in the role of Lord and Master. He guides Tish through sexual initiation, and he is responsible for the change she undergoes, the religious conversion in the creation of their love religion. He initiates the action, calms her fears, baptizes her, and brings her forth anew (160).

In addition, Harris, in "The Eye as Weapon in *If Beale Street Could Talk*," in *Critical Essays on James Baldwin*, ed. Fred L. Standley and Nancy V. Burt (Boston: G. K. Hall & Co., 1988), also touches on this theme of Fonny as "Lord." She states, "Tish records of Fonny: 'he called me by the thunder at my ear,' which brings to mind immediately the lines of the spiritual, 'Steal Away' ('My Lord, He calls me, He calls me by the thunder/The trumpet sounds within my soul/I ain't got long to stay here.') As her lord calls her, Tish is 'being changed' (the conversion)" (213–14).

109. Harris, *Black Women in the Fiction of James Baldwin*, 161, 163. Harris, on page 161, claims: "No woman in the novel is complete without the intellectual and emotional support of a man or a male figure, on either a real level or symbolic one."

110. Harris, *Black Women in the Fiction of James Baldwin*, 157–58.

111. Baldwin, *If Beale Street Could Talk*, 404; Harris, *Black Women in the Fiction of James Baldwin*, 157, 160.

112. Baldwin, *If Beale Street Could Talk*, 380, 442; Harris, *Black Women in the Fiction of James Baldwin*, 158–59.

113. Baldwin, *If Beale Street Could Talk*, 439, 464; Harris, *Black Women in the Fiction of James Baldwin*, 159.

114. Harris, *Black Women in the Fiction of James Baldwin*, 158–59.

115. Baldwin, *If Beale Street Could Talk*, 408–9; Harris discusses this passage on page 160 of *Black Women in the Fiction of James Baldwin*.

116. This quote is worth offering in full. Harris, in *Black Women in the Fiction of James Baldwin*, states: "Even the freest of Baldwin's black women, such as Ernestine in *Beale Street* and Julia in *Just Above My Head*, are initially not free of conformity, and, at some level, to male definitions of them. Finally, and most important, they are not free of the creator who continues to draw in their potential for growth on the short rein of possibility" (11). This quote, found later in Harris's text is also relevant. Referring to the women in *Beale Street*, she states: "Though most are free of the masculine God, they are ultimately not truly free of domination, because their happiness and fulfillment are tied to their lives with male figures. It is a limitation in their conception that they seek for no more and ask no questions about the way things are. Good they do and good feelings they inspire are short-circuited by the fact that they have never heard of freedom from men and never desired to know of it" (163).

117. David Leeming, *James Baldwin: A Biography* (New York: Henry Holt & Company, 1994), 314; Matthew Brim, in the "conclusion" of his work *James Baldwin and the Queer Imagination*, offers an excellent examination of the "underrepresentation" and "unrepresentability" of black lesbians in Baldwin's work (156), in addition to a broader engagement of Baldwin's sexism. He does so through an examination of Baldwin's dialogues with Nikki Giovanni and Audre Lorde.

118. James Baldwin and Nikki Giovanni, *A Dialogue* (Philadelphia: J.B. Lippincott, 1973), 34–35, https://search.alexanderstreet.com/view/work/bibliographic_entity%7C document%7C4390032; Brim, in *James Baldwin and the Queer Imagination*, states: "The question of how 'his' child came to be 'produced' from the black woman's body seems to have little to do with her sex, her relationship to it, or her sexuality. Rather, the black man's innate ownership of the child and of the black woman's body that bears the child operates as the pressure point for Baldwin, the point of his own unique violation" (164).

119. Baldwin and Giovanni, *A Dialogue*, 34–41.

120. Baldwin and Giovanni, *A Dialogue*, 41.

121. Baldwin and Giovanni, *A Dialogue*, 34–41. Matt Brim, in *James Baldwin and the Queer Imagination*, supports this point, arguing: "For Baldwin, however, the mistreatment of black women by black men provides commentary not primarily on black men's relationship with black women but on black men's situation vis-à-vis the racial disparity with white men" (164).

122. Baldwin and Giovanni, *A Dialogue*, 38.

123. Baldwin and Giovanni, *A Dialogue*, 41–42.

124. Baldwin and Giovanni, *A Dialogue*, 46–47.

125. Baldwin and Giovanni, *A Dialogue*, 50.

126. Baldwin and Giovanni, *A Dialogue*, 47–48.

127. Baldwin and Giovanni, *A Dialogue*, 53.

128. Baldwin and Giovanni, *A Dialogue*, 61–62.

129. Baldwin and Giovanni, *A Dialogue*, 63.

130. All quotes from Baldwin's exchange with Lorde are taken from James Baldwin and Audre Lorde, "Revolutionary Hope: A Conversation Between James Baldwin and Audre Lorde," *The Culture*, accessed March 21, 2019, http://theculture .forharriet.com/2014/03/revolutionary-hope-conversation-between.html. The website does not provide pagination for the conversation, and the original manuscript was not available.

131. Baldwin, "Everybody's Protest Novel," 17.

132. Baldwin, *No Name in the Street*, 432.

133. Wynter, "Unsettling the Coloniality of Being," 268, emphasis mine.

134. Joseph Vogel, *James Baldwin and the 1980s: Witnessing the Reagan Era* (Champaign: University Illinois Press, 2018), 54.

135. Baldwin, "Freaks and the American Ideal of Manhood," 814.

136. Baldwin, "Freaks and the American Ideal of Manhood," 814.

137. Baldwin, "Freaks and the American Ideal of Manhood," 814–15.

138. Vogel, *James Baldwin and the 1980s*, 59.

139. Vogel, *James Baldwin and the 1980s*, 51.

140. Vogel, *James Baldwin and the 1980s*, 51–52, 58–59.

141. Baldwin, "Freaks and the American Ideal of Manhood," 815.

142. Baldwin, "Freaks and the American Ideal of Manhood," 828.

143. Baldwin, "Freaks and the American Ideal of Manhood," 823.

144. Baldwin, "Freaks and the American Ideal of Manhood," 819.

145. Ashon Crawley, *Blackpentecostal Breath: The Aesthetics of Possibility* (New York: Fordham University Press, 2017), 2.

146. Leeming, *James Baldwin: A Biography*, 377.

147. Leeming, *James Baldwin: A Biography*, 376.

148. Leeming, *James Baldwin: A Biography*, 377.

149. Leeming, *James Baldwin: A Biography*.

150. Baldwin, "Freaks and the American Ideal of Manhood," 827.

151. Vogel, *James Baldwin and the 1980s*, 60.

152. Leeming, *James Baldwin: A Biography*, 378.

153. Hardy, *James Baldwin's God*, 47, 73.

154. Baldwin, "Everybody's Protest Novel," 16–17.

155. Baldwin, "Freaks and the American Ideal of Manhood," 814–15.

Chapter 5. Jimmy's (A)Theology: Toward a Black Agnostic Mysticism

1. El Kornegay, Jr., *A Queering of Black Theology: James Baldwin's Blues Project and Gospel Prose* (New York: Palgrave Macmillan, 2013), 2–3, 153 (fn. 2).

2. Joe McKnight, "That's Why They Crucified Him: An Interview with James Cone," *The Revealer: A Review of Religion & Media*, June 21, 2012, https://the revealer.org/thats-why-they-crucified-him-an-interview-with-james-cone/; See also Kornegay, *A Queering of Black Theology*, 2–3.

3. James H. Cone, *Said I Wasn't Gonna Tell Nobody* (Maryknoll, NY: Orbis Books, 2018), 150.

4. Kornegay, *A Queering of Black Theology*, 2–5. In this section, Kornegay also discusses the four major problems caused by Baldwin's "erasure" in and for the discourse of black liberation theology. Kornegay returns to the subject on pages 92–96.

5. Those monographs include: Clarence E. Hardy III, *James Baldwin's God: Sex, Hope, and Crisis in Black Holiness Culture* (Knoxville: The University of Tennessee Press, 2003); Kornegay, *A Queering of Black Theology*; and Josiah Ulysses Young III, *James Baldwin's Understanding of God: Overwhelming Desire and Joy* (New York: Palgrave Macmillan, 2014).

6. Ashon T. Crawley, *Blackpentecostal Breath: The Aesthetics of Possibility* (New York: Fordham University Press, 2017), 11–12.

7. I borrow this language of "refusal" from Michael A Sells's work *Mystical Languages of Unsaying* (Chicago: The University of Chicago Press, 1994), 2.

8. I am indebted to Ashon T. Crawley's work, *The Lonely Letters* (Durham, NC, Duke University Press, 2020) for helping me see the importance of "feeling" in

Baldwin's mysticism. In one section in which Crawley discusses the Baldwin-like characteristics of the 2016 film *Moonlight*, he states: "Yet *Moonlight* could've been James Baldwin's, could've been his fictional narrative. And this is because *Moonlight*, like Baldwin's work, is all about feeling. And in that way, like Baldwin's work, it's also, then, about blackness, religion, and the failure to find sanctuary in the most ordinary, everyday, supposedly safe places" (106).

9. See *The Lonely Letters* for Crawley's most robust treatment of mysticism. By "otherwise," I am building on Crawley's concept offered in *Blackpentecostal Breath*. He states, "Otherwise, as word—otherwise possibilities, as phrase—announces the fact of infinite alternatives to what *is*. And what *is* is about being, about existence, about ontology. But if infinite alternatives exist, if otherwise possibility is a resource that is never exhausted, what *is*, what exists, is but one of many" (2).

10. For an example of how Ashon Crawley uses the language of "sociality," see his essay "Susceptibility," *GLQ: A Journal of Lesbian and Gay Studies* 27, no. 1 (2021): 11, muse.jhu.edu/article/777706.

11. José Esteban Muñoz, *Disidentifications: Queers of Color and the Performance of Politics* (Minneapolis: The University of Minnesota Press, 1999).

12. James Baldwin, "To Crush a Serpent," in *The Cross of Redemption: Uncollected Writings*, ed. Randall Kenan (New York: Vintage International, 2011), 203.

13. David Leeming, *James Baldwin: A Biography* (New York: Henry Holt & Company, 1994), 384.

14. Crawley, *The Lonely Letters*, 95.

15. Leeming, *James Baldwin: A Biography*, 384; Leeming notes a similar statement made by Baldwin in a letter to his friend Cyndie Packard (378): "To Cyndie, Baldwin wrote about the 'journey' that he was undergoing. As he experienced 'the stillness at the center' of the night, he said, he listened to the darkness and felt that 'something' was 'listening to me'" (379).

16. James Baldwin, "In Search of a Majority: An Address," in *James Baldwin: Collected Essays*, ed. Toni Morrison (New York: Library of America, 1998), 220.

17. Young, *James Baldwin's Understanding of God*, 2.

18. Young, *James Baldwin's Understanding of God*, 191–94. Young also mentions Baldwin's letter to Cyndie Packard, which contains the language of "something," and his conversation with David Leeming in which Baldwin spoke of "something out there" (191–92). In another section of the book, Young states: "What kept him going? Perhaps it was his understanding of 'God,' his faith in something deep inside him—something *like fire . . . something that can change you*. I think that it was that 'something' which thrashed him on the dusty church floor one summer's night, releasing the light in him" (77).

19. Young, *James Baldwin's Understanding of God*, 9, 191–94. Young, on page 9 and in part on pages 192 and 194, highlights Baldwin's now famous statement on love in his interview with Colin MacInnes and James Mossman:

> I believe in . . . I believe in love. . . . I believe we can save each other. In fact I think we must save each other. I don't depend on anyone else to do it. . . . I don't mean anything passive. I mean something active, something more like

a fire, like the wind, something which can change you. I mean energy. I mean a passionate belief, a passionate knowledge of what a human being can do, and become, what a human being can do to change the world in which he finds himself (James Baldwin and James Mossman, "Race, Hate, Sex, and Colour: A Conversation with James Baldwin and Colin MacInnes" in *Conversations with James Baldwin*, ed. Fred L. Standley and Louis H. Pratt (Jackson: University Press of Mississippi, 1989), 48.

20. Young, *James Baldwin's Understanding of God*, 192.

21. Young, *James Baldwin's Understanding of God*, 18. See also page 5; In addition, Christopher Z. Hobson in *James Baldwin and the Heavenly City: Prophecy, Apocalypse, and Doubt* (East Lansing: Michigan State University Press, 2018), also highlight's Baldwin's conversation with Leeming in regard to his lack of belief in god, and refers to Baldwin's view of god as "quasi-Feuerbachian" (4).

22. Ludwig Feuerbach, *The Essence of Christianity*, trans. George Eliot (New York: Harper & Brothers, 1957), 12.

23. Feuerbach, *The Essence of Christianity*, 18–19.

24. Feuerbach, *The Essence of Christianity*.

25. Feuerbach, *The Essence of Christianity*, 18–21.

26. Feuerbach, *The Essence of Christianity*, 19.

27. Young, in *James Baldwin's Understanding of God*, states: "God for Feuerbach is thus the *future*-bound totality of humankind—the apotheosis of human potential and, sadly, our ongoing capacity to maim ourselves too. From everything I have written in this book, it is clear to me that James Baldwin would agree. God is the self and the sum total of other selves" (195).

28. Young, *James Baldwin's Understanding of God*, 101.

29. It is in relation to this essay, "Preservation of Innocence," that Young, in *James Baldwin's Understanding of God*, notes Baldwin's "Feuerbach-like" tendencies (18). See pages 17–18 for Young's discussion of this essay.

30. James Baldwin, "Preservation of Innocence," in *James Baldwin: Collected Essays*, 596.

31. Baldwin, "Preservation of Innocence," 594.

32. Baldwin, "Preservation of Innocence," 595–96.

33. Baldwin, "Preservation of Innocence," 596.

34. *Our Protestant Heritage*, "The Meaning of the Birmingham Tragedy, 1963," aired September 15, 1963, 1:29 to 2:24, https://digital.history.pcusa.org/islandora/object/islandora:71692. Emphasis mine.

35. Baldwin, through the character Hall Montana, expresses this sentiment in *Just Above My Head*, in *James Baldwin: Later Novels*, ed. Darryl Pinckney (New York: The Library of America, 2015). During a conversation between the characters Hall and Sidney, Sidney posits that white people have stolen "everything they own" from the rest of the world, including "God." Hall reflects on this statement, thinking: "Gods who could be stolen and then stolen back did not interest me at all . . . As far as I was concerned, it was all a lie, from top to bottom: and, since we had built it, only we could dare it down. That energy called divine is really human need,

translated, and if that God we have created needs patience with us, how much more than patience do we need with God!" (814–15).

36. Hardy, *James Baldwin's God*, 80.

37. James Baldwin, "White Racism or World Community?," in *James Baldwin: Collected Essays*, 755.

38. James Baldwin, *The Fire Next Time*, in *James Baldwin: Collected Essays*, 314.

39. Baldwin, "In Search of a Majority," 220, emphasis mine.

40. Crawley, *Blackpentecostal Breath*, 2.

41. James Baldwin, *The Devil Finds Work*, in *James Baldwin: Collected Essays*, 565–66.

42. Baldwin, *The Devil Finds Work*, 565.

43. Baldwin, *The Devil Finds Work*, 565.

44. Baldwin, *The Devil Finds Work*, 565; Baldwin, *The Fire Next Time*, 304.

45. Baldwin, *Devil Find's Work*, 566.

46. Baldwin, *The Devil Finds Work*, 565.

47. Baldwin, *The Devil Finds Work*, 566.

48. Leeming, in *James Baldwin: A Biography*, notes that Baldwin once wrote to his mother that he "was still in the service of some power for good beyond himself, that his mission was sacred" (115).

49. "Unnameable" or "unnameability" is language borrowed from Sells, *Mystical Languages of Unsaying*.

50. Sells, *Mystical Languages of Unsaying*, 2.

51. Sells, *Mystical Languages of Unsaying*.

52. Vincent W. Lloyd, *Religion of the Field Negro: On Black Secularism and Black Theology* (New York: Fordham University Press, 2018), 40.

53. Leeming, *James Baldwin: A Biography*, 384, emphasis mine.

54. William James, *The Varieties of Religious Experience* (Mineola, NY: Dover Publications, 2002), 379–80.

55. James, *The Varieties of Religious Experience*, 380.

56. James, *The Varieties of Religious Experience*.

57. James, *The Varieties of Religious Experience*.

58. James, *The Varieties of Religious Experience*.

59. James, *The Varieties of Religious Experience*, 381.

60. James, *The Varieties of Religious Experience*.

61. Baldwin, *The Devil Finds Work*, 566.

62. Baldwin, "To Crush a Serpent," 203.

63. Joy R. Bostic, *African American Female Mysticism: Nineteenth-Century Religious Activism* (New York: Palgrave Macmillan, 2013), 38. Bostic also discusses William James's "four marks" of mysticism on page 37.

64. Bostic, *African American Female Mysticism*, xvi, 43–44.

65. Bostic, *African American Female Mysticism*, 43.

66. Douglas Field, *All Those Strangers: The Art and Lives of James Baldwin* (New York: Oxford University Press, 2015), 85–86.

67. Crawley, *Blackpentecostal Breath*, 9–11.

68. Crawley, *Blackpentecostal Breath*, 5.

69. Crawley, *Blackpentecostal Breath*, 4.

70. Crawley, "Susceptibility," 11.

71. Crawley, *Blackpentecostal Breath*, 4.

72. Crawley, *The Lonely Letters*, 70.

73. Crawley, *The Lonely Letters*, 108.

74. Crawley, *The Lonely Letters*.

75. Crawley, *The Lonely Letters*, 10.

76. Crawley, *Blackpentecostal Breath*, 4.

77. Crawley, *The Lonely Letters*, 42.

78. Crawley, *Blackpentecostal Breath*, 4.

79. Leeming, in *James Baldwin: A Biography*, notes Baldwin's commitment to sensuality. He states, "He was a man who laughed a lot and who knew how to make others laugh. And while clearly obsessed by what he saw as a witnessing role, he was just as committed to the life of the senses; when he ate a meal, smoked a cigarette, sipped a scotch, or touched another human being, he did so with deep pleasure that was evident and with an incomparable elegance and care" (xii); For Baldwin's own take on the "sensual," see pages 310–12 of *The Fire Next Time*.

80. Baldwin, "To Crush a Serpent," 203, emphasis mine.

81. Like Young, in *James Baldwin's Understanding of God*, I do not believe Baldwin is expressing a belief in god in this passage. Young is spot on in stating: "I can only assume here that Baldwin, writing of 'God' in the last year of his life (1987), is not referring to a biblical 'God,' an alabaster, or an ebony 'God.' He is, it seems to me, reaffirming his credo: *'I believe in love . . . I believe we can save each other . . . we must save each other'*" (191).

82. Baldwin, "To Crush a Serpent," 203.

83. Crawley, *The Lonely Letters*, 94.

84. Crawley, *The Lonely Letters*, 95.

85. Crawley, "Susceptibility," 11.

86. Crawley, "Susceptibility"; Fred Moten, in his work "Blackness and Nothingness: Mysticism in the Flesh," *The South Atlantic Quarterly* 112, no. 4 (2013), https://doi.org/10.1215/00382876-2345261, makes a similar point. He states, "What I assert is this: that black life—which is as surely to say *life* as black thought is to say *thought*—is irreducibly social" (739).

87. Crawley, *The Lonely Letters*, 30–31.

88. See Crawley's *Blackpentecostal Breath* for further discussion of "categorical distinction."

89. Charles H. Long, *Significations: Signs, Symbols, and Images in the Interpretation of Religion* (Aurora, CO: The Davies Group, 1995), 7.

90. Beyond that, Baldwin also shows the ways in which "salvation," i.e., genuine human connection / sociality, might be found for white people *if* they are able to truly *hear, touch, commune with* black life (which would, in fact, mean the end of their whiteness). See the closing section of this study's Chapter 2 for a substantive discussion of this idea.

91. Crawley, "Susceptibility," 17.
92. Baldwin, *The Fire Next Time*, 306.
93. Baldwin, *The Fire Next Time*.
94. Baldwin, *The Fire Next Time*, 310–11.
95. Crawley, *The Lonely Letters*, 147.
96. Baldwin, "To Crush a Serpent," 203.
97. Field, *All Those Strangers*, 96.
98. James Baldwin, *No Name in the Street*, in *James Baldwin: Collected Essays*, 366.
99. James, *The Varieties of Religious Experience*, 382–83.
100. Saadi A. Simawe, "What Is in a Sound? The Metaphysics and Politics of Music in *The Amen Corner*," in *Re-Viewing James Baldwin: Things Not Seen* (Philadelphia: Temple University Press, 2000), 17, emphasis mine.
101. See Chapter 2 of this study for a discussion of how music communicates suffering, and suffering becomes the means through which community is knit together. This quote from the character Hall Montana, in *Just Above My Head*, captures this sentiment. Hall states:

> Niggers can sing gospel as no other people can because they aren't singing gospel—if you see what I mean. When a nigger quotes the Gospel, he is not quoting: he is telling you what happened to him today, and what is certainly going to happen to you tomorrow: it may be that it has already happened to you, and that you, poor soul, don't know it. In which case, *Lord, have mercy!* Our suffering is our bridge to one another. Everyone must cross this bridge, or die while he still lives—but this is not a political, still less, a popular apprehension (611).

102. See Chapter 2 of this study for a discussion of the relationship of blackness to "tone"/sound in the work of Baldwin, Crawley, and Ed Pavlić.
103. Baldwin, *The Fire Next Time*, 310–11.
104. Crawley, "Susceptibility," 12.
105. Crawley, "Susceptibility," 13.
106. See Chapter 2 of this study for a discussion of how Baldwin grounds blackness in sound/"tone."
107. Crawley, "Susceptibility," 13.
108. Hardy, *James Baldwin's God*, 58.
109. Baldwin, "To Crush a Serpent," 203.
110. Baldwin, "To Crush a Serpent."
111. Crawley, "Susceptibility," 11.
112. Crawley, *The Lonely Letters*, 21.
113. Crawley, *The Lonely Letters*.
114. Sylvester A. Johnson, *African American Religions, 1500–2000: Colonialism, Democracy, and Freedom* (New York: Cambridge University Press, 2015), 51.
115. Again, this language of refusal is borrowed from Sells, *Mystical Languages of Unsaying*, 2.
116. Crawley, *The Lonely Letters*, 147.

Coda

1. A version of this "Coda" originally appeared as the conclusion of Christopher Hunt's, "'Somebody Touched Me:' Disidentification, Conversion, and the Promise of Queer Transformation in James Baldwin's Fiction," *Black Theology: An International Journal* 21, no. 3 (2023): 221–22, https://doi:10.1080/14769948.2023.2255774.

2. José Esteban Muñoz, *Disidentifications: Queers of Color and the Performance of Politics* (Minneapolis: The University of Minnesota Press, 1999).

3. James Baldwin, "The Price of the Ticket," in *James Baldwin: Collected Essays,* ed. Toni Morrison (New York: The Library of America, 1998), 839.

4. Sylvester Johnson, *The Myth of Ham in Nineteenth-Century American Christianity: Race, Heathens, and the People of God* (New York: Palgrave Macmillan, 2004).

5. James Baldwin and Richard Goldstein, "'Go the Way Your Blood Beats:' An Interview with James Baldwin," in *James Baldwin: The Last Interview and Other Conversations* (New York: Melville House Publishing, 2014), 73.

6. David Leeming, *James Baldwin: A Biography* (New York: Henry Holt & Company, 1994), 384.

7. Michael A. Sells, *Mystical Languages of Unsaying* (Chicago: The University of Chicago Press, 1994).

8. James Baldwin, "In Search of a Majority: An Address," in *James Baldwin: Collected Essays,* 220.

9. James Baldwin, "Freaks and the American Ideal of Manhood," in *James Baldwin: Collected Essays.*

10. Please see my engagement of the work of Josiah Ulysses Young in Chapter 3 of this text for a full discussion of the relationship of the black child to, to quote Young, "Baldwin's hope that we can make the world better than it is." Josiah Ulysses Young III, *James Baldwin's Understanding of God: Overwhelming Desire and Joy* (New York: Palgrave Macmillan, 2014), 161.

11. See chapter seven of Anthony B. Pinn's *Terror and Triumph: The Nature of Black Religion* (Minneapolis: Fortress Press, 2003), for a discussion of the meaning of "complex subjectivity."

12. Ashon T. Crawley, *Blackpentecostal Breath: The Aesthetics of Possibility* (New York: Fordham University Press, 2017), 2.

13. Baldwin and Goldstein, "Go the Way Your Blood Beats," 73.

14. Crawley, *Blackpentecostal Breath,* 11.

15. Crawley, *Blackpentecostal Breath,* 11–12

16. This quote by Douglas Field, in *All Those Strangers: The Art and Lives of James Baldwin* (New York: Oxford University Press, 2015) resonates with my claim: "In Baldwin's writing transcendence or ecstasy frequently occurs outside of religious worship; it is most likely to be found in the communion of friends and lovers, through playing or listening to music or making love. These moments are, as Clarence Hardy observes, imbued with 'a very nearly religious cadence'" (85). In addition, this quote from David Leeming, in *James Baldwin: A Biography,* also resonates: "And while

clearly obsessed by what he saw as a witnessing role, he was just as committed to the life of the senses; when he ate a meal, smoked a cigarette, sipped on a scotch, or touched another human being, he did so with deep pleasure that was evident and with an incomparable elegance and care" (xii).

17. Muñoz, *Disidentifications*, 31.
18. Muñoz, *Disidentifications*.
19. Muñoz, *Disidentifications*, 12.
20. Crawley, *Blackpentecostal Breath*, 4, 17–18.

Bibliography

Baldwin, James. *The Amen Corner*. New York: Vintage Books, 1998.

———. "Anti-Semitism and Black Power." In *The Cross of Redemption: Uncollected Writings*, edited by Randall Kenan, 250–53. New York: Vintage Books, 2011.

———. "Civil Rights—James Baldwin—Interview—Mavis on Four." Interview by Mavis Nicholson, *Mavis on Four*, February 12, 1987, Thames Television, video. https://www.youtube.com/watch?v=YUMrEDNiy3I.

———. "*The Black Scholar* Interviews James Baldwin." In *Conversations with James Baldwin*, edited by Fred L. Standley and Louis H. Pratt, 142–58. Jackson: University Press of Mississippi, 1989.

———. *The Devil Finds Work*. In *James Baldwin: Collected Essays*, edited by Toni Morrison, 477–572. New York: The Library of America, 1998.

———. "Equal in Paris." In *James Baldwin: Collected Essays*, edited by Toni Morrison, 101–16. New York: The Library of America, 1998.

———. "Everybody's Protest Novel." In *James Baldwin: Collected Essays*, edited by Toni Morrison, 11–18. New York: The Library of America, 1998.

———. *The Evidence of Things Not Seen*. New York: Henry Holt & Company, 1995.

———. *The Fire Next Time*. In *James Baldwin: Collected Essays*, edited by Toni Morrison, 287–347. New York: The Library of America, 1998.

———. "Freaks and the American Ideal of Manhood." In *James Baldwin: Collected Essays*, edited by Toni Morrison, 814–29. New York: The Library of America, 1998.

———. *Go Tell It on the Mountain*. In *James Baldwin: Early Novels and Stories*, edited by Toni Morrison, 1–215. New York: The Library of America, 1998.

———. *If Beale Street Could Talk*. In *James Baldwin: Later Novels*, edited by Darryl Pinckney, 363–509. New York: The Library of America, 2015.

———. "In Search of a Majority: An Address." In *James Baldwin: Collected Essays*, edited by Toni Morrison, 215–21. New York: The Library of America, 1998.

———. *Just Above My Head*. In *James Baldwin: Later Novels*, edited by Darryl Pinckney, 511–1039. New York: The Library of America, 2015.

———. "Many Thousands Gone." In *James Baldwin: Collected Essays*, edited by Toni Morrison, 19–34. New York: The Library of America, 1998.

———. "Mass Culture and the Creative Artist: Some Personal Notes." In *The Cross of Redemption: Uncollected Writings*, edited by Randall Kenan, 3–7. New York: Vintage International, 2011.

———. *No Name in the Street*. In *James Baldwin: Collected Essays*, edited Toni Morrison, 349–475. New York: The Library of America, 1998.

———. *Nobody Knows My Name*. In *James Baldwin: Collected Essays*, edited by Toni Morrison, 131–285. New York: The Library of America, 1998.

———. "Notes for the Amen Corner," in *The Amen Corner*. New York: Vintage Books, 1998.

———. "Notes of a Native Son." In *James Baldwin: Collected Essays*, edited by Toni Morrison, 63–84. New York: The Library of America, 1998.

———. "Notes on the House of Bondage." In *James Baldwin: Collected Essays*, edited by Toni Morrison, 799–807. New York: The Library of America, 1998.

———. "Preservation of Innocence." In *James Baldwin: Collected Essays*, edited by Toni Morrison, 594–600. New York: The Library of America, 1998.

———. "The Price of the Ticket." In *James Baldwin: Collected Essays*, edited by Toni Morrison, 830–42. New York: The Library of America, 1998.

———. "Stranger in the Village." In *James Baldwin: Collected Essays*, edited by Toni Morrison, 117-29. New York: The Library of America, 1998

———. "A Talk to Teachers." In *James Baldwin: Collected Essays*, edited by Toni Morrison, 678–86. New York: The Library of America, 1998.

———. *Tell Me How Long the Train's Been Gone*. In *James Baldwin: Later Novels*, edited by Darryl Pinckney, 1–362. New York: The Library of America, 2015.

———. "To Crush a Serpent." In *The Cross of Redemption: Uncollected Writings*, edited by Randall Kenan, 195–204. New York: Vintage International, 2011.

———. "The Uses of the Blues." In *The Cross of Redemption: Uncollected Writings*, edited by Randall Kenan, 70–81. New York: Vintage International, 2011.

———. "White Racism or World Community?" In *James Baldwin: Collected Essays*, edited by Toni Morrison, 749–56. New York: The Library of America, 1998.

Baldwin, James, and Kenneth B. Clark. "A Conversation with James Baldwin." In *Conversations with James Baldwin*, edited by Fred L. Standley and Louis H. Pratt, 38–45. Jackson: University Press of Mississippi, 1989.

Baldwin, James, and David C. Estes. "An Interview with James Baldwin." In *Conversations with James Baldwin*, edited by Fred L. Standley and Louis H. Pratt, 270–80. Jackson: University Press of Mississippi, 1989.

Baldwin, James, and Nikki Giovanni, *A Dialogue*. Philadelphia: J.B. Lippincott, 1973. https://search.alexanderstreet.com/view/work/bibliographic_entity%7C bibliographic_details%7C4390030.

Baldwin, James, and Richard Goldstein. "'Go the Way Your Blood Beats:' An
    Interview with James Baldwin." In *James Baldwin: The Last Interview and Other
    Conversations*, 55–74. New York: Melville House Publishing, 2014.
Baldwin, James, and Jewell Handy Gresham. "James Baldwin Comes Home." In
    Conversations with James Baldwin, edited by Fred L. Standley and Louis H. Pratt,
    159–67. Jackson: University Press of Mississippi, 1989.
Baldwin, James, and Audre Lorde. "Revolutionary Hope: A Conversation Between
    James Baldwin and Audre Lorde." *The Culture*. http://theculture.forharriet.com
    /2014/03/revolutionary-hope-conversation-between.html.
Baldwin, James, and Margaret Mead. *A Rap on Race*. New York: Dell Publishing,
    1971.
Baldwin, James, and James Mossman. "Race, Hate, Sex, and Colour: A Conversation
    with James Baldwin and Colin MacInnes." In *Conversations with James Baldwin*,
    edited by Fred L. Standley and Louis H. Pratt, 46–58. Jackson: University Press of
    Mississippi, 1989.
Baldwin, James, and Studs Terkel, "An Interview with James Baldwin." In
    Conversations with James Baldwin, edited by Fred L. Standley and Louis H.
    Pratt, 3–23. Jackson: University Press of Mississippi, 1989.
Birt, Robert. "Existence, Identity, and Liberation." In *Existence in Black: An
    Anthology of Black Existential Philosophy*, edited by Lewis R. Gordon, 205–13.
    New York: Routledge, 1997.
Blount, Brian K. *Can I Get a Witness? Reading Revelation Through African American
    Culture*. Louisville, KY: Westminster John Knox Press, 2005.
Bostic, Joy R. *African American Female Mysticism: Nineteenth-Century Religious
    Activism*. New York: Palgrave Macmillan, 2013.
Brim, Matt. *James Baldwin and the Queer Imagination*. Ann Arbor: University of
    Michigan Press, 2014.
Camus, Albert. *The Myth of Sisyphus and Other Essays*. Translated by Justin
    O'Brien. New York: Vintage International, 1991.
Carter, J. Kameron. *The Anarchy of Black Religion: A Mystic Song*. Durham, NC:
    Duke University Press, 2023.
———. *Race: A Theological Account*. New York: Oxford University Press, 2008.
Cone, James H. *Black Theology and Black Power*. Maryknoll, NY: Orbis Books, 1997.
———. *Said I Wasn't Gonna Tell Nobody*. Maryknoll, NY: Orbis Books, 2018.
Crawley, Ashon T. *Blackpentecostal Breath: The Aesthetics of Possibility*. New York:
    Fordham University Press, 2017.
———. *The Lonely Letters*. Durham, NC: Duke University Press, 2020.
———. "Susceptibility." *GLQ: A Journal of Lesbian and Gay Studies* 27, no. 1 (2021):
    11–38. muse.jhu.edu/article/777706.
Day, Keri. *Azuza Reimagined: A Radical Vision of Religious and Democratic
    Belonging*. Stanford, CA: Stanford University Press, 2022.
Douglas, Kelly Brown. *What's Faith Got to Do with It? Black Bodies/Christian Souls*.
    Maryknoll, NY: Orbis Books, 2005.

Edelman, Lee. *No Future: Queer Theory and the Death Drive.* Durham, NC: Duke
University Press, 2004.

Ferguson, Roderick. *Aberrations in Black: Toward a Queer of Color Critique.*
Minneapolis: University of Minnesota Press, 2004.

———. "The Nightmares of the Heteronormative." *Cultural Values* 4, no. 4 (October
2000), 419–44. https://doi:10.1080/14797580009367210.

Feuerbach, Ludwig. *The Essence of Christianity.* Translated by George Eliot. New
York: Harper & Brothers, 1957.

Field, Douglas. *All Those Strangers: The Art and Lives of James Baldwin.* New York:
Oxford University Press, 2015.

Glaude, Eddie S., Jr. *Begin Again: James Baldwin's America and Its Urgent Lessons
for Our Own.* New York: Crown Publishing, 2020.

Gordon, Lewis R. *Bad Faith and Antiblack Racism.* New York: Humanity Books, 1995.

———. *Existentia Africana: Understanding Africana Existential Thought.* New
York: Routledge, 2000.

Hall, Donald, E. *Queer Theories.* New York: Palgrave Macmillan, 2003.

Hardy, Clarence E., III. *James Baldwin's God: Sex, Hope, and Crisis in Black
Holiness Culture.* Knoxville: The University of Tennessee Press, 2003.

Harris, Trudier. *Black Women in the Fiction of James Baldwin.* Knoxville: The
University of Tennessee Press, 1985.

———. "The Eye as Weapon in *If Beale Street Could Talk.*" In *Critical Essays on
James Baldwin,* edited by Fred L. Standley and Nancy V. Burt, 204–16. Boston:
G. K. Hall & Co., 1988.

Heng, Geraldine. "The Invention of Race in the European Middle Ages I: Race
Studies, Modernity, and the Middle Ages." *Literature Compass* 8, no. 5 (2011):
315–31. https://doi.org/10.1111/j.1741-4113.2011.00790.x.

———. "The Invention of Race in the European Middle Ages II: Locations of
Medieval Race." *Literature Compass* 8, no. 5 (2011): 332–50. https://doi.org/10.1111
/j.1741-4113.2011.00795.x.

Hobson, Christopher Z. *James Baldwin and the Heavenly City: Prophecy, Apocalypse,
and Doubt.* East Lansing: Michigan State University Press, 2018.

Horn, Rosa A. "What is Holiness? A Complete Life in Christ." In *Daughters of
Thunder: Black Women Preachers and Their Sermons, 1850–1979* by Bettye
Collier Thomas, 189–93. San Francisco: Jossey-Bass, 1998.

Howard-Brook, Wes, and Anthony Gwyther. *Unveiling Empire: Reading Revelation
Then and Now.* Maryknoll, NY: Orbis Books, 1999.

Hunt, Christopher. "'Somebody Touched Me': Disidentification, Conversion, and
the Promise of Queer Transformation in James Baldwin's Fiction." *Black
Theology: An International Journal* 21, no. 3 (2023): 205–23. https://doi:10.1080
/14769948.2023.2255774.

"James Baldwin BBC Bookshelf Program Interview (1963)." *Bookstand* on *BBC,*
1963. 29:36. https://worldhistoryarchive.wordpress.com/2018/02/07/james-baldwin
-bbc-bookshelf-program-interview-1963/.

James Baldwin: The Price of the Ticket. American Masters series. PBS, 1990. 1 hr., 27 min. https://www.kanopy.com/en/coloradocollege/watch/video/116250.

James, William. *The Varieties of Religious Experience.* Mineola, NY: Dover Publications, 2002.

Jennings, Willie James. *The Christian Imagination: Theology and the Origins of Race.* New Haven, CT: Yale University Press, 2010.

Johnson, Sylvester A. *African American Religions, 1500–2000: Colonialism, Democracy, and Freedom.* New York: Cambridge University Press, 2015.

———. *The Myth of Ham in Nineteenth-Century American Christianity: Race, Heathens, and the People of God.* New York: Palgrave Macmillan, 2004.

Kornegay, El, Jr. *A Queering of Black Theology: James Baldwin's Blues Project and Gospel Prose.* New York: Palgrave Macmillan, 2013.

Leeming, David. *James Baldwin: A Biography.* New York: Henry Holt & Company, 1994.

Lloyd, Vincent W. *Religion of the Field Negro: On Black Secularism and Black Theology.* New York: Fordham University Press, 2018.

Long, Charles H. *Significations: Signs, Symbols, and Images in the Interpretation of Religion.* Aurora, CO: The Davies Group, 1995.

Lum, Kathryn Gin. *Heathen: Religion and Race in American History.* Cambridge, MA: Harvard University Press, 2022.

Lynch, Michael F. "A Glimpse of the Hidden God: Dialectical Vision in Baldwin's *Go Tell It on the Mountain.*" In *New Essays on Go Tell It on the Mountain,* edited by Trudier Harris, 29–57. Cambridge: Cambridge University Press, 1996.

———. "Staying Out of the Temple: Baldwin, the African American Church, and *The Amen Corner.*" In *Re-Viewing James Baldwin: Things Not Seen,* edited by D. Quentin Miller, 33–71. Philadelphia: Temple University Press, 2000.

McKnight, Joe. "That's Why They Crucified Him: An Interview with James Cone." *The Revealer: A Review of Religion & Media,* June 21, 2012. https://therevealer.org/thats-why-they-crucified-him-an-interview-with-james-cone/.

Mitchem, Preston. "'I Am Not Your Negro' Erased the Sexuality of James Baldwin. What if it Wins an Oscar?," *ThinkProgress,* February 26, 2017. https://archive.thinkprogress.org/i-am-not-your-negro-erased-sexuality-baldwin-3b68fb881421/.

Moltmann, Jürgen. *Theology of Hope: On the Ground and Implications of Christian Eschatology.* Translated by James W. Leitch. Minneapolis: Fortress Press, 1993.

Moraga, Cherríe, and Gloria Anzaldúa, eds. *This Bridge Called My Back.* 4th edition. Albany: SUNY Press, 2015.

Moten, Fred. "Blackness and Nothingness: Mysticism in the Flesh." *The South Atlantic Quarterly* 112, no. 4 (Fall 2013): 737–80. https://doi.org/10.1215/00382876-2345261.

"(1965) The Moynihan Report: The Negro Family, the Case for National Action," *The Black Past.* https://www.blackpast.org/african-american-history/moynihan-report-1965/.

Mullen, Bill V. *James Baldwin: Living in Fire.* London: Pluto Press, 2019.

Muñoz, José Esteban. *Cruising Utopia: The Then and There of Queer Futurity.* 10th
      anniversary edition. New York: NYU Press, 2019.
———. *Disidentifications: Queers of Color and the Performance of Politics.*
      Minneapolis: University of Minnesota Press, 1999.
Oliver, Michael. "James Baldwin and the 'Lie of Whiteness:' Toward an Ethic of
      Culpability, Complicity, and Confession." *Religions* 12, no. 6 (2021): 447. https://
      doi.org/10.3390/rel12060447.
Our Protestant Heritage. "The Meaning of the Birmingham Tragedy, 1963." Aired
      September 15, 1963. https://digital.history.pcusa.org/islandora/object/islandora
      :71692. 29:35.
Pavlić, Ed. *Who Can Afford to Improvise? James Baldwin and Black Music, the Lyric,
      and the Listeners.* New York: Fordham University Press, 2016.
Pêcheux, Michel. *Language, Semantics, and Ideology.* New York: St. Martin's Press,
      1982.
Pinn, Anthony B. *The End of God-Talk: An African American Humanist Theology.*
      New York: Oxford University Press, 2012.
———. *Terror and Triumph: The Nature of Black Religion.* Minneapolis: Fortress
      Press, 2003.
———. *Varieties of African American Religious Experience: Toward a Comparative
      Black Theology.* 20th anniversary edition. Minneapolis: Fortress Press, 2017.
Pinn, Anthony B., ed. *By These Hands: A Documentary History of African American
      Humanism.* New York: NYU Press, 2001.
Raboteau, Albert J. *Slave Religion: The "Invisible Institution" in the Antebellum
      South.* updated edition. New York: Oxford University Press, 2004.
Runions, Erin. *The Babylon Complex: Theopolitical Fantasies of War, Sex, and
      Sovereignty.* New York: Fordham University Press, 2014.
Sanders, Cheryl J. *Saints in Exile: The Holiness-Pentecostal Experience in African
      American Religion and Culture.* New York: Oxford University Press, 1996.
Schwartz, Regina M. *The Curse of Cain: The Violent Legacy of Monotheism.* Chicago:
      The University of Chicago Press, 1997.
Sells, Michael A. *Mystical Languages of Unsaying.* Chicago: The University of
      Chicago Press, 1994.
Sneed, Roger A. *Representations of Homosexuality: Black Liberation Theology and
      Cultural Criticism.* New York: Palgrave Macmillan, 2010.
Simawe, Saadi A. "What Is in a Sound? The Metaphysics and Politics of Music in
      The Amen Corner." In *Re-Viewing James Baldwin: Things Not Seen,* edited by
      D. Quentin Miller, 12–32. Philadelphia: Temple University Press, 2000.
Smithsonian. National Museum of African American History & Culture. "James
      Baldwin Digital Resource Guide." https://nmaahc.si.edu/explore/exhibitions
      /chez-baldwin/digital-resource-guide.
Spillers, Hortense J. "Mama's Baby, Papa's Maybe: An American Grammar Book."
      In *Black, White, and in Color: Essays on American Literature and Culture,*
      203–29. Chicago: The University of Chicago Press, 2003.

Thomas, Eric A. "The Futures Outside: Apocalyptic Epilogue Unveiled as Africana Queer Prologue." In *Sexual Disorientations: Queer Temporalities, Affects, Theologies*, edited by Kent L. Brintnall, Joseph A. Marchal, and Stephen D. Moore, 90–112. New York: Fordham University Press, 2018.

Vogel, Joseph. *James Baldwin and the 1980s: Witnessing the Reagan Era*. Champaign: University of Illinois Press, 2018.

Weisenfeld, Judith. *New World A-Coming: Black Religion and Racial Identity During the Great Migration*. New York: NYU Press, 2016.

West, Cornel. "Philosophy and the Afro-American Experience." In *Blackwell Companions to Philosophy: A Companion to African-American Philosophy*, edited by Tommy L. Lott and John P. Pittman, 7–32. Malden: Blackwell Publishing, 2006. https://doi.org/10.1002/9780470751640.ch1.

———. *Race Matters*. Boston: Beacon Press, 1993.

Wilderson, Frank B. *Afropessimism*. New York: Liveright Publishing, 2020.

Wright, Michelle M. "'Alas Poor Richard!' Transatlantic Baldwin, the Politics of Forgetting, and the Project of Modernity." In *James Baldwin Now*, edited by Dwight A. McBride, 208–32. New York: NYU Press, 1999).

Wynter, Sylvia. "On How We Mistook the Map for the Territory, and Reimprisoned Ourselves in Our Unbearable Wrongness of Being, of *Desêtre*: Black Studies Toward the Human Project." In *I Am Because We Are: Readings in Africana Philosophy*, revised edition. Edited by Fred Lee Hord (Mzee Lasana Okpara) and Jonathan Lee Scott, 267–80. Amherst and Boston: University of Massachusetts Press, 2016.

———. "Unsettling the Coloniality of Being/Power/Truth/Freedom: Towards the Human, After Man, Its Overrepresentation—An Argument." *CR: The New Centennial Review* 3, no. 3 (2003): 257–337. http://www.jstor.org/stable/41949874.

Young, Josiah Ulysses, III. *James Baldwin's Understanding of God: Overwhelming Desire and Joy*. New York: Palgrave Macmillan, 2014.

Zaborowska, Magdalena J. *Me and My House: James Baldwin's Last Decade in France*. Durham, NC: Duke University Press, 2018.

Index

absurd, philosophical category of, 79–80
Abyssinian Baptist Church, 19
aesthetic, mysticism rooted in, 144–45
affective, mysticism rooted in, 142–43
African American Female Mysticism: Nineteenth-Century Religious Activism (Bostic), 138
African American Protestantism, 18
African American Religions, 1500–2000: Colonialism, Democracy, and Freedom (Johnson), 50, 146
agnostic, mysticism rooted in, 145–47
"'Alas Poor Richard!' Transatlantic Baldwin, the Politics of Forgetting, and the Project of Modernity" (Wright), 46–47
All Those Strangers: The Art and Lives of James Baldwin (Field), 1, 39
Amen Corner, The (Baldwin): answering Macedonian call, 24; Baldwinian salvation in, 26–27; critique of sanctified church in, 22–23; David narrative in, 27–30; disidentifying praxis in, 23; disillusionment with institution of church in, 169n84; examining Margaret in, 115–18; exchanging love of human beings for love of god, 26–27; godless lifestyle in, 24–25; metaphysics and politics of music in, 144–46; plot of, 22–23; queering meaning of salvation in, 24; reading, 22
androgynous, reclamation of, 103
androgyny, idea of, 126–28
"Anti-Semitism and Black Power" (Baldwin), 67
Anzaldúa, Gloria, 2

apophasis, 136
apophatic discourse, relationship to, 135–37
asubjectivity, 8
autobiography, rehearsal for fiction, 4–6

Babylon, juxtaposition with, 81–83
Baldwin, David, 77–79
Baldwin, James, vii–viii, 149–51; accusations of pessimism, 80–84; apophatic "something" of, 135–37; arts luring, 28–29; and autobiography as rehearsal for fiction, 4–6; black feminist check on, 119–25; and Blackpentecostalism, 68; both Baldwins, 6; construction of God by, 131–35; deconstruction of God by, 131–35; disidentifying with notion of "personhood," 44–73; Douglas Field on, 1; dramatic portrayal of conversion experience of, 20–21; encountering "true religion," 68–69; eschatological "promise" of, 84–87; examining black music/tone, 63–72; examining literature as religious critique and vision, 8–9; failure of universal "Man" of, 103–11; fixation of, 17–18; gospel prose of, 34–35; and Hamitic rhetoric, 52–54; human complexity according to, 8; importance of confession, 171n100; inner vocabulary of, 84; masculinity in nonfiction of, 111–14; mysticism of, 140–47; negative assessment of black women, 112–13; "New Jerusalem," vision of, 74–101; paradoxical nature of language concerning god, 132–33; problem of sexism in, 102–29; problem of women and femininity in fiction of,

Christopher W. Hunt is Assistant Professor of Religion at Colorado College.

www.ingramcontent.com/pod-product-compliance
Lightning Source LLC
Jackson TN
JSHW080158141224
75386JS00029B/915

JIMMY'S FAITH

Jimmy's Faith

JAMES BALDWIN, DISIDENTIFICATION,

AND THE QUEER POSSIBILITIES OF BLACK RELIGION

Christopher W. Hunt

FORDHAM UNIVERSITY PRESS   NEW YORK 2025

Library of Congress Cataloging-in-Publication Data available online
at https://catalog.loc.gov.

Printed in the United States of America
27 26 25   5 4 3 2 1
First edition